The Reader's
Repentance

The Reader's Repentance

WOMEN PREACHERS, WOMEN WRITERS,
AND NINETEENTH-CENTURY
SOCIAL DISCOURSE

Christine L. Krueger

THE UNIVERSITY OF CHICAGO PRESS
CHICAGO AND LONDON

Contents

Acknowledgments

I am grateful to U. C. Knoepflmacher and Margaret A. Doody for the care they took with this project at the dissertation stage, and their continued encouragement throughout its development. My colleagues Brian Abel Ragen, Jeffrey Spear, Camilla Nilles, Russ Reising, Michael Gillespie, and John Boly have made suggestions and raised questions based on their attentive readings of my manuscript which contributed enormously to the process of revision. Alan Thomas has conscientiously guided this manuscript through the press and shown much appreciated sensitivity to the anxieties of producing one's first book. Donna Foran provided valuable editorial assistance. Karen Ford supplied crucial technical help as well as timely personal support.

An ACLS grant for recent recipients of the Ph.D. and a Monticello Fellowship at the Newberry Library enabled me to devote an academic year to research and revision. That year was spent at the Newberry Library, where I benefited from discussions with other Fellows, particularly Barbara Freedman and Barbara Foley. Travel to the Methodist Archives at the John Rylands University Library of Manchester was funded by grants from the Princeton University Department of English, the Princeton Women's Studies Program, and Marquette University.

I would especially like to thank Claudia L. Johnson and Catherine L. McClenahan, both for their extraordinary intellectual generosity and their inexhaustible loyalty. Finally, I am deeply grateful to my parents, William and Lillian Krueger, for their unfailing support and faith in my work.

Abbreviations and Editions Used

AB   George Eliot, *Adam Bede,* intro. Stephen Gill (Harmondsworth: Penguin, 1980).

CB   Elizabeth Gaskell, *The Life of Charlotte Brontë,* ed. Alan Shelston (Harmondsworth: Penguin, 1975).

CW   Hannah More, *Coelebs in Search of a Wife,* vols. 11–12 in *The Works of Hannah More,* 18 vols. (London: Cadell and Davies, 1818).

FH   George Eliot, *Felix Holt,* ed. Peter Coveney (Harmondsworth: Penguin, 1973).

HF   Charlotte Elizabeth Tonna, *Helen Fleetwood,* vol. 1 in *The Works of Charlotte Elizabeth Tonna,* 2 vols., intro. H. B. Stowe (New York: M. W. Dodd, 1848).

IC   Hannah More, *Inflexible Captive,* vol. 4 in *The Works of Hannah More,* 18 vols. (London: Cadell and Davies, 1818).

JR   George Eliot, "Janet's Repentance," in *Scenes of Clerical Life,* ed. David Lodge (Harmondsworth: Penguin, 1973).

LL   Elizabeth Gaskell, "Lizzy Leigh," in *Cousin Phillis and Other Tales,* ed. Angus Easson (Oxford: Oxford University Press, 1981).

LM   Elizabeth Gaskell, "The Three Eras of Libby Marsh," vol. 2 in *The Works of Mrs. Gaskell,* 7 vols., ed. A. W. Ward (New York: AMS Press, 1972).

MB   Elizabeth Gaskell, *Mary Barton* (London: Everyman, 1971).

NS   Elizabeth Gaskell, *North and South*, vol. 4 in *The Works of Mrs. Gaskell*, 7 vols., ed. A. W. Ward (New York: AMS Press, 1972).

P   Hannah More, *Percy*, vol. 4 in *The Works of Hannah More*, 18 vols. (London: Cadell and Davies, 1818).

Perils   Charlotte Elizabeth Tonna, *Perils of the Nation: An Appeal to the Legislature, the Clergy, and the Higher and Middle Classes* (London: Seeley, Burnside and Seeley, 1848).

R   Elizabeth Gaskell, *Ruth* (London: Everyman, 1982).

Rom   George Eliot, *Romola*, ed. Andrew Sanders (Harmondsworth: Penguin, 1980).

SL   Elizabeth Gaskell, *Sylvia's Lovers*, ed. Andrew Sanders (Oxford: Oxford University Press, 1982).

WW   Charlotte Elizabeth Tonna, *The Wrongs of Women*, vol. 2 in *The Works of Charlotte Elizabeth Tonna*, 2 vols., intro. H. B. Stowe (New York: M. W. Dodd, 1848).

Part One
The Preachers

Introduction

"Sir, a woman preaching is like a dog walking on its hind
legs. It is not done well; but you are surprised to find it
done at all."

—Dr. Johnson

Britain's lady novelists are our great Evangelists of Reconciliation.

—Reviewer of Elizabeth Gaskell's *Ruth*

Dancing dogs and evangelists of reconciliation—both are
men's anxious descriptions of women who presumed to call
them to repent. Johnson, who could praise Hannah More's
verse and admire the piety of Isaac Watts, dismisses the combination of female speech and spiritual authority as unnatural
and grotesque. Almost a century later, the reviewer of *Ruth* indicates the cultural centrality women preachers had achieved
by 1853, but in so doing attempts to recuperate Gaskell's condemnation of Victorian sexual hypocrisy as "reconciliation"
and construes the prophet as a relatively harmless "evangelist."
Despite the misogynistic resourcefulness of both writers in
devising methods for ridiculing or circumscribing female authority, they testify to women's empowerment in the evangelical tradition. Eighteenth-century evangelicalism fostered the
emergence of female orators and writers of remarkable authority, whose legacy shaped social discourse throughout the
Victorian period and enabled female novelists—most notably
Elizabeth Gaskell and George Eliot—to be recognized as social
critics.

The evangelistic features of nineteenth-century social discourse—its secular adaptations of the sermon form, homiletic
rhetoric, and goal of converting readers from various social
and political sins—have long attracted critics' attention.[1] They
have described authors as prophets and as "Victorian sages."

"progressive," "conservative" vs. "liberal") obscure women's relation to power in a patriarchal society, where collusion has strategic value and where even limited rebellions are often carried out covertly. Women's preaching supplies a context crucial to understanding the development of social discourses by women writers in a society ruled by men.

First, writers in this preaching tradition demonstrate that women are not caught inextricably between the patriarchal rock and hard place: doomed either to internalize the beliefs that oppress them or to become hysterics. Evangelical women's interpretations of scripture offer striking instances of feminist reading. The fact that male writers and readers understood a discourse to legitimate their primacy did not prevent female writers and readers from interpreting the same discourse in a very different fashion and even appropriating its cultural authority for feminist purposes.[5] The fact that women's public speech, including calls for social reform, flourished within the context of a religious discourse suggests that the patriarchal domination of that discourse does not amount to monolithic control. Women's success in manipulating the evangelical idelect offers a prime example of what Elaine Showalter has called the double-voiced discourse of women's writing, where, in this case, explicit theological orthodoxy becomes implicit social rebellion. Following the models of the female preachers, women writers not only seized the opportunities offered them by evangelical teaching and practice to appropriate interpretive and literary authority, but also sought to make their feminized social gospel prevail, calling on male readers to repent.

The paradoxical relationship of female speakers and writers to patriarchal discourse cannot be overemphasized, but whereas in many instances that paradox has been interpreted as collapsing into immasculation, the practices of women preachers offer an example of genuine dialectic and opposition.[6] Undeniably, the myths of ideal womanhood that served to silence women in the eighteenth and nineteenth centuries relied on the authority of Christian teaching.[7] Nancy Armstrong has analyzed this tradition as a primary force in the domestication of women, encouraging female writers only insofar as they constructed female desire in line with the needs of bourgeois patriarchy.[8] Paul could be cited for the most explicit injunction against women's public speech, writing in 1 Timothy "Let the woman learn in silence with all subjection. But I suffer not a woman to teach, nor to usurp authority over the man, but to be in silence" (2:11–12). Paul's teaching on wifely submission is likewise notorious, rendering women as silent, relative creatures. As Thomas Timpson wrote in 1834: "Subjection of the wife to the husband is certainly enjoined in the institutes of Christianity; but this is perfectly rational. For in the ordinary affairs of life, it is indispensably requisite that one should be the representative, and the chief agent. From the natural constitution of woman, it is manifest that she could not take that office; but the injunction by no means argues inferiority of nature or of right, only a different department of occupation and sphere of action."[9]

Women preachers and writers mounted vigorous resistance to domestic ideology on the basis of scripture and evangelical teaching. Scripture could validate myths of ideal domestic womanhood only if its own ideological conflicts were suppressed, for scripture texts might also be adduced in support of sexual, racial, and class equality, and to justify revolution. Leonore Davidoff and Catherine Hall, in their detailed account of religious ideology and the construction of gender roles in the period from 1780 to 1850, formulate the contradiction succinctly: "the crucial distinction was between spiritual equality and social subordination."[10] What I will argue is that, more often than has been acknowledged, evangelical women rejected this distinction, or at least developed rhetorical strategies for eluding its implications. Christian women pointed to the Hebrew judge Deborah, Queen Esther, or Sarah—who laughed at God—as precedents for divinely sanctioned female speech, in opposition to patriarchal authority. Women preachers reminded their enemies that at Pentecost Peter had quoted the prophet Joel, who described an era of special blessing as one in which "thy sons and daughters shall prophesy." Moreover, Paul himself provided the rallying cry for many liberation movements, including early feminism, by exclaiming that in Christ "there is neither Jew nor Greek, there is neither bond nor free, there is neither male nor female" (Gal. 3:28).

These gaps in the scriptural armor of masculine ideology

needed to be concealed by esoteric methods of exegesis, a clerical monopoly on preaching, and limits on the spread of literacy. When evangelicals attacked these deterrents to scripture reading as obstacles to their pentecostal mission to save all souls, regardless of sex, class, or race, they appeared to be clearing the way for future appropriations of scripture for subversive purposes. Eighteenth-century Englishmen well remembered the incendiary role scripture had played in their own civil war, viewing even the Methodists—whom modern historians generally categorize as reactionary—as the heirs of the revolutionary Independents, reviving democratic, antiauthoritarian sentiments along with private scripture study and domestic piety. "It was not surprising that there was a radical wing within Methodism," Bernard Semmel remarks in *The Methodist Revolution*, "for . . . Methodism, despite the Tory sympathies of its founder, was the disseminator of a popular religion with a strongly egalitarian tendency. Its principal characteristics—in the eyes of its enemies—were those which the genteel associated with the lower orders."[11] Evangelical hermeneutics produced an ideology that was in fact contradictory, torn between the ideal of spiritual equality and divinely sanctioned patriarchy, disclosing scripture's vexed representation of authority. The consequences of this paradox were not limited to class but had a profound impact where gender intersects with literary authority.[12]

Evangelicals believed scripture to be radically accessible. Attacking the mystification of scripture that demanded of "legitimate" readers expertise available to a select few, they maintained that God would reveal to babes what he concealed from the wise. Indeed, scripture itself imposed on the individual a duty to attend to that Word, the authority to interpret it, and the duty to spread it—to speak for God. Anglican Evangelicals and Methodists made this argument without abandoning their belief that scripture was the divinely inspired Word of God, and in so doing perpetuated a paradoxical view of discursive authority.

From the women preachers of the eighteenth century to the Victorian novelists who were their heirs, women's writings testify to their ability to recognize the ideological conflicts in scripture that were suppressed in the patriarchal feminine ideal, and to interpret scripture as offering divinely sanctioned challenges to masculine authority. Contradictions within their culture's myth of ideal womanhood were often made apparent to women of the eighteenth and nineteenth centuries through their reading of scripture and application of its egalitarian doctrines to their social and political circumstances. Women adduced scripture in defense of equality between the sexes or for precedents of female political power, interpreted parables as denunciations of women's sexual and economic exploitation, and validated marginalized voices in terms of "spiritual gifts." As the principal catechists of their daughters and, in middle-class families, their female servants, women established their own discursive traditions; they formed communities in which they could entertain the more radical implications of their beliefs and in public they could vilify their critics as "pharisees" and "sinners." Most important, finding in scripture calls to essentially literary vocations as preachers, prophets, and evangelists, women writers could re-envision women's lives and represent them authoritatively. These women were revising and subverting the dominant Christian ideology, and thereby reconstructing social discourse.

With its reliance on scriptural authority, claim to immediate divine inspiration, and dialogic stance towards an audience as potential converts, the evangelical ideolect provided women writers, severely constrained by the discursive limits of propriety, with effective rhetorical tactics in their struggle for access to authoritative language, supplying at once camouflage and firepower. Patricia Meyer Spacks's claims for the conventions of spiritual autobiography are more broadly applicable to uses of the evangelical ideolect, which "declar[es] the writer's total conformity with a religious orthodoxy. Behind the screen of such conformity [s]he may find the freedom to render intimate details of [her] psychic experience, even discovering unexpected meanings for that experience as [s]he fits it into the established mold,"[13] or to promulgate her personal vision of women's talents and rights. The ambiguity of the term "repentance" in women's socioreligious discourse succinctly illustrates my point. Presenting themselves as prophets armed with scriptural authority, women could presume to construct their audience as sinners and define sinfulness in feminist terms: as tyranny over wives and daughters, persecution of "fallen women," or exploitation of female workers. Another sense of a reader's repentance appears in George Eliot's story "Janet's

Repentance." For Janet, repentance means the liberation of her own voice, and represents a rather timid instance of what by 1857 had become a trope in women's writing for other women: confession as vindication. Women preachers sought to convert their enemies from the misogyny Dr. Johnson's notorious remark reveals, but also to liberate the voices of other women, enjoining them to "repent" of their silence.[14]

Thus understood, authorship in no way constituted an unmitigated blessing for otherwise silenced women. Less attractive was the tendency encouraged by the prophetic role to see one's self as merely a passive medium for a divine message, which persisted through George Eliot's claim that her writing expressed her "inner voices." Women preachers referred to themselves as "vessels," "mouths," and "temples" of the Word. Moreover, the legitimacy of the woman preacher's fruits depended on the precarious sanction of the Holy Spirit, who was imagined to have engendered her message. Confident of that sanction, women preachers referred to one another as "Mothers of Israel," charged with the task of calling God's children to repentance. However, without it they became fallen women. Indeed, the Methodist women preachers endured the same *ad feminam* attacks on their chastity and modesty that we associate with writers from Wollstonecraft to Eliot.

Nevertheless, despite the fact that these women described themselves as vessels for the Word, it was of course the woman preacher herself who deployed the most persuasive language in the culture, what Elizabeth Gaskell's character, George Wilson, called "Bible words." While male Romantic writers were developing decidedly masculine metaphors for inspiration and authorship,[15] evangelical symbolism provided women, as well as men, with a means of representing themselves as authors. Margaret Homans, who analyzes the use of these metaphors by various female writers in the nineteenth century, considers women writers' description of themselves as vessels or as bearing the Word to be evidence of all women's essentially passive relation to language.[16] I would agree that this imagery is potentially debilitating, but the evangelists' uses of these images constitute important and influential exceptions. Male as well as female preachers applied this imagery to their authorship, modeling themselves on the Old Testament prophets with whom this language originates. When Mary Bosanquet speaks of herself as "bear[ing] the vessels of the Lord," she is quoting Isaiah 52:11, where the prophet enjoins the Israelites to throw off the yoke of oppression. As a Christian and an evangelist, Bosanquet *bears* the vessels of the Lord (she does not even identify with the vessel); that is, she has inherited the gift and responsibility to prophesy. Further, as I shall argue, women preachers could adopt such imagery to disguise their subversive power rather than to eschew it.

Women preachers wielded this power shrewdly. Not only did scripture provide them with authoritative texts by which to condemn the pharisaical attitudes of their persecutors, but even more important, with texts to liberate women. They exploited the paradoxical foundation of evangelical hermeneutics to appropriate the language of God the Father in order to subvert the authority of their temporal masters. This fruitful but precarious role was the legacy inherited by the female social preachers of the nineteenth century.

The history of women's literary empowerment that follows from this model offers a more nuanced picture of the eighteenth- and nineteenth-century literary landscape by recovering women preachers, like Mary Bosanquet Fletcher, Sarah Crosby, and Joanna Southcott, who were famous among their contemporaries. By establishing female precursors for women writers who have been considered originary, it restores important "links in the chain that bound one generation to the next,"[17] which in turn raises new questions about influence and self-consciousness, inviting reassessments of both "major" and "minor" writers. In selecting authors and texts for this study I attempt to illustrate the literary and political consequences of this revision, necessarily in a preliminary fashion. I have chosen to focus primarily on Methodist women preachers, although some other sects, most notably the Quakers, also had female preachers. In part, that choice was dictated by practical matters. First, a substantial record of their public voices remains—not many sermons, but published writings in genres such as epistles, advice literature, memoirs, and biographies in which literary authority is somewhat effaced. More interesting, however, are their extant private writings—letters and diaries—which provide evidence of women's resistance to and manipulation of domesticating ideologies, often from within the domestic sphere itself. Second, Methodist women preachers attracted large audiences and public attention during their lifetimes, and their reputations survived into the nineteenth century in biographies, and in some histories of Methodism. They include women from the working and middle classes, gathered for the most part around the provincial communities so important in the fiction of More, Tonna, Gaskell, and Eliot. But I have also chosen them because, like their sect, the Methodist women preachers are politically ambiguous. Their public discourse reflected the conflicted ideology of evangelicalism that attempted to embrace democratic ideas while remaining committed to patriarchy. This ambiguous status enabled them to survive patriarchal censorship and contribute to the formation of women's public voices and to the fascinating duplicity of nineteenth-century social criticism by women.

Throughout the period during which women were becoming active as preachers, the discursive conventions of social discourse, its production, and, particularly, what constituted appropriate public speech, were the subject of passionate debate. Members of the ruling class were striving to secure their domination by countering the leveling effects of evangelical linguistic practices with language theories aimed at strengthening political and legal barriers to the speech of the disenfranchised. Olivia Smith cites a trend in linguistic theory from the mid-eighteenth century on, expressed in such influential works as Johnson's *Dictionary* (1755), the first comprehensive grammar of English by Bishop Robert Lowth (1762), and James Harris's *Hermes* (1751), of increasingly vehement hostility to vulgar vernacular language coupled with the attempt to establish a hegemonic English, based on rules derived from Latin that only thinly disguised the class interests of these classically educated men.[18] In the 1790s, members of the House of Commons called on these theories to justify rejecting hundreds of progressive petitions on the grounds that, as William Wilberforce put it in 1793, their writers had failed to "address the House in decent and respectful language."[19]

The political undercurrent that had always been a part of attacks on Methodists' simple (vulgar) language and extension of linguistic authority to vulgar speakers rose to a fever pitch in the decades following the French Revolution. Accusing Methodists and other sectarians of despising learning, sanctioning preaching by laymen, and authorizing the supremacy of individual conscience, the Reverend T. E. Owen wrote in his preface to *Methodism Unmasked, or The Progress of Puritanism*:

> My intention . . . is to prove, by the following Extracts, what I have before asserted, "that Sectarists of all kinds are," (and ever have been, since the time of the Reformation) "either blind instruments, or wilful [sic] tools, in the hands of Anarchists and Atheists," that their aim is not a reform in religion, but a total overthrow of our Religious and Political Constitutions, and a revolution in these dominions, similar to that which has deluged France with blood, and brought upon many millions irreparable ruin.[20]

The task of constructing an impenetrable hegemonic social discourse that denied the authority of political dissent became a point of paramount importance in maintaining national stability. This imperative coincides with the rise of social science and a new clerisy of experts who would likewise attempt to consolidate political and discursive authority.

Ridding social discourse of religious rhetoric and placing it on a solid scientific foundation would appear to have been associated with progressive politics. However, it was not Mary Wollstonecraft or Thomas Paine, but the conservative par excellence, Edmund Burke, who favored disentangling political and religious discourses on the grounds that volatile Christian theology tended to inflame sentiments inappropriate to the calm reason required to settle difficult, abstract questions of political philosophy. By contrast with the conventions of evangelism, which offered a set of authoritative discursive practices accessible to any Christian at least, social science reasserted the elitist barriers to public debate once guarded primarily by the clergy. This new clerisy of experts based its authority on an alleged objectivity and a neutral-seeming foundation of empirical evidence. Their discursive practices, from the arcane laws of political economy to the quasi-religious hierarchies of social statics, identified them for women writers as the new pharisees.

The survival of women's public voices depended on their ability to preserve the alternative constructions of social reality that evangelicalism had first made possible. Women writers from Hannah More to George Eliot insisted on maintaining the connection between religious and social discourses—

casting social problems in spiritual terms, despite ideological contradictions—because Christianity legitimated women's participation in the political debate while secular philosophy sought to exclude them.

A few points should be made about my selection of authors to illustrate the impact of female preaching on women writers of social discourse. Although it may be argued that the precedent of female preaching was on the order of a cultural given for all women writing social fiction in the nineteenth century, I have chosen to focus on four authors in order to discuss their writing with sufficient specificity to notice subtle literary practices. In this way, I hope to suggest strategies for reading other writers in terms of preaching conventions. The group of writers I treat—Hannah More, Charlotte Elizabeth Tonna, Elizabeth Gaskell, and George Eliot—not only indicates the changes and continuities within women's preaching during the nineteenth century, but also represents the diversity of political, religious, and literary opinions accommodated by the tradition. My choice was also made with reference to our literary canon. Some of the reasons that More and Tonna remain in the ranks of "also wrote," while other writers are revived, appear suspect in the light of their roles in adapting the practices of female preachers to social fiction. As for the major writers, Gaskell and Eliot, this recontextualization is crucial to any effort to address the patriarchal misreadings that have characterized criticism of their novels.

Hannah More became a prophet to her nation in a time of extraordinary crisis. Like the women preachers, she identified herself with patriarchal authority, employing many of the preachers' strategies to attain political power in a vigorously reactionary period. Although she is remembered today almost exclusively as a reactionary,[21] More undoubtedly represents the best example in this period of a women writer whose work insinuates subversion while overtly preaching on behalf of the patriarchy. From her early plays through her immensely influential *Cheap Repository Tracts* (1795–98) to her controversial novel, *Coelebs in Search of a Wife* (1809), authoritarian, unitary texts give way to alternative perspectives and marginal voices. More achieved her success not merely through her popular political alliances, which have long been noted, but thanks to literary innovations that stemmed from her evangelical beliefs: insisting on the continuity of private and public virtue against the notion of separate spheres; privileging simple, concrete language over the ornate or abstract; imbuing vulgar dialects with authority; and most important, recognizing the political implications of the diffusion of narrative authority in the novel.

Among the many women writing social-problem fiction in the first three decades of the nineteenth century, Charlotte Elizabeth Tonna (1790–1846) did the most to adapt the women preachers' legacy to the demands of her industrial society and the special problems it posed for women. Tonna situated herself squarely in the tradition of evangelical social writing by women, responding to what she saw as its embattled status with influential literary innovations. She accomplished this by combining evangelical and novelistic techniques to challenge the privileged language of social science that had come to dominate the description of social realities. A direct line of influence can be traced from Hannah More, through Charlotte Elizabeth Tonna, to Elizabeth Gaskell. Tonna, who visited More several times at Cowslip Green in the 1820s, called herself a disciple of the author of the *Cheap Repository Tracts*. In turn, *Helen Fleetwood* (1841), "the first English novel completely devoted to the life of industrial proletarians,"[22] was a major source for Elizabeth Gaskell's first social-problem novel, *Mary Barton* (1848).[23] Thanks to Gaskell's evangelistic mission, the Victorian writers inherited models of social realism.

Elizabeth Gaskell, Harriet Martineau, Charlotte Brontë, and George Eliot were hardly without precedent as female social writers, but they should be seen as quite conscious of both the benefits and handicaps of their status as literary daughters.[24] Considering these writers in the context of the female-dominated preaching tradition rather than in relation to Dickens, Kingsley, or Disraeli, reveals a new landscape of literary history as well as affording a crucial perspective on their conception of authorship, literary strategies, and sense of audience. This recontextualization would yield insights into the career of Charlotte Brontë, who, I believe, undertook *Shirley* reluctantly because she resisted the co-optation as an "evangelist of reconciliation" that the Victorian conventions of female preaching made inevitable, and that of Harriet Martineau, who employed the evangelical ideolect and preacher's role in order to "sanctify" a materialist philosophy. In each case, it reveals an intricate web of subtexts. I have chosen, however, to focus on Elizabeth Gaskell and George Eliot.

The extreme contradictions which have marked literary and political assessments of Gaskell's social fiction stem in part from an ignorance of her response to the preaching tradition. Of the principal female social-problem novelists, Elizabeth Gaskell not only employed the evangelical idiom with great success, appropriating it for feminist goals, but she appears to have internalized the evangelical mission as the informing metaphor in her career as author. That tradition provided her with a vocation—a "higher calling"—that enabled her to loosen the stranglehold of "natural duties." Further, it suggested strategies for subverting the privileged languages that made up social discourse in the 1840s. The languages of statistics, law, economics, and social science dominated that discourse with their alleged objectivity, but Gaskell maintained the priority of the individual spirit over the social law as the authoritative interpreter of reality. She considered her audience to be in need of conversion, finally realizing that misogyny was their most stubborn vice. Though she was originally empowered by the evangelical mission, Gaskell would recognize the irreconcilability of God's law with man's, accepting the role of fallen woman in order to appropriate transcendent authority for a female discourse.

Her *Life of Charlotte Brontë* (1857) might be seen as Gaskell's last attempt to preach to the pharisees on behalf of a sister. Through reading, editing, and incorporating Brontë's personal papers into her own narrative, Gaskell had entered into a conversation with a female-dominated literary community, like that shared among the Methodist women preachers. The "confession" Brontë elicited by this dialogue was of Gaskell's failure to fulfill her evangelistic calling: rather than reconcile women's history with the opinion of "Good men," her duty was to liberate voices men had silenced. *Sylvia's Lovers* (1863) reveals precisely this recognition: "I'm speaking like a women," Sylvia exclaims, "like a women as finds out she's been cheated by men as she trusted, and as has no help for it. It's me as has been wronged, and as has to bear it" (*SL*, pp. 443–44).

In her efforts to liberate the female voice, Elizabeth Gaskell, whose experience of authorship was so thoroughly infused with the vocation and voices of women's preaching, came to discover, as no woman preacher before her, the intractability of a more subtle misogynistic resistance to feminizing social discourse. The woman preacher's jeremiad would always be vulnerable to the same patriarchal interpretations that blunted the egalitarian imperatives of scripture: she would be "cheated by men as she trusted." Eventually convinced of the futility of preaching to the patriarchy, Gaskell would pursue the separatist potential of the evangelical discourse. By appropriating her authority without regard for patriarchal legitimacy, Gaskell took on the subversive voice of the fallen woman—the mother of illegitimate fruit. But all this would occur well into the literary career of an author whose fame had come as a preacher.

George Eliot's position on the "Woman Question" has overtaken her religious beliefs as the topic of greatest interest, and most passionate disagreement, among critics of her fiction. While critics once fought to claim Eliot for their particular theological or philosophical camp, the battle has now shifted to the field of feminist criticism, where her novels spark debates about the very nature of our enterprise. Gillian Beer, in attempting to distance herself from Ellen Moers, Elaine Showalter, and others who have voiced objections to the novels' sexism, ends up restating the grounds for suspecting that criteria of artistic merit are themselves ideologically charged. Having argued that "theories of literature which result in blame for the most creatively achieving of women will raise questions about their own sufficiency," Beer immediately draws attention to the question-begging of this claim with the qualification "though we should also ask questions with a contrary bias about the adequacy of the criteria according to which we judge works of literature."[25] Clearly, the author-idolatry that would forbid critical analyses of a "great novel's" political content is unacceptable, not only because it assumes the possibility of an apolitical aesthetic judgment that renders some novels "great," but particularly, with respect to novels by women, because it implies that the fragile reputation of a female author cannot endure such scrutiny. Furthermore, even with her qualification, Beer maintains a dominant canon intact, merely querying the criteria for admission.

The need for a critical analysis that ties the political vision of George Eliot's novels to the acclaim they have earned her is nowhere more evident than in the intersection of religious beliefs and the Woman Question as it shaped her understanding of authorship and the specific qualities of her fiction. Her novelistic treatments of evangelicalism are legendary, while her particular interest in women preachers has been relegated to the status of one curious fact: the possible model for Dinah Morris. Valentine Cunningham, in his discussion of *Adam Bede*, helps us to go beyond proposing the obvious—but insufficiently examined—model for Dinah, Eliot's Methodist preacher aunt, Elizabeth Evans, to name Mary Bosanquet Fletcher and Sarah Crósby as other famous women preachers who might have influenced Eliot's creation.[26] What remains to be considered is that, as authors and public figures, these women preachers were models for George Eliot herself. Eliot creates the most memorable woman preacher in fiction—Dinah Morris—but by undermining that character, and the preachers Savonarola and Felix Holt, prevents the creation of a better.

Eliot's stance towards Dinah, and the preachers who stand behind her, bears out Sandra Gilbert's contention that, for Eliot, "the terror of the female precursor is not that she is an emblem of power but, rather, that when she achieves her greatest strength, her power becomes self-subverting: in the moment of psychic transformation that is the moment of creativity, the literary mother, even more than the literal one, becomes the 'stern daughter of God,' who paradoxically proclaims her 'allegiance to the law' she herself appears to have violated."[27] Eliot exposes the hierarchical power structure which inheres in the sermon form, setting one voice in authority over all others, claiming omniscience, seeking as its end conversion of its audience from bondage to sin, but achieving instead submission to a kind of Carlylean hero's power over the ignorant imagination.

Yet such power clearly tempted George Eliot. Masked by her critique of sermonizing—the very rhetorical mode that first established Eliot as a "Victorian sage"—is a vital concern with legitimacy. Her own narrators assume the characteristics she attributes to Dinah's sermon. "Out of history itself," U. C. Knoepflmacher asserts, George Eliot "was forced to create in her later novels a power corresponding to the exacting Miltonic God she had rejected."[28] Gilbert argues that the "embedded fantasies of female, and sometimes even matriarchal, autonomy," which she finds in *Romola* and *Middlemarch*, "clearly function as covertly compensatory gestures towards liberation from father-daughter scripts elaborated in works like *Silas Marner*."[29] I would add that, despite her profound attraction to the women preachers' tradition, Eliot, unlike Gaskell, would refuse to risk as a writer the *ad feminam* attacks on the prophet as fallen woman that she endured personally, finally renouncing her female precursors in favor of Feuerbach and Comte to become a preacher of patriarchy—an evangelist of reconciliation. In effect, George Eliot helps to return the woman preacher to the status of "dancing dog," the legacy that literary historians have inherited. Eliot herself, and women for a century before her, had been empowered as authors of the social discourse by a call to "repent" of their own silence. Eliot did not relinquish the task of calling her readers to repentance, but the feminist subtext of that call as it was made in "Janet's Repentance" is increasingly reconciled with the dominant voice of her Feuerbachian narrators, urging her readers to act in silent obedience to historical forces.

The ideological and discursive contradictions that mark the women's preaching tradition eventually collapsed. My account of that tradition, from the eighteenth-century preachers, through Hannah More and Charlotte Elizabeth Tonna, to Elizabeth Gaskell and George Eliot, attempts to explain why those contradictions were so fruitful. In our eagerness to claim the great Victorian women writers as the foremothers of contemporary feminist writing, the temptation has been either to ignore their reactionary tendencies or to express dismay that such talented, forward-looking women all too often merely internalized the benighted attitudes of their age. What I hope to show in this study is that the preacher's role did at one time empower them. This was the crucial contribution evangelical Christianity made to the history of women's writing.

This study is divided into two parts. The first part, devoted to women preachers, is organized according to conceptual headings marking principal features in the model of female literary empowerment I am seeking to describe. To some extent the chapters follow one another chronologically, from the callings of the earliest preachers in the mid-eighteenth century to the early nineteenth-century biographies, written to memorialize women's preaching after it had been outlawed by the Methodist hierarchy. However, many of these stages were played out simultaneously in the lives of various preachers over several generations. In the chapters in part 2 I give particular attention to the beginning of each author's career, assessing the role that a spiritual calling to a literary vocation played in enabling More, Tonna, Gaskell, and Eliot to justify their rejection or revision of women's domestic duties. I also consider the function of male mentors in sanctioning, as well as controlling, women's writing in a manner patterned on the relationship between female preachers and ordained clergymen. In the case of each writer I discuss not only biographical data but, more important, her early writing in terms of the evangelical model of inspiration and authorship developed in part 1. The body of each chapter consists of readings of each writer's major contributions to social discourse in terms of evangelical hermeneutics and rhetoric and their impact on the writer's feminism.

One

"Wise and Holy Women"
The Methodist Women Preachers

Like their sect, the Methodist women preachers are politically ambiguous: revolutionary and progressive in living out their vocation, appropriating their culture's most powerful language to exhort their hearers to repent; strictly conservative in treating that vocation as an extraordinary call, an exception rather than a fundamental challenge to constituted patriarchal authority. Their history is a complicated one in which abject submission might be used to justify remarkable female authority, or radically subversive doctrines be defended in terms of religious duty. As early as the 1760s, preachers such as Mary Bosanquet (Mrs. Fletcher, 1739–1816), Sarah Crosby (1729–1804), and scores of other Methodist women often proclaimed a more subversive message than did their avowedly radical sisters later in the eighteenth century, yet they rarely presented themselves as a special-interest group within their sect, articulating the woman's point of view. They had found within Methodism a patriarchal structure that supplied the means by which its own authority could be exploited by the disenfranchised—it offered the silenced a voice. In taking advantage of that power they refrained from any overt attempt to usurp it. In this ambiguous status lies the reason for their success and, hence, their contribution to the formation of women's public voices in the nineteenth century.

Like John Wesley (1703–91) and George Whitefield (1714–70), women preachers could rationalize their activities by claiming that they sought to revive the established religion, not rebel against it. The two consummate orators began the Methodist movement because they perceived that other Church of England clergy were failing to preach the gospel adequately, neglecting their prophetic and pastoral duties to effect conversions and bring lost sheep into the fold. They were inspired by the same scriptural texts that soon after prompted women to become evangelists. To these reformers, the Anglican church seemed intent on reducing scripture to a static, exclusive discourse. Originally, they did not set up a rival hierarchy that would recreate the power structure of the Anglican church; neither, however, did they deny the apostolic source of clerical power, as many dissenting sects had done. Methodists retained the familiar doctrines and many practices of the established church, and would have remained within it had Methodist preachers not been denied Church of England pulpits.[1] The women who became preachers could apply this logic not only in their dealings with critics of Methodism, but within their own sect. As evangelists, women could be seen as occupying the high moral ground, matching or exceeding their brethren in fulfilling an orthodox duty to bring sinners to repentance, even when they sought their enemies' repentance from misogynistic attitudes.

The source of the women preachers' vexed relation to power, specifically linguistic power, lies in the paradoxical nature of evangelical hermeneutics and practices, the fundamental features of Methodism itself. The scripturally authorized individualism and practical piety that had inspired Puritan zealots to regicide, reemerged as an apparently apolitical spirituality in the writings of such evangelical High Anglican divines as the Reverend William Law. His "Serious Call to a Devout and Holy Life" (1726), the text Samuel Johnson cited as responsible for his conversion and John Wesley considered to have been the seed of Methodism, exhorted its readers to personal scripture study and active evangelism. Law was no incendiary. His advocacy of such activities without reference to their volatility would seem incongruous coming from an ordained clergyman of the established church had it not been for the understanding of scripture on which it was based.

Evangelical hermeneutics, the driving force behind Law's call and Wesley's revival, holds scripture to be divinely inspired—the Word of God. Scripture itself imposes on the in-

dividual a duty to attend to that Word, the authority to interpret it, and the duty to spread it—to speak for God. A
paradoxical view of linguistic authority results, requiring a her-
meneutical miracle of the Holy Spirit, which transcends ordinary epistemological categories by means of faith. As Paul
writes in Corinthians,

> Now we have received, not the spirit of the world,
> but the spirit which is of God; that we might know
> the things that are freely given to us of God. . . .
> But the natural man receiveth not the things of the
> Spirit of God: for they are foolishness unto him:
> neither can he know them, because they are spir-
> itually discerned. But he that is spiritual judgeth all
> things, yet he himself is judged of no man. For who
> hath known the mind of the Lord, that he may in-
> struct him? But we have the mind of Christ. (1 Cor.
> 2:12, 14–16)

This like-mindedness with Christ enables the faithful to transcend the worldly wisdom of sinners, a teaching which could
mean very different things to William Law, believing in the divinely ordained status quo, and to the disenfranchised, discovering their own moral authority as believers. To the former
such a text might suggest a beautifully economic technique for
achieving ideological conformity, to the latter an invitation to
dismiss any authority that conflicts with the individual's spiritual judgment. For women, specifically, it could encourage the
rejection of the foolishness of men, in the name of Christ.

Clearly, such an identification of Christ's will with an individual woman's was made by the eminent preacher Sarah Crosby,
when she wrote to her friend and protégé Frances Mortimer:

> Look up then my Dear, Expect Jesus to Bless you
> *now* with Pardon, Peace, & Love, &c. for the king-
> dom of GOD cometh not with observation; But; we
> *listen* while Heaven Springs up in our Hearts. This
> simple attention to Jesus, to hear Him inly Speak; is
> what you My Dear, want more of: yr mind has been
> too much Dissipated, & drawn from the One thing
> needful, by Reading & attending too much, to the

various opinions of Good men. Now harken to
Jesus: *"this word is Truth"* wch will make you free indeed . . . for the wisdom of this World is foolishness
with GOD. But the word is Truth. O! make use of all
the understanding, & Reason with wch GOD has
blest you, to search the sacred word. Believe the
Promises therein contained, and strive to practice
all the Precepts, & you shall Daily feel by lively Experience, that the Precious word of GOD is *Truth.*[2]

Crosby urges her correspondent to abandon the knowledge of
men and claim for herself the liberating teachings of the Bible:
"*'this word is Truth* wch will make you free.'" This message will
not be mediated by temporal authorities, but will "Spring up in
[the] Hearts" of those who "search the sacred word," bringing
to bear upon it their own "understanding and Reason." The
authority to interpret scriptural "Promises" according to
women's desires would allow them to escape a rigidly defined
female destiny. Most notably Paul, writing to the Galatians,
provides women with the text Mary Wollstonecraft would cite
in *The Rights of Woman*—"in Christ there is neither male nor
female"—guaranteeing their spiritual equality before God.
More important for the history of women's writing, the Spirit
enables women to do as Crosby does here, to appropriate the
language of scripture in order to invest their own speech with
authority.

Women who practiced such methods of exegesis and evangelism were only applying what had been taught them by clergymen like Law and Wesley. The central theme of the Methodist
revival—that the simple gospel message was accessible to all
who read and heard with an open heart—effectively promoted
private scripture interpretation and application, thus granting
to the individual the authority to discern God's will for herself.
Wesley remained enough a high churchman to insist on the importance of traditional guides to scripture study. However, he
may not have foreseen the consequence, that he obligated his
converts to acquire mastery over a greater number of texts
than scripture study alone would have allowed. Indeed, they
were urged to pursue their reading beyond the Bible to commentaries, and finally into texts of general knowledge.

Furthermore, Methodism impressed upon its converts the duty not only to listen but to speak. The very process of evangelism by which women as well as men were converted was ostensibly dialogic in structure: the convert had to respond to the evangelist's message with a confession. Paul describes that process in Romans:

> But what saith it? The word is nigh thee, even in thy mouth, and in thy heart: that is, the word of faith, which we preach; That if thou shalt confess with thy mouth the Lord Jesus, and shalt believe in thine heart that God hath raised him from the dead, thou shalt be saved.
> For with the heart man believeth unto righteousness; and with the mouth confession is made unto salvation. For the scripture saith, Whosoever believeth on him shall not be ashamed. (Rom. 10:8–11)

Confession could mean salvation in more ways than Paul may have anticipated. For the convert whose voice had been silent, whose story had never been told, the confession presented an opportunity for ecstatic self-revelation, and even for self-justification, all expressed in the authoritative language of scripture. As the dramatic and liberating confessions of Elizabeth Gaskell's Ruth, or George Eliot's Hetty Sorrel illustrate, these Victorian writers continued to recognize the potential of evangelical dialogism to empower women's voices. The necessity of confession—to testify to the workings of God's grace in one's life—only began with conversion, imposing on the believer, no matter how inarticulate or marginal, a lifelong duty to "speak the truth that [was] in [her]."

Ordinary intellectual faculties, or institutionally recognized training ("man's wisdom"), did not qualify a believer to give testimony but rather "spiritual gifts." Paul speaks of spiritual gifts in two letters, Romans and Corinthians. As Methodists were quick to point out, he describes them as bestowed on all people by God for the benefit of all (1 Cor. 12:7). One might be gifted as a prophet, another as a minister, teacher, ruler, miracle-worker, helper, healer, one who exhorts or speaks in tongues (Rom. 12:6–8; 1 Cor. 12:28). Whatever the gift, Paul enjoins his readers to exercise it in obedience to God's will for the entire congregation (1 Cor. 12:28). The Holy Spirit bestowed gifts on whomever it willed—including the poor, the uneducated, and women; the vocations such gifts imply empowered the laity of all stations. Among the early Christian leaders, whose mission was primarily evangelical, were a substantial number of women who exercised gifts of prophecy, preaching, and pastoral ministry. Priscilla, Aquila, as well as the Old Testament prophetesses, were oft-cited precedents for Methodist women preachers. This teaching removed a significant obstacle to women's authoritative public speech.

Indeed, as evangelism shifted the emphasis of Christian piety away from sacraments toward language, women might be perceived as possessing superior spiritual gifts. Law argued in "A Serious Call" that "women possessed a *finer sense*, a *readier apprehension*, and *gentler dispositions*" than men.[3] "All which tempers," he claimed, "if they were truly improved by *proper* studies, and *sober* methods of education, would in all probability carry them to greater heights of piety, than are to be found amongst the generality of men."[4] Law believed such reforms would produce a renaissance of female sainthood: "The *Church* has formerly had *eminent saints* in that sex, and it may reasonably be thought, that it is purely owning to their *poor* and *vain* education, that the honour of their sex is for the *most part* confined to *former ages*."[5] The argument for improvements in women's education on evangelical grounds had considerable impact and would later be made by women of such diverse ideologies as Mary Wollstonecraft and Hannah More. Law not only claims that women are educable, but that they are temperamentally better suited to learning Christian truths than are men. Works like Law's contributed to the rising level of literacy among women, and thereby their intellectual empowerment. In light of this fact, women evangelists should not be considered so freakish an aberration as Dr. Johnson's notorious remark might suggest. The origin of their call and the education that enabled them to answer it can be traced back to the same work that converted Johnson. Richardson's Clarissa possesses the virtues as well as the skills requisite for a woman preacher. And Sarah Scott, in *Journey Through All the Stages of Life* (1745), disguises her heroine as an Anglican clergyman and has her preach a charity sermon, brilliant for its unusual sympathy and insight.

At the same time, the institutional authority that upheld the doctrine of spiritual gifts and gave it cultural legitimacy could seek to prescribe what these newly empowered voices were allowed to say. Despite—or perhaps because of—Law's high valuation of women's powers, his formulation is fraught with the rhetoric of control and discipline. It is not surprising that dependent, powerless women would possess "a *finer sense*, a *readier apprehension*, and *gentler dispositions*" to be "improved by *proper* studies, and *sober* methods of education" than men, who might be accustomed to having their own way. Potentially hysterical women should be controlled by sober masters, their energies directed into proper channels. It was not until women answered the call to public ministry, fulfilling the destiny Law predicted for them, to rise "to greater heights of piety, than are to be found amongst the generality of men," that they began to recognize these more subtle and intractable obstacles to their intellectual freedom, and evade them by devising the rhetorical strategies that would eventually produce the remarkable duplicity of nineteenth-century social discourse by women.

Methodism had opened a way for women's linguistic empowerment. The women who took advantage were, for the most part, middle-class, educated, articulate, and well-bred; in many cases they were the daughters, wives, or siblings of Anglican clergymen.[6] As a matter of religious duty, and often with the assistance of clergymen, women set out to claim the intellectual mastery for which they were ripe. In 1790 John Wesley responded to a female convert's request for a program of reading by publishing a "Female Course of Study" in the *Arminian Magazine*. This document reflects the degree of intellectual mastery that had been encouraged in women as a matter of Christian duty. Wesley begins by enjoining his correspondent, a Miss L———, to pursue knowledge of God. Everything one can know of God, he asserts, is to be found in the Bible, and it would be wise to spend "at least two hours every day, in reading and mediating upon" it.[7] However, he then suggests two commentaries: Mr. Henry's ("if you would save yourself the trouble of thinking"), and the "Explanatory Notes" ("if you would only be assisted in thinking").[8] Then follows his rather embarrassed instruction of orphan children, in aiding institutions of benevolence; and while their once gay companions were amusing themselves with parties, or crowding the theatre, these women were found in the house of God, or spending an hour in meetings for social prayer, and religious fellowship."[18] It seems noteworthy that most of the edifying female activities mentioned by Sutcliffe should have involved words—reading, writing, conversing, instructing—activities that would exercise their rhetorical powers.

This represents a significant advance over earlier evangelicals' emphasis on women's education, based on the conviction that evangelism must begin at home, where mothers had the duty to catechize their children. Just over a decade before William Law advocated pious education for women, Daniel Defoe, in his popular *Family Instructor* (1715), had called on parents to become ministers in their own homes.[19] In that work, mothers were depicted leading prayer, directing scripture study, and teaching Christian doctrine to their children. *The Family Instructor* illustrates the importance attached to the mother's religious duties, as well as the ability of young children of either sex to act as "preachers" to their siblings. Leonore Davidoff and Catherine Hall have documented the persistence and elaboration of women's duties as domestic catechists well into the nineteenth century, emphasizing the role such practices played in confining women to the domestic sphere by burdening them with ever greater maternal responsibilities.[20] However, it is important to notice that women frequently extended their activities outside their families, and even eschewed literal maternity altogether for a public ministry by construing "the family" as a spiritual rather than biological structure. Methodists, who encouraged the revival of family prayers and parents' catechezing of their children,[21] and modeled their own worship on these practices, helped pave the way for this move on the part of women preachers.

Susanna Wesley (1669–1742), John's mother, who lived out the ideal described in the *Family Instructor*, must be acknowledged for contributing to women's transition from familial to public ministries. With her clergyman husband away on business, or in debtors' prison, Susanna took charge of her own domestic ministry. When her husband objected to her practices, she wrote the following reply:

As to its looking particular, I grant it does, and so
does almost every thing that is serious, or that may
in any degree advance the glory of God, or the salvation of souls, if it be performed out of a pulpit, or in
the way of common conversation; because in our
corrupt age, the utmost care and diligence have
been used to banish all discourse of God, or spiritual
concerns, out of society; as if religion were never to
appear out of the closet, and we were to be ashamed
of nothing so much as, of professing ourselves to be
Christians.

To your second [objection] I reply, that, as I am a
woman, I am also mistress of a large family. And
though the superior charge of the souls contained
in it lies upon you, as head of the family, and as their
minister, yet in your absence I cannot but look upon
every soul you leave under my care, as a talent committed to me under a trust, by the great Lord of all
the families of heaven and earth; and if I am unfaithful to him or to you, in neglecting to improve
these talents, how shall I answer unto him when he
shall command me to render an account of my stewardship.[22]

Rather than violating her Christian duty, Wesley saw herself
as fulfilling it. Wesley laces her letter with scriptural allusion,
enlisting God in support of her practices. God's ways are not
man's ways, so it should not surprise her husband that the
Lord's work looks "particular" according to secular standards.
Wesley well knows that the implication of being too "ashamed"
to profess Christ means that he will not own us. Further, she
reminds her husband of their family's extraordinary circumstances justifying her ministry: in his absence, duties of domestic piety fall on her. Wesley concludes by citing the parable of
the talents, which was commonly interpreted as referring to
spiritual gifts. Opportunities for evangelism and the power to
evangelize came from God, and could not be ignored without
peril to one's soul.

From the description of her practice, which follows, Wesley's
talents soon came to be exercised on others in addition to her
children.

itual mentor, encouraged her in *"Holy Obedience* to the Divine Commandments," but also in attending class meetings over her mother's objections. On March 2, 1781, Crosby wrote to her dear Miss Mortimer,

> May you ever be strengthened to persevere in the good way; that you may never need the support of *Opinion,* that you can never fall.
>
> Yet I can't advise Dr Miss M to say much abt. it to those you meet with to oblige yr. Mother; nor to *Her* neither: for I believe our Lord will ease you of that trial, when He sees it most for yr. good. but as I suppose Mrs. W.[alton?] and Miss R[itchie?] have no objection to yr. meeting in their class, with out being what is call'd *joined,* I wod. advise you, to take no notice of yr. Mother, but meet with *them* at *all* opportunityes.[27]

Crosby appears to waffle on the question of a mother's authority to control her daughter's religious practices: at first, she dismisses objections as mere worldly wisdom ("opinions"), but then seems to acknowledge Frances's duty to oblige her mother, recommending duplicity as a means of avoiding conflict, and finally reasserts her exhortation that Frances ignore any authority that poses an obstacle to her intercourse with holy women. Interestingly, this dilemma may be more difficult to resolve as it pits one woman's authority against another's.

However, Methodist women had embarked on a course of liberation which they could not easily reverse. In Mary Bosanquet's case, her pious challenge to her father's authority culminated in her exodus from her parents' home.

> One day my father said to me: "There is a particular promise which I require of you; that is, that you will never attempt to make your brothers what you call a Christian." I answered, (looking to the Lord,) "I think, sir, I dare not consent to that." He replied, "Then you force me to put you out of my house." I answered, "Yes, sir, according to your views of things, I acknowledge it; and, if I may but have your approval, no situation will be disagreeable." He

replied, "There are many things in your present situation which must be, I should think, very uncomfortable." This I acknowledged, and added that if he would but say he approved of my removal, I would take a lodging which I had heard of at Mrs. Gold's, in Hoxton-square; but that no suffering could incline me to leave him, except by his free consent. He replied with some emotion, "I do not know that you ever disobliged me willfully in your life, but only in these fancies; and my children shall always have a home in my house."[28]

This exchange illustrates the power evangelical piety could afford a woman in such a struggle. Though Mr. Bosanquet attempts to denigrate his daughter's convictions with such language as "what you call a Christian" and "these fancies," nevertheless he betrays his fear of the threat posed by the ultimate father—God—to the patriarchy he here strives to preserve. In her response, impressively shrewd and thoroughly orthodox, Mary refuses to confine that power to private devotions, retaining the option of extending that influence into the legal and economic heart of the family—its sons. She gets exactly what she wants, and by appearing to acknowledge his will in obeying God's ("if I may have your approval" or "no suffering could incline me to leave him, *except by his free consent*"), secures her father's blessing to boot. She has, in effect, gone over her father's head by "look[ing] to the Lord." Bosanquet escapes to a relatively independent existence, with the timely receipt of a maintenance at her majority. In 1761, at age twenty-two, she was the mistress of her own Spartan lodgings, armed with the confidence that she was doing God's will.

The value of a strategy by which women could secure some liberty without forfeiting patriarchal sanction cannot be underestimated. Young Methodists of both sexes endured persecution from unconverted parents, but daughters were socially and economically more vulnerable than sons, and obtained from their faith the courage and the means to take that greater risk in defying their parents. Her stance as an obedient servant of Christ saved Bosanquet from the exclusion that would normally have followed upon a woman's rebellion against patriarchal authority. The Bosanquets had not demanded her departure; in fact, her father offered her money after she had left home, an offer which she refused. Though temporarily estranged from her family, Bosanquet was spared the additional social and legal ostracism that would have accompanied a break from the established church. She had not set herself up to dispute the wisdom of orthodoxy nor the legitimacy of constituted authority, as a dissenter would have done. Rather, she was obeying orthodox teaching more fully than her family would allow. In so doing Bosanquet enjoyed the patronage and protection of ordained Anglican clergy, including Wesley himself, and of powerful Methodist sympathizers of her own class. The memoirs of many eminent Methodist women relate similar domestic debates. They would be replayed by women writers such as Emily Brontë and George Eliot throughout the nineteenth century.

Having once identified a disjunction between the temporal power that had defined their role as daughters and the divine power that had supposedly ordained that role, women went on to question the validity of other allegedly "natural" duties—specifically those of wife and mother. While they did not reject them outright as mere social conventions, most were careful to exempt themselves by arguing that their devotion to higher duties justified—indeed demanded—their unmarried state. Daughters who had acquired some authority were hardly eager to give up that power to a husband. Among the major women preachers, Sarah Crosby and Sarah Ryan were widowed young and never remarried, Bosanquet and Ritchie married late, and Elizabeth Hurrel, Hannah Ball, Ann Lutton, Mary Tooth, Ann Tripp, and many others remained spinsters. More often than not, they appear to have chosen to remain single, and customarily spoke of marriage as an impediment to their vocations.

As the traditional definitions of feminine essence gave way to the possibilities sanctioned by spiritual gifts, women had literally to reimagine womanhood. What did it mean to be a female minister, teacher, ruler, a miracle-worker, healer, or one who exhorts or speaks in tongues? Not surprisingly, these women, who had already been empowered by scripture, turned to the Bible not only for role models but also for a lexicon of images which describe an analogously disenfranchised people—the Israelites—chosen by God to escape their bondage. While still living under her father's roof, Mary Bosanquet dismissed marriage and motherhood as her appointed destiny with the help of scripture and the encouragement of Sarah Crosby. A conversation with Crosby confirmed the eighteen-year-old Bosanquet in her rejection of a suitor and in her decision to commit herself to God. "I went to meet her [Crosby] in the spirit of prayer and expectation," Bosanquet recorded.

> She simply related what God had done for her soul. The words she spoke were clothed with power, and my convictions of the necessity of holiness were much increased. The affair of the gentlemen was obliterated from my mind; and the prospect of a life wholly devoted to God drank up every other consideration.[29]

A few days later, she wrote the following to Crosby:

> The Lord hath indeed been merciful above all I can ask or think. I am more drawn to prayer. I find a more earnest pursuit of holiness than ever; but what most stirs me up is, I seem to hear the Lord calling to me in these words, "Depart ye, depart ye, go ye out hence, touch not the unclean thing, be clean, ye that bear the vessels of the Lord."[30]

Just as Bosanquet here reimagines herself as a woman, we must reassess the value of any sexual construction of this imagery that would foreclose the possibility of female empowerment. Clearly, linking the obliteration of "the affair of the gentleman" from her mind with the injunction "touch not the unclean thing" suggests Bosanquet's rejection of the phallus. But she does so not in order to eschew power, to become a passive "vessel" of divine will, but because she possesses a superior source of power. The voice that "stirs [her] up" to avoid "the unclean thing" likewise calls her to an active role, to "bear the vessels of the Lord." The distinction between the literal meaning of this phrase, indicating a rejection of heterosexuality and maternity, and its metaphorical significance is crucial. Bosanquet rejects the roles of wife and mother that would reduce her to a literal vessel on the basis of her vocation to bear symbolic "vessels of the Lord." In the chapter from second Isaiah where the writer anticipates the Israelites' departure from the unclean land of their oppressors, he refers to the vessels of the ark, an important locus of cultural power, which the Israelites will carry in triumph back to Palestine.[31] By analogy, Bosanquet describes herself on the brink of liberation from servitude and deliverance to a position of power.

Bosanquet married at age forty-two, after she was already recognized as a Methodist leader, and was (perhaps) past child-bearing age. She formed a preaching partnership with her husband, the Reverend John Fletcher, one of Wesley's most famous preachers, and eventual leader of the Methodist Connexion. Sarah Mallet Boyce, Frances Mortimer Pawson, and Ann Freeman managed similar joint ministries with their husbands. Nevertheless, the mixed blessings of even so congenial a marriage can be detected in Elizabeth Evans's remarks on her own marriage.

> Oh what things occured to distress my mind, those that formerly thought I did wrong in preaching now said I was fighting against God, and the door for usefulness was then wide open. I could not see my way clear to marry, and only eternity can clear up this point to me, however, I am fully persuaded that I could not have had a more suitable companion, as he loved the Lord's blessed work from his heart, and did not only preach himself, but make every way he possibly could for me. Blessed be the Lord I felt the very day I was married as though I married not, I was enabled to pursue my way and at every convenient opportunity to speak in the name of the Lord, I met with very little persecution or opposition when I had a friend to plead my cause, and the word of God broke out and we had most powerful times.[32]

For Dinah Morris in *Adam Bede*, the character George Eliot modeled on her aunt, Elizabeth Evans, marriage coincided with the Methodist Connexion's decision to forbid women's preaching. With historical hindsight, George Eliot saw that marriage might mean silence for the preacher.

Wives, more so than daughters, were at the mercy of masculine authority in a culture that denied them economic independence, and forbade divorce. When Grace Murray converted to Methodism, her husband threatened to have her confined to a madhouse[33]—not an unprecedented male response to female independence.[34] Alexander Murray never made good his threat, for he died at sea shortly thereafter. Grace Murray passed through her trials first as a persecuted wife, and then as a widow, with the help of her Methodist friends, including John Wesley, who appointed her as his housekeeper in Newcastle. He later assigned her the task of organizing classes for female converts in the north of England. But her eventual success was ultimately attributable to the timely death of her husband.

Only when temporal authority could be completely transcended, that is, only when women became men's unqualified equals in the next life, would they be safe from persecution. Ann Tripp, who did not have complete success in warding off unwanted suitors with the Word of God, expressed sentiments familiar to readers of women's writing from Wollstonecraft's to George Eliot's. She closes a letter to Mary Bosanquet describing the troublesome attentions paid her by a married member of one of her classes by exclaiming, "how happy those who are got where men nor devils cannot disturb them."[35] For most Methodist women, such were the first of many experiences with the conflict between what was termed the "natural duties" of their sex and the higher duties to which evangelical teaching appeared to be calling them.

Two

The Community of Women
of the Word

Though not immune from intrusion by uninvited men, Methodist women came closer than many of their contemporaries to creating an autonomous community of women, capable of exerting influence outside their circle. Their solidarity with one another and society's recognition of their mission made this independence possible. Such friendships were especially important to women when their activities expanded beyond the boundaries that described feminine duties. Together these women overcame the anxieties their new public role caused them and encouraged one another to persist in their evangelical mission. Methodist organization was essential to the formation and maintenance of women's communities. Between visits by itinerant preachers, Methodist congregations sustained themselves through small-group meetings which became a formal part of the Methodist structure. These groups were generally segregated by sex. Groups called "classes" were intended primarily for people who had felt a call to repent and reform, but had not yet fully committed themselves to doing so. "Band" was the term applied to groups of more established Christians who had practiced their faith for a longer period of time. Both types generally included hymn singing, prayer, scripture reading, testimony from the members, examination of recent converts, and occasional exhortation by the group's leader. Classes usually met in a member's home and could be especially appealing to unmarried women as surrogate families. Groups like those described by John Lyth, meeting for scripture reading and prayer, solidified contacts between Methodist women.

Bosanquet, Crosby, Ritchie, Pawson, and others, who became the major women preachers, met in Methodist class meetings and continued to have frequent contact, in conversation and by letter, concentrated as they were around the Methodist centers of Leeds, Bristol, and York.

In a culture that looked on displays of learning as prideful, classes and bands were important not only because they brought women together, but because they gave them the opportunity to speak. The male clergy's intellectual and oratorical gifts were honed during their university experiences; for many women, however, the testimony and spontaneous prayer, essential parts of such meetings, were their first experiences with speaking in public on matters of faith. Further, free from male censors, they could explore the implications of their evangelical beliefs on controversial issues of female behavior and power.

In forming their communities, women were able to forge bonds and create social structures that valorized the qualities which masculine culture had denied them. Bosanquet's first contact with Mrs. Downes's (née Furley) circle in the 1750s was formative. Through Downes she met Sarah Crosby, Mary Clark, and Sarah Ryan, who would become her fast friend and assistant when she founded Cross Hall School.

Bosanquet justified her choice of the chronically ill Ryan to be her associate in terms that those familiar with Gaskell's or Eliot's fictional sisterhoods should recognize. Between herself and Ryan Bosanquet believed that

> The Lord had given us to feel that union which even death itself could not dissolve. I have often thought on those words of Solomon, "A faithful friend is the medicine of life; and he that fears the Lord shall find him."[1]

To objections to her choice she answered,

> I did not choose at all. I stood still, saw, and followed the order of God. And if my means had been enlarged in money, and lessened in grace, what should I have gained by that? I acknowledge I neither gained honour, gold, nor indulgence to the

flesh, by uniting myself to a sickly persecuted saint;
but I gained such a spiritual helper as I shall eter-
nally praise God for. Many are the advocates of
friendship. Many will say, with Dr. Young,
"Poor is the friendless master of a world.
A world in purchase for a friend is gain."
But they refute the sacrifice demanded by that
friendship, and forget the following lines:—
"But for whom blossoms this elysian flower?
Can gold gain friendship? Impudence of hope!
As well mere man an angel might beget.
Love, and love only, is the loan for love.
Delusive pride repress—
Nor hope to find a friend, but who hath found
A friend in thee."[2]

Bosanquet explicitly rejects the qualities for which men valued
women: wealth, social standing, comfort, sexual gratification.
She substitutes the model of friendship.

Ideally, power in these friendships would serve to empower
rather than exploit the weaker member. In December 1773,
Frances Mortimer (later Pawson), who had taken steps towards
Methodism, was told by her friend, Mrs. Car, that "the Lord
was preparing [Mortimer] to be a mother in Israel."[3] A few
months later, Sarah Crosby would begin to fulfill that prophecy. Mortimer recorded in her journal for June 19, 1774:

> I met Mrs. Crosby, an eminently pious woman, at
> Leeds, at Mrs. Buckle's; she seemed much inter-
> ested in my welfare, and gave me many instructions,
> and advised me particularly to pray with simplicity,
> and to request the Lord to teach me to come to him
> will all the simplicity of a little child. She desired my
> good, not only on my own account, but with a view to
> the good it would prove to others.[4]

By 1780, Crosby was recommending other women to Miss
Mortimer's care, asking her to take them to class meetings, and
supporting them in their opposition to their parents.[5] Four
years later, Crosby would be addressing Pawson as one Mother
in Israel to another. The influence of such relationships on

later women writers can be seen in the sisterly solidarity between Gaskell's Mrs. Leigh and Susan Palmer, Mary Barton and Esther, or between George Eliot's Dinah Morris and Hetty Sorrel, or Romola and Tessa—fictional sisterhoods that had a utopian appeal to writers who worked largely without the benefit of collegial support from other women.

Bosanquet's Cross Hall, Madeley, became a hub of the Methodist women's community; over the years it was home to Sarah Ryan, Sarah Crosby, Sarah Lawrence, and Mary Tooth, and was frequently visited by Elizabeth Ritchie, Susanna Knapp, and others. Ann Tripp and Elizabeth Ritchie lived together in Leeds, where they ran a shop that helped to support the work of various Methodist women preachers. Wesley's own houses were home to a number of Methodist women, as well. Sarah Ryan, Grace Murray Bennet, Elizabeth Ritchie, and Susanna Knapp each went on to independent ministries after a term as Wesley's housekeeper. These circles of women, then, were veritable Cranfords, whose influence, however, extended well beyond their borders.

Fortunately, some evidence of the intellectual activities of these groups has survived that reveals first their fledgling attempts at public speech, and then the increasingly radical conclusions they drew from scripture, as well as their efforts to develop a dual discourse—one by which they could become the equals of male preachers, but also through which they could convey their beliefs to other women. What can be determined with certainty from these records is that women encouraged one another to engage privately in discussions of doctrine and religious practice, which in public would have been construed as preaching.

Frances Mortimer Pawson, a sort of Boswell in her circle, recorded some of the conversations of the "holy women" who inspired her. Pawson's diary entry for October 3, 1787, offers her response to lively, pious conversation.

> To-day the spirit of prayer rested upon me for two hours, that I might be useful and fill the place Providence had assigned me, with acceptance. My privileges are great, and I feel myself but as a little child compared with those wise and holy women with whom I have the happiness to converse.[6]

tially publishable, and many women seem to have written them with a dual audience in mind. Indeed, among the first Methodist women to gain access to a public forum was Anne Dutton, who assisted George Whitefield in answering his correspondence during the 1730s and 40s, and thus exercised her evangelistic gift as a writer rather than as a preacher.[11] Dutton's career as a Methodist writer to some extent predicts the way in which evangelical women would take up their pens when they were pressed to give up preaching.

From the beginning of her association with Whitefield's Methodists in the 1730s, Dutton considered writing to be her sacred duty. Most of her work was anonymous: she wrote and edited for Whitefield. However, like her Wesleyan Methodist sisters, Dutton relied on the letter to allow her to exercise her oratorical powers publicly, in print. For example, in her *Letter from Mrs. Anne Dutton to the Reverend Mr. G. Whitefield* (1743), Dutton takes the occasion of the preacher's visit to Bristol to publish an indirect exhortation to the faithful, including substantial portions of exegesis:

> *If we say we have no sin* (says the Apostle John) *we Deceive ourselves, and the Truth is not in us* 1 John 1.8. And says the Holy Ghost by *Solomon, There is not a just Man upon Earth that doeth good, and sinneth not,* Eccles. 7.20. . . . *Teaching them, that denying ungodliness and wordly* [sic] *lusts, they should live soberly, righteously, and godly in* this present World, Tit. 2.11, 12. The word *Teaching,* being in the present Tense, denotes the constant Work of Divine Grace upon the Subjects thereof, while they are in the World. The Word *Denying,* denotes the constant Duty, and Business of Christians, so long as they are in this present World. And the Teaching of Grace, to deny ungodliness, and the denying, of the same, both being of equal *Duration* with the stay of Christians in this present World; do necessarily imply the Being, and Solicitations of Ungodliness, and worldly Lusts in their Souls, even so long as they are in the Body, in this present World, To *deny* a Person or Thing, supposes the Being, and Solicitations of that Person or

Thing. So to deny ungodliness and worldly Lusts, suppose the Being, and Solicitations thereof. And as a Christians *Work,* his constant Work, lies in a continual *denying* of ungodliness, and worldly lusts; it must undeniably suppose the Being, and solicitations of Sin, so long as they are in this World. Thus, 2 *Cor. 7.1. Having these Promises (dearly beloved) let us* Cleanse *ourselves from all filthiness of the Flesh and Spirit,* perfecting *Holiness in the Fear of God* Doth necessarily suppose our present *Impurity* and *Imperfection,* both in the Soul and Body, while in this Life.[12]

What sort of letter is this? What begins as an evangelistic plea for the conversion of Bristol's population develops into a theological argument against perfectionism. Her model seems to be the epistles of Paul. By addressing herself to Whitefield, Dutton could assume his protection. And, though she is clearly preaching, Dutton's status remains that of pious female correspondent. Almost a century later, women would continue to employ such oblique techniques to disguise their polemics.

Conscious of this potential for publication, women preachers studded their correspondence with biblical quotations and paraphrases which they used to illustrate or gloss events in their own lives. They frequently quoted hymns and pious poetry, especially that of Edward Young, whom Agnes Bulmer named the favorite of Methodist readers.[13] Sarah Crosby concluded an especially exhortative letter to Frances Mortimer Pawson, "I may surely add, (without ostentation to My Dear Mrs Pawson) the words of our Sweet poet; viz: My Heart is full of Christ, and longs its Glorious Maker to endite."[14] Her parenthetical remark suggests that Crosby felt self-conscious about this literary effect. By contrast, Ann Freeman went so far as to cast her epistles to friends and relatives in heroic couplets. After her death, her husband published a number of these letters with Freeman's memoirs.[15] However, their letters reveal that most women preachers spoke most freely and forcefully in what Gaskell's character George Wilson called "Bible language."[16]

Wesley carried on extensive correspondences with Crosby, Bosanquet, Ritchie, and, later, Susanna Knapp. Ritchie and

Knapp spoke of Wesley as their "father," Wesley called Knapp "Sukie" in his correspondence, and a number of Ritchie's, Bosanquet's and other women's letters, as well as Wesley's encouraging and sometimes affectionate responses, were published in the *Arminian Magazine* in the 1780s and 90s. His exchanges with Crosby were so frequent that Mrs. Wesley broke into his desk, stole his papers, and warned him to stop writing to her. He did not. Wesley might be seen as an honorary member of this community of women, and up to a point acted as its advocate in public. Yet, despite Wesley's support of his female converts, correspondence with him offered a meager chance to gain access to a public forum. Rather, women's voices would emerge most significantly in an oral tradition.

Three

Mothers in Israel:
Preachers in the Patriarchy

The call to evangelize enabled women preachers successfully to challenge the male monopoly on moral and religious power. As Mary Bosanquet had done in her own family, they refused to confine themselves to addressing other women and children, and sought to evangelize the patriarchy itself. Great crowds of both men and women thronged to hear women preachers, and many people were converted by them. Bosanquet recorded as many as two thousand attending one of her meetings at Huddersfield. Elizabeth Evans had dramatic success in her gallows ministry and among Yorkshire villagers.[1] Mary Barritt, a highly successful and active traveling evangelist, awed the Methodist hierarchy with the conversions effected by her preaching. Direct results were crucial to women preachers, and Wesley considered the fruits of their labors the surest confirmation of their calling. After hearing Barritt speak, William Seagar, a pillar of the Connexion, told the Reverend Lancelot Harrison, "It is at the peril of your soul that you meddle with Mary Barritt; God is with her—fruit is appearing wherever she goes."[2] As evangelists, women attained recognition from the patriarchy as "Mothers in Israel."

However, the term "Mothers in Israel" when applied to women in the public sphere, or more precisely a patriarchal "Israel" as opposed to a community of women, suggests the way in which their authority might be circumscribed. Rather than identifying women as a group with the Israelites seeking liberation from political oppression, Mothers of Israel might find themselves preaching on behalf of the patriarchy, at least insofar as they acknowledged the extraordinary nature of their activities and thereby reaffirmed women's subservience to male authority.

Indeed, the course of many women preachers' careers through the ranks of the Methodist sect reveals the compromises that made their success possible. The similarity between the activities of a class leader, the first position of authority in which women were officially sanctioned, and the duties of patriarchally defined motherhood facilitated men's acceptance of female class leaders and bolstered the leaders' confidence. But these women understood that the similarity was in fact deceptive. They had invoked the term "Mother in Israel" when remarking on one another's astonishing power, associating themselves with such leaders as the judge Deborah, who was not a mother at all, with Sarah, who laughed at God, and with prophetesses. The political, moral, and religious influence of such women differed considerably from the influence a virtually enslaved wife had over her children. Yet in its ambiguity, the term "Mother of Israel" provided women with a useful image with which to ease their entry into a public ministry.

In their move from mothers in the house to Mothers in Israel, then, women might gain power within the patriarchal organization of Methodism because they did not overtly contest its authority. At the same time, women did not abandon the important female discourse they had established but used that base to create a subversive discourse in which they sought feminist aims as well. Slowly, a dual discourse would emerge from these strategies: one, a jeremiad calling the patriarchy to repentance, the other a dialogue among women in an atmosphere of linguistic separatism. That latter dialogue demanded that women behave ever more shrewdly to mask their activities from male censorship. Methodist evangelical practice proved useful in effecting the former: the immediacy of testimony afforded women direct access to an audience, making their speech much more difficult to censor even in mixed company; the eloquence and sincerity of women's testimony forced the hierarchy to recognize their spiritual gift as evangelists, leading to their assignment as class leaders and, eventually, to the sanctioning of women as itinerant preachers. What had begun as testimony to God's work in the life of an individual became prophecy of God's will for the community.

Not surprisingly, women preachers' diaries reveal that some approached their new opportunities for a public ministry with a combination of excitement and fear. Grace Bennet remarked several times on her hesitation to speak. In the following passage, she seems at once to blame herself, her company, Christian teaching, and Satan for her silence.

> We are bidden to be swift to hear and slow to *Speik*—but sometimes we forget our ears go into our Tongues as the philosopher said—I have been blamed for not speaking much in Company—I may be blameworthy I cannot say—but I must confess—some speeking so much have laid an Embargo upon my to which has been the cause of my not speaking what I ought—perhaps Satan may have hindered too.[3]

Despite Bennet's ambivalence about her obligation to testify, one thing is clear: others of the company were sufficiently enthusiastic to prevent this more reserved member from getting a word in edgewise. Mary Hewett, a Quaker who had converted to Methodism, noted in her journal both her call and the anxiety it caused her.

> I believe, at that period, I received a commission to testify to my fellow creatures what God had done for my soul. . . . After many combats with the enemy and struggles with my own heart; I gave an exhortation at a prayer meeting, at Daw's-Green, on the 7th of the 3rd mo. 1824; about which time, the Lord was pleased to deepen his work with me. . . .[4]

As their oratorical gifts became evident, Susanna Wesley's son John found women to be ideally suited to the role of class leader because this role appeared consistent both with the natural duties of their sex and the evangelical mission of Methodism. The class meeting closely resembled domestic conversation, and though the exchanges between a leader and class members were governed by the meeting's goals, they nonetheless were intimate dialogues on edifying topics as one might find recommended in *The Family Instructor*. The leader's role in classes and bands was that of pastoral counselor, questioning members about the state of their consciences and their progress in the struggle against sinfulness. The leader could admonish, encourage, and exhort. Women who might never have imagined themselves as preachers emerged naturally as class and band leaders. That role simply required them to transfer to the public sphere activities that they or other women were already performing in their homes. Women's gifts as teachers, pastors, and preachers were revealed in the class setting. Agnes Bulmer wrote of Methodist classes that "their principle [was] founded in the sympathies of human nature, and recognized throughout the oracles of God. Social feelings [were] thus enlisted into the service of religion; the more difficult and abstract ministrations of the pulpit [were] brought down to special states and circumstances."[5] Recognition of a spiritual gift caused many women to consider speaking a duty, and assignment to class leadership commonly forced them to overcome any misgivings they may have had about their public voices.

The calling described in the journals of Sibyl Best, Sarah Cox, and Sarah Mallet reveals its ability to empower the most timid or reluctant woman. Sibyl Best made the connection between obedience to the Holy Spirit's call and her own salvation.

> When I found the impression of God's spirit, urging me to preach the Gospel, my heart was ready to sink within me. O how did I struggle with my own weakness. But at last I was as clear of my call by the spirit of God, as I was of my own conversion, that *I must preach or perish*. And glory be to his holy name, he did bless my weak endeavours.[6]

Paraphrasing her diary, Zechariah Taft elaborates on Cox's call.

> How she reasoned in her mind against it, and for a long season resisted the powerful leadings and convictions of the Holy Spirit to this duty, till she found there was a necessity laid upon her, and a woe unto her if she obeyed not. This was a conversation in

season, and one sister finding that she durst no longer delay least [sic] she should endanger her own salvation, she attempted to "preach the unsearchable riches of Christ." When first she stood before a congregation, she dared not to look them in the face, and when she repaired to the place of preaching, she generally did it as secretly as possible; but she looked to the Lord and he saved her from the native timidity of her heart.[7]

Taft stresses that Cox was motivated not by impudence but by obedience, which required her to answer the divine call. Though he does not mention precedents for her situation, Taft might have chosen Moses ("I *am* not eloquent . . . but I *am* slow of speech, and of a slow tongue," Ex. 4:10), or Jeremiah ("I am in derision daily, every one mocketh me. . . . But *his word* was in my heart as a burning fire shut up in my bones, and I was weary with forbearing, and I could not *stay*," Jer. 20:7,8).

The evangelical calling became so commonly accepted as a means for sympathetic male preachers to deal with the problem of women preachers, that when Elizabeth Evans experienced her call in the 1790s, she attributed it to the Reverend Mr. Bramwell.

> *Mr. Bramwell observed in his sermon, "why are there not more Women Preachers? because they are not faithful to their call."* I concluded if ever the Lord called me I would be faithful; and almost immediately *I felt it my duty to call sinners to repentance.* . . . I felt assured that if I did not preach I never could be happy, for I was sensible it was the will of God.[8]

As Mothers in Israel, women saw it as their duty to call their sinful nation to repentance. The evangelical call provided women with an acceptable image of authorship, figuring them as God's chosen representatives, rather than as impudent radicals. However, the popularity of the reluctant prophet strategy also forced perfectly able and confident women to cite an anxiety attack as a validation of their calling. Sarah Mallet's behavior during the illnesses which eventually confirmed her in her calling offers an extreme example of this problem. As an

adolescent, Mallet was subject to seizures in which she halluci-
nated that she was before a congregation, and therefore
preached, though she appeared to witnesses to be "utterly
senseless." Wesley met with her at Long Stratton in 1786, and
was impressed with the sincerity of her call. On October 27,
1787, Joseph Harper gave her a permit to preach "' by order of
Mr. Wesley and the Conference.'"[9] By this time, Mallet's
preaching style had become more orthodox—indeed too orthodox. "My way of preaching from the first is to take a text
and divide it, and speak from the different heads. For many
years, when we had but few chapels in this country, I preached
in the open air and in barns and wagons," she recorded in her
memoirs.[10] Despite the fact that the activity she now described
corresponds exactly with Wesley's definition of preaching, to
which the "grand objection" applied, it was Mallet's virtual
possession which continued to elicit sympathetic attention.
Although other women did not manifest Mallet's physical
behavior, they did recognize the value of such charism in con-
vincing Wesley and other Methodist leaders of their sincerity.
Zechariah Taft believed that the irresistibility of the Spirit's call
was among the most powerful arguments to be made on behalf
of women's preaching.[11] Most of Taft's biographical sketches
include the woman's struggle with her prophetic call, and her
eventual surrender to the will of God.

Further, not only a woman's calling, it was implied, but also
the very substance of her message came from God. This was a
mixed blessing. It helped legitimate that message, but it might
encourage women preachers to present themselves as passive
mediums for a divine message. Ann Gilbert, for example,
spoke of herself as an "instrument" "constrained" to call sinners to repentance.

> I would have done and suffered anything on their
> account if I might have been the instrument of their
> conversion. I have poured out my soul both in pub-
> lic and private on their behalf. In the year 1771
> going one day to preaching in the adjoining village,
> the preacher happened not to come; I therefore
> gave out a hymn and went to prayer according to my
> usual custom; I then told the people they need not

be disappointed, for the Lord was present to bless them. Immediately I received such a manifestation of the love and power of God that I was *constrained* to entreat and beseech them to repent and turn to the Lord. All the people were melted into tears, and many were convinced of sin.[12]

Gilbert clearly meant to imply that God was present first to her, and then through her; her words were inspired prophecy. Sarah Crosby likewise considered herself a channel for divine grace. After meeting a band, she recorded on Sunday, May 1, 1768:

Full of faith and expectation, I met the band, Jesus made me his mouth unto the people, and poured the spirit of love, zeal and wisdom upon me, for their instruction. In the last prayer, he so abundantly revealed his glory to the eye of my faith, as melted soul before him and them; they caught the holy flame, while tears of love overflowed my eyes. Oh! The great, the glorious love, wherewith the Father himself loveth us! A taste causeth my soul to melt in desire and love before him.[13]

Over forty years later, Susanna Knapp echoed Crosby:

I think this evening I can set my witness as to the truth of those words, "I will pour out my spirit upon all flesh, and your sons and daughters shall prophesy." Glory be to the Lord! I have found the Spirit of God with me while at prayer with the little company. Surely I have felt something of what it is to be a temple of God, and to have God take up His abode with me. Glory, glory be to the triune God for ever and ever! Amen.[14]

Crosby's metonomy ("a mouth") and the imagery used by all three women describe a distinctive model of authorship, resembling closely only that of Blake among their contemporaries. The woman orator is neither mirror nor lamp, to borrow Abrams's terms, but medium. These women are filled as vessels; the spirit is poured out on them; their message overflows.

Though the similarity to Wordsworth's "spontaneous overflow of powerful emotion" seems inescapable, it is important to notice that the inspiration does not well up from within, as in the masculine Romantic model. Instead, its source is wholly other: words burst forth as wine from a flask that is filled too full; or, as a sort of birth of divinely engendered progeny. In this very important sense, these childless women bore fruit. Like Mary they gave birth to the Word.[15]

Eventually the trials of Old Testament prophets and New Testament evangelists helped women to explain their own self-doubts and persecutions by their enemies. Jeremiah, Moses, and Paul each had a profound sense of his unworthiness, and each knew rejection. But these trials finally confirmed their calling; they were called to suffer for the Word of God. The journals and letters of women preachers abound in reflections on their own weakness and persecution. To withstand such difficulties could become a source of strength and confirm that God was their inspiration and defense. Mary Bosanquet, who experienced her calling in a dream,[16] confronted almost constant challenges to her call and anxiety about it. She was frequently ridiculed, sometimes threatened with violence, and often stricken with fear when speaking in public. Her memoirs (May 28, 1774), make clear that she saw her preaching as a test of her faith.

> This day I set apart for prayer, to inquire of the Lord, why I am so held in bondage about speaking in public. It cannot be expressed what I suffer—it is known only to God what trials I go through in that respect. Lord, give me more humility, and then I shall not care for anything but thee! There are a variety of reasons why it is such a cross. The other day one told me "He was sure I must be an impudent woman; no modest woman, he was sure, could proceed thus." Ah! how glad would nature be to find out—Thou, Lord, doest [sic] not require it! Mr. William Bramah observed today, "The reason why your witness is not more clear, is because you do not glorify God by believing, and more freely declaring what he hath done for your soul." He spake much of these words, "What things so ever ye ask in prayer,

believe that ye receive them, and ye shall have them." His words came with power, and my soul got a farther hold on Jesus. I do see that by his death he hath purchased perfect salvation for *all who believe* and that we receive it in proportion as we thus believe. "Be it unto you according to your faith," is the word of the Lord. Then I will, I do cast my whole soul on thee! O let me find *salvation as walls and bulwarks!*[17]

Here weakness becomes strength—"Lord give me more humility"—just as it did for Jeremiah and Paul. Unlike these male precursors, however, women preachers suffered *ad feminam* attacks on their chastity, and in order to overcome anxieties caused by accusations that she was an impudent, immodest woman, Bosanquet recalled the words of a preacher who exhorted her to speak not less, but more freely.

The evangelical calling proved a mixed blessing. It enabled women to establish their talents before men as well as women, forcing many powerful Methodist clergy to admit their remarkable, and often superior abilities to evangelize. But they also forfeited the luxury of a wholly private female discourse, not susceptible to male criticism. Fearful of such criticism, women themselves, whose classes had grown into sizable congregations, were the first to express concern that in addressing their classes they violated Paul's injunction against women preaching, or "gave offense." As Paul was the source for the liberating teaching of spiritual gifts, he likewise was responsible for a very troublesome restriction on the exercise of one gift by one sex. "I suffer not a woman to teach," Paul writes, "nor to usurp authority over the man, but to be in silence" (1 Tim. 2:12). This text was the locus of bitter debate and the source of painful anxiety among Methodists. Grace Walton sought Wesley's advice when outsiders began walking into her class meetings, apparently desiring instruction. She feared that Wesley might disapprove of her speaking, since her addresses increasingly resembled preaching. Wesley advised her on September 8, 1761:

> If a few persons come in when you are meeting, either enlarge four or five minutes on the question you had, with a short exhortation (perhaps five or

six minutes, sing and pray). I think, and always, its meaning is this: "I suffer not a woman to teach in a congregation, nor thereby to assert authority over the man. . . God has invested with this perogative [sic]. . . . "[18]

In February of the same year, Wesley had offered Sarah Crosby an escape from the Pauline injunction cited to Grace Walton. When a group asked her to preach, she should "say 'you lay me under a great difficulty; The Methodists do not allow women preachers; neither do I take upon me any such character. But I will just nakedly tell you what is in my heart.' This will obviate in a great measure the grand objection. . . . "[19]

Elizabeth Ritchie, among the earliest women class leaders, felt some anxiety about fulfilling her duties. So too did Mary Lyth who, in 1828, after having had considerable experience as a class leader, continued to suffer from doubts.

> As I went to meet my class it was suggested, as it was also the last time, "who hath required this at your hand?" Is it from the enemy? or am I in a wrong position? The people seem to prosper, and the Lord gives me liberty among them; but often has a cloud gathered over my spirit when I have been going to meet them. O Lord, remove my doubts, and guide me by Thy counsel. I wish to sink into Thy will; use me or lay me aside; only let Thy will be done.[20]

In the decade that followed, Wesley tried various strategies to avoid making a clear decision on the issue, thereby setting important precedents for subverting the enemies of women's public speech. Given that the "grand objection" applied only to women preaching, Wesley strove to define preaching as narrowly as possible. Wesley took preaching to mean a very specific rhetorical form: taking a scripture text, dividing it, and speaking on its various heads.[21] He distinguished it from leading prayer, giving testimony, expounding, and even exhorting, thereby preserving for women a considerable variety of rhetorical powers.

Nevertheless, by overtly denying them the authority to interpret scripture, Wesley, who had encouraged women's speech by undermining the patriarchal control of authoritative language, placed women in a double bind. Lay preachers of both sexes worried about the self-expression required by testimony. Was it inspired by God or Satan? Was it orthodox? Was it edifying? Was one guilty of enthusiasm? These anxieties could be alleviated by grounding testimony or prayer in scripture. But Wesley severely limited women's privilege of invoking scripture to guarantee the veracity and value of their testimony. In order to overcome this dilemma and legitimate their preaching—and their appropriation of scripture—women preachers had to emphasize their spiritual gift at the expense of their own talents, characterizing themselves as passive mediums rather than self-conscious polemicists. The impact of these strategies would be felt long into the next century and be reflected in women writers' sense of vocation, choice of genre, and most significantly, in the voices they would adopt.

Four

Speaking in Tongues:
The Rhetoric of the Women Preachers

Like the apostles at Pentecost, women preachers had been called out into the world, where in a sense they too confronted people of diverse languages. "The world" was a patriarchally constituted linguistic community in which women's speech was foreign and threatening. Indeed, as Dr. Johnson's comparison of a woman preaching to a dog walking on its hind legs indicates, men might find a woman preaching to be grotesque and incomprehensible. To achieve their remarkable success in this sphere, women had to accomplish for themselves the miracle of Pentecost, whereby the Spirit had enabled people to understand a language that was not their own. Scripture itself proved the most effective language with which to overcome the misogynist's spiritual deafness and bring him to repentance. Women preachers had to choose their ethos, modes of rhetoric, and genres strategically in order to appropriate scripture to exhort their fallen brethren. After all, a woman's preaching style was evidence not only of how she perceived her role (preacher, teacher, prophet, etc.), but of the state of her soul and her relationship to God. What I wish to consider in this chapter are the "tongues" in which women preached to the patriarchy.

The two principal discursive strategies adopted by women preachers to address their patriarchal audience were the ethos of prophecy and the ethos of simplicity. The preacher could modulate between the emphatic and oracular at one extreme, the earnest and childlike at the other. She had to sound sincere, but not enthusiastic; simple, but not uninspired. These voices reflect the complicated relation of women's oratory to the literary tradition. Prophecy generally implies an authoritarian, exclusionary discourse, the prophet's unequivocal condemnation of the sins of the age and demand for reform. Paradoxically, women assumed prophetic authority to call for the liberation of silenced voices. George Eliot, with her range of authorial stances, would continue to struggle with the same contradiction.[1] Simplicity and sincerity of language (the revival's legacy to the Romantics) and the related concern with realism (the inheritance it bequeathed to the Victorian novelists) had heightened significance for women preachers as they challenged the authority of "experts" to construct reality. In 1848, in *Mary Barton*, Elizabeth Gaskell would still be denying any expertise in Political Economy and urging her simple desire to "write truthfully" as ample qualification to represent "the idea [she had] formed of the state of feeling among too many of the factory-people in Manchester."

By assuming the role of prophet, women preachers came closest to achieving the same authority in public to employ scripture that they had enjoyed among other women. The role had obvious attractions for women. Their claim to a prophetic gift was certainly more easily defended than that of preaching, and afforded them a great deal of freedom. Paul's injunction against women preaching did not clearly pertain to their prophesying; indeed, scripture not only offered precedents, but it even spoke of women's prophetic gift as a sign of God's blessing.[2] The promise in Joel (2:28), quoted by Peter in his Pentecost sermon (Acts 2:17), was one of the scripture passages often adduced in defenses of women's preaching: "and thy sons and *daughters* shall prophesy." Scripture recorded the prophetic gifts of Deborah, Pricilla, Anna, and Huldah. Moreover, the voice of the prophet manifested the divine origin of its inspiration in profoundly powerful oracular, exhortative rhetoric, releasing women from the confines of decorous feminine speech. Despite the enabling possibilities of prophecy, it also could undermine a woman preacher, figuring her as a passive medium for a divine message, often requiring her to fabricate a crisis that called for a prophetess, laying her open to charges of enthusiasm. Yet, not until the role had gained for many women extraordinary moral and rhetorical power, did they discover that they were vulnerable as prophets too.

Ironically, it was the demand for simplicity, potentially a constraint on women's prophetic voice that lay at the heart of Methodism's original evangelical mission, which proved useful. God revealed himself directly and plainly in scripture and in believers' lives, hence, the most effective means of evangelizing was to repeat the gospel truth in the simplest terms possible. The austere beauty of plain-style homiletics was the result. All Methodist preachers would have understood that they were to avoid obscuring God's message with rhetorical embellishments; women preachers would also have wished to avoid the appearance of attracting attention to themselves as speakers. Crosby certainly took to heart Wesley's advice to "speak nakedly what [was] in [her] heart," and passed it on to Frances Mortimer. Time and again, Crosby reminds Mortimer to be simple as a child in understanding and expression. "I believe My Dr. Fr. does admire simplicity in Others," she wrote on June 17, 1780.

> & *I* May Say, *you* are *Simple* in communicating your Mind; but the way of Simple Faith or looking to Jesus, & casting yr. helpless Soul upon Him who only is able to help you, as yet you have not learn'd, as I cod. wish you had. . . . Pray Him to simplify, & Breath His Spirit into yr. Soul.[3]

This ethos of simplicity could be enabling as well as confining. It might force women to present themselves as childlike, or helpless. However, simplicity of language, implying clarity and distinctness of ideas to the male descendants of Locke, might also mean something quite different to women, whose speech had been marginalized as vulgar, ignorant, originating in the heart rather than the head. First, it privileged speech that was not mediated by "the wisdom of men," but came directly from a woman's mind, thereby allowing a woman to be the sole judge of her own authority to interpret scripture. Second, it validated modes of speech other than the male elite's as appropriate for expressions of the divine word. Both the rhetoric of prophecy and the rhetoric of simplicity came to dominate social-problem writing by women.

By combining the ethos of prophecy and the ethos of simplicity women preachers succeeded in appropriating the powerful language of scripture in order to bring about repentance. Frances Mortimer described Crosby's use of these voices for public prayer in this way:

> She used to begin prayer with the simplicity of a little child, and then rise to the language of a mother of Israel. Thus she prayed with the Spirit and with the understanding.

Mortimer's description, aligning simplicity with the Spirit and prophecy with the understanding, reveals the shrewd logic of the preachers' strategy: simplicity would confer on their speech and authority of divine inspiration and prophecy the moral authority of a judge, like Deborah.

The exact nature of the preachers' voices must, for the most part, be inferred from their journal accounts, from letters, and from strictures on their practices, since very few examples of their preaching were ever published. An example of Crosby's ecstatic preaching voice can be found in a letter she wrote to Mortimer on January 6, 1775:

> Beare with me My Dear Miss Mortimer for out of the *abundance* of the Heart, the mouth will speak and my Precious Lord has with the New Year, given me a New degree of His Love. His light shines upon my *Path*, & His Love flows in to my *Heart* and if I shd. not *Praise Him*, the stones might well cry out. But I will Praise my Maker while I've Bredth, &e. Glory, Glory be to His dear name forever!

Crosby reiterates the account of inspiration we have seen before: the gifts of the Spirit demand her praise. *Humilitas* enables her confident application to her own emphatic speech of Luke 19:40, where Jesus defends his disciples' rejoicing, saying "if these should hold their peace, the stones would immediately cry out." Her style, imitating the emphases and cadences of the spoken word, provides us with a sample of the preaching voice of one of the Methodists' most successful women preachers.[4] One can infer from this passage what Mortimer described as language of a Mother of Israel.

Wesley's warnings to Crosby indicate that she was no more restrained in her public speech, and that other women surpassed her power. As early as 1769, Wesley had written to Sarah Crosby, citing the unfortunate example of a woman who had failed to heed his warning:

> I advise you, as I did Grace Walton formerly, (1) Pray in private or public as much as you can. (2) Even in public prayer you may properly enough intermix *short exhortations* with prayer; but keep as far from what is called preaching as you can: therefore never take a text; never speak in a continued discourse without some break, about four or five minutes. Tell the people, "We shall have another *prayer-meeting* at such a time and place." If Hannah Harrison had followed these few directions, she might have been as useful now as ever.[5]

This stricture testifies to the oratorical power women were exercising in public. Wesley may have hoped to distract Crosby from exhorting her immediate audience by directing her to pray to God instead, but women preachers simply turned public prayer into indirect exhortations. As Frances Mortimer's description quoted above indicates, Crosby took full advantage of public prayer. Anne Cutler, too, found an outlet in charismatic prayer. "I cannot be happy unless I cry for sinners. . . . I see the world going to destruction, and I am burdened till I pour out my soul to God for them."[6] Clearly, the content of her passionate prayer included a denunciation of the behaviors that were leading the world to destruction, and a plea that God bring the sinners in her audience to repentance.

Wesley's advice that Crosby keep her exhortations short suggests that women preachers had given him cause to disrupt their extended, coherent arguments. She is to avoid the authoritative language of preaching, and never take a text. That is, announce a scripture text and proceed to interpret it. Of course, that injunction did not preclude quotation, as we have seen, an equally effective method of appropriating scripture.

As a last resort, Wesley alludes to the ill-fated preaching career of Hannah Harrison, whose defiance of the hierarchy's restriction brought about a suppression so severe that no record of her activities has survived.

Wesley might attempt to tone down female voices if they could not be silenced, but he was not to expect much cooperation from women. Though it was clearly impossible for a John Wesley or a George Whitefield to address crowds at decorous conversational pitch, nevertheless, Wesley warned women field preachers to confine themselves to acceptable feminine tones. Wesley urged Crosby to avoid "shrieking." We know that many women failed to restrain themselves, because they recorded in their journals justifications for raising their voices. Her profound need to pray overcame, in Anne Cutler's mind, the accusation that she spoke too loudly. "I have tried to pray differently, but am always less confident. I would do anything to please if it did not hurt my own soul; but I am in this way the most free from wanderings, and have the greatest confidence."[7]

By deceptive choices of nomenclature, genre, and audience, women eluded threats against their preaching. Bosanquet records a rather testy defense of her method of handling these problems. When detractors ask

> "Why do you not give out, I am to preach? Why call it a meeting?" I answer, Because that suits my design best. First, it is less ostentatious. Secondly, It leaves me at liberty to speak more or less, as I feel myself led. Thirdly, It gives less offence to those who watch for it. . . . Besides, I do nothing but what Mr. Wesley approves.[8]

Recall, this is the same woman who, forty years earlier, had secured the blessings of the father she was defying. Her claim to Wesley's approval was strictly true; she had manipulated his restrictions to her benefit.

For Margaret Davidson, posture as well as nomenclature offered protection. An Irish preacher, whose testimony was made especially impressive by her blindness,[9] Davidson recorded in her memoirs that she would never "presume to stand up as an exhorter, lest any should take occasion to say that I assumed the character of a preacher, which would hurt the cause of God."[10]

Some women limited their speaking to genres approved by Wesley. Alice Cambridge, among the first women to preach in Ireland, preferred engaging her listeners in dialogues, "draw[ing] inferences from their own catechism and from the hymns with which they were affected."[11] Elizabeth Ritchie was also known for her evangelism in small class meetings.

Women whose classes and prayer meetings had awakened a sense of vocation justified their preaching by citing the range of unfortunates, from orphans to their unredeemed peers, who made up their audiences. Grace Bennet, who had originally been so reluctant to speak in classes, confessed a strong desire to evangelize the unsaved:

> how was my Heart affected with seeing the Club walk at Chapel to day—to see so many Souls and perhaps not one of them knows the Lord that bought them—I could have gone into the midst of them to call them to repentance—had much to do with myself not to do it O poor souls perish for want of knowledge. Some may say ought women to preach—I answer—if there is no man that knows the way to salvation ought a woman suffer souls to perish?
>
> I think not—yet I should think it my bound and Duty to cry aloud. if this is vile—I wode be vile Still—If I could pluck sinners from Hell—I know God wode approve of it.[12]

Bennet here reiterates Susanna Wesley's argument that stewardship imposed upon her a duty to speak.

Early in her career, Bosanquet had avoided the "grand objection" to women's preaching by confining her audience to women and children. "From the time I was seventeen," she wrote in her memoirs, "some drawing toward the care of children dwelt on my mind. I felt the same desire now as at that time to become in every sense a servant to the Church."[13] This tack guaranteed she had complete independence: "We determined, however, to take none but destitute orphans that no one might interrupt our plan of education."[14] Bosanquet began by educating orphans, and soon found herself an itinerant preacher. Wesley referred to the dependents Bosanquet housed and instructed as her "family." Hannah Ball also became famous for her ministry to children, founding many Sunday schools.[15] Though she also preached to sailors and prisoners, she mentioned instructing only children in her memoirs.

As their success suggests, Crosby, Bosanquet, Barritt, and others had created powerful voices, which temporarily, at least, secured their place among the Methodists. Recognizing the fruits of their preaching, Wesley formulated a characteristically Methodistical resolution to the women-preacher issue. Writing to Sarah Crosby in 1777, Wesley reasoned, "The difference between us and the Quakers in this respect is manifest. They flatly deny the rule itself, although it stands clear in the Bible [1 Tim. 2:12]. We allow the rule, only we believe that it admits of some exceptions."[16] By positing an extraordinary call, Wesley hoped to be able to maintain strict scriptural conservatism while sanctioning the dangerously progressive practice of women preaching. Crosby, Bosanquet, and others concurred in this strangely antifeminist sanction of their right as women. Women as a class were to remain silent.

This delicate balance could not last. Mary Bosanquet, for example, claimed that her extraordinary call justified her extraordinary behavior.[17] Bosanquet's reputation as an evangelist to orphans and widows brought her to the attention of Methodist congregations, and she regularly attracted large crowds to her "preaching house" at Madeley. Whatever she may have called her activity there, it quite clearly fit Wesley's definition of preaching. Looking back on her long career, Bosanquet (then Mrs. Fletcher) described her practice to Mary Barritt Taft in a letter dated November 28, 1803.

> When I was in Yorkshire, for near fourteen years, I went about a good deal, and had many meetings both there and in other parts. The same also after I came hither [Madeley]; but *now* my breath is very short, and, many complaints render me unable to travel; I therefore feel the Lord leads me to apply to what little I can do in my own preaching room,

> where the congregation increases, and many come
> from far, and I am, through mercy, at present car-
> ried through six or seven meetings in a week, of dif-
> ferent sorts. For some years, I was often led to speak
> from a text, of late I feel greater approbation in
> what we can *expounding*, taking a part or whole of a
> chapter, and speaking on it. . . . My Sally's [Ryan]
> usual way was to read some pious author, and stop
> and apply it as the Lord gave her utterance. But ev-
> eryone must follow their own order and the Lord
> hath promised "I will instruct thee in the way
> though shalt go."[18]

Inspired by activities such as Bosanquet describes, women
preachers beginning their ministries in the 1780s became increasingly unwilling to conform to Wesley's restrictions. Soon
they would begin to feminize social discourse.

Five

Publishing the Word

Even more than public speaking, publishing their writing marked women preachers' entry into male-dominated social discourses, crucial if actual women were to have any place in men's history, or, more important, if they were to produce their own history. Yet publication placed women preachers in a double bind between satisfying the demands of a patriarchal censor with immediate control over their writing and the needs of a wider female readership that could be reached and converted by publishing the Word. For the Methodist women preachers that meant, among other things, that they had to convince the Methodist clergy who controlled the sect's presses to publish their work. That these women ever penetrated the solidly male-controlled domain of Methodist publishing, and continued to do so even after they were banished from preaching, testifies to their own sophistication in manipulating the evangelical idiom. At the same time, women preachers tried to maintain the same intimate, dialogic relationship with their readers that they had formed with their converts. Their writings, therefore, most often took the form of epistles or dialogues addressed to other women. These publications and their histories offer remarkable examples of women's interaction with masculine authority and manipulation of patriarchal ideology.

Though later women writers could more easily avail themselves of a powerful prophetic voice, women preachers had limited opportunity to display their oratorical skills in print. Their controversial status would have excluded such writings from consideration by many conservative Methodist editors and printers. Consequently, few overtly polemical works by women were published. Those of which there is any record at all are now extremely rare. Significantly, such works as Sarah Cox's *Plea for Religion*, and Francis Pawson's *Letters on Relative Duties*[1] are not included in the collection of the Methodist Archives. By strategic choice of genre, audience, and rhetoric, these women could convince a sympathetic publisher to accept their writings. That is, in order to get their writings into print, women preachers often employed the same techniques they had used to secure an audience for their preaching.

Pawson mentions this project of her later years, *Letters on Relative Duties*, in her journal entry for February 14, 1807. Her pamphlets were addressed to her friend Mrs. Reece, and distributed in the preaching circuits. As the title of Pawson's work suggests, the letter, unlike the sermon, was an acceptable genre for women writers. It was associated with a private rather than a public discourse; it implied that its author was responding to a request—engaging in a dialogue—rather than presuming to speak without invitation. The letter writer could select her audience quite carefully by addressing herself to a woman friend, a sympathetic clergyman, or women generally, thereby escaping the attention of some critics and avoiding the appearance of engaging in polemics. However, as with the Pauline epistles, letters could convey an authoritative message. Many examples of such subterfuge have survived.

Spiritual Letters, a collection of Hester Ann Rogers's edifying correspondence, was published in 1803, and sold in the Methodist preaching houses in Ireland.[2] Like Crosby, Rogers saw correspondence as an opportunity to evangelize, filling many letters with exhortations and scriptural allusions, and developing others into full-fledged sermons with a text, divisio, and powerful rhetoric. Rogers transformed the gestures of ordinary correspondence between friends into an occasion to preach. Encouraging a depressed friend, she wrote:

> this, I say, is a time to take the advice of God, by his prophet:—*Who is among you that feareth the Lord, that obeyeth the voice of his servant, that walketh in darkness and hath no light? Let him trust in the name of the Lord, and stay upon his God.*[3]

This is a prime example of a woman writer's appropriation of privileged language in an intimate discourse, recommending "the advice of God" as if he were a personal friend.

Mary Bosanquet employed a similar strategy in her pamphlet *Jesus, Altogether Lovely: or a Letter to some of the Single Women in the Methodist Society* (1766). In this work, essentially a sermon on the text "Blessed are the pure in heart, for they shall see God,"[4] Bosanquet urged women to consider renouncing marriage and devoting themselves wholly to God's service. She recognized that her message might offend some of her readers, yet hoped for an audience fit though few. "It is not my business to please," Bosanquet wrote,

> I am only to do all I can for your souls, simply commiting it to that God, whose I am, and whom I desire in all things to obey. I here apply myself to those, whose desire it is, to care only *how they may please the Lord*; and for that reason, make it their cry day and night, that they may be preserved from every snare, and singly live to Jesus.[5]

In a world where women's purpose was "to please" men, Bosanquet issues her readers a remarkable challenge to please the Lord instead. "Singly" here equates singleheartedness with the unmarried state in which women answer only to the authority of the Lord. Bosanquet then confesses to her sympathetic—and chosen—audience the pleasure they can expect from singlehearted devotion to Jesus.

> To *you*, who are able to receive this saying, I will speak the inmost sentiments of my heart. Whatever others are, *you* are called to the glorious privileges of a single life, O cast them not behind you; nor, having beheld the beauties of the lovely Jesus, now forget, that he is fairer than the sons of men. I shall not attempt to enumerate the particular advantages of your situations: I am not persuading you to it; I need not. All your soul stretches itself out, after the entire devotion to him, whom having *seen* you love; and your heart bounds within you while you say to every presenting object
> A nobler Lord for mine I claim,

plied to Dinah's ministry in *Adam Bede*, for that ministry is intended to bring about the same liberation of women's voices Bosanquet enjoyed as a preacher addressing other females. In *Jesus Altogether Lovely*, quoted above, Bosanquet had written "To *you* . . . I will speak the inmost sentiments of my heart." Here, too, she wishes other women to discover their own voices in confession. This is precisely the service of verbal empowerment Dinah performs for Hetty, and all female evangelists for their audiences. Female evangelists merely needed an occasion to expand their efforts outside their religious circles and begin the task of reforming the notion of duty for the entire society. As their activities intensified through the 1780s and 90s, so did those of their opponents.

From the first, opponents of women's preaching sought to suppress records of their activities and successes if they could not forbid the practice itself. Zechariah Taft, in the Preface to volume 1 of *Biographical Sketches of the Lives and Public Ministry of Various Holy Women* (1825), wrote that

> A great deal of pains has been taken to preserve in printed records, some account of the labours and success of those *men*, whom God has honoured by putting them into the ministry; while many *females*, whose praise was in all the churches while they lived, have been suffered to drop into oblivion, and their pre-eminent labours, and success in the conversion of souls to remain as destitute of any public record as though they had never existed; or if any account of their exemplary piety is preserved, their public labours are either suppressed or passed over in silence. It is very easy to account for this, the great majority of Biographers and Editors of Magazines are enemies to females preaching, so that we have very little concerning their labours.[10]

Wesley's letters and journals make clear that while he would sanction women's preaching, every available subterfuge was to be enlisted to disguise that fact from the less tolerant. As we have seen, he was especially careful to call their preaching anything—prayer, exhortation, amplification, testimony—but what it was, and counseled them to do likewise. Under such circumstances he was unlikely to encourage published evidence of his leniency under the heading "Sermon." The few polemical writings by these women appeared as open letters frequently addressed to other women,[11] a technique which allowed them to avoid censorship by those opposed to women's preaching.

After Wesley's death, the attack on women preachers began in earnest. Provoked by the successful preaching of Alice Cambridge and Mrs. George Brown to the soldiers and their families in the barracks at Charles Fort, Ireland, the Conference of 1802 debated the question of women preaching. The result was a resolution "that it is contrary both to Scripture and prudence that women should preach or exhort in public."[12] As a deterrent to further disobedience, the Conference decided to exclude from Methodist meetings all women who continued to preach.[13] This is the step which curtailed Dinah Morris's preaching in *Adam Bede*. But the likes of Alice Cambridge were unwilling to abandon their call so easily. As Taft put it, "many, very many [women] . . . suffered a *martyrdom* of conflicting passions, arising from a *sense of their duty to God* on the one hand, *and of opposition from men* on the other."[14] Elizabeth Hurrell, for one, succumbed to the Connexion, and never overcame the sense that she had betrayed her calling. As a young woman, Hurrell had been sanctioned by Wesley and preached with great success. Zechariah Taft commented on Hurrell that "she possessed a wonderful ability of conveying her ideas and feelings with scriptural accuracy, and often manifested such strength of thought and felicity of expression as were irresistibly impressive." As an old woman in her final illness, Hurrell wrote, "O that I but had my time to live again, I would not bury my talent as I have done."[15] Without their champion, John Wesley, the women no longer had access to power, and an ever dwindling number took up the cross when Bosanquet's generation died.

Shortly after the deaths of the first generation of women preachers, their memoirs and biographies began to appear. Such publications were numerous, encouraged as they were by the Puritan practice of spiritual autobiography and the hagiographic biography adopted by the Methodists. However, they are not always the best records of women's preaching activity. They tend to be formulaic, following the pattern and employing the terminology of the Pauline spiritual journey (conviction, repentance, conversion, justification, and sanctification), and lack description of events not pertaining directly to the progress of the soul. What is more, this biographical material is affected by the controversy among Methodists over women's preaching. The reliability of a woman's memoirs or biography depends on the editor's or biographer's opinion of women's preaching. Any manuscripts a woman preacher left behind were at the mercy of friends and relatives, of editors, biographers, and publishers. If any among this group were hostile to women's preaching, that aspect of her life simply disappeared. Their treatment in the *Arminian Magazine* (later the *Methodist Magazine*), provides a barometer of one official Methodist attitude towards women preachers. The *Arminian Magazine* was never especially explicit about the practices of such preachers. Yet, while Wesley was alive, the magazine reprinted letters to him by Bosanquet, Ritchie, and others, in which they reported on the success of Methodist evangelism in their area and asked for advice for their own ministries.[16] Occasionally a writer would refer to some innocuous example of a woman preaching, as in the obituary of the pious Ann Brooks, who, when a child at school, was said to have "turn[ed] preacher to her little companions."[17] Women preachers lost their most influential advocate when John Wesley died in 1791. Among his successors, who also controlled the Methodist presses and periodicals, women found no comparable champion.[18] As editor of the *Methodist Magazine*, Jabez Bunting expressed his disapproval of such practice by omitting any mention of a woman's preaching activity from her obituary.[19]

Cases of suppression abound. Letters and brief biographical accounts are all that survive of Sarah Crosby, who, along with Mary Bosanquet Fletcher, was the most prominent woman preacher of the revival. Zechariah Taft, husband of the preacher Mary Barritt, and champion of women's preaching, remarked with regret in his biographical sketch of Crosby that, although she left behind a memoir of over three hundred pages, the only account of her life had been a brief article in the *Methodist Magazine*.[20] The letters of Crosby's close friend Ann Tripp, to whom she had bequeathed her manuscript, gives some indication of its fate.

Crosby died in November 1804. On June 13, 1805, Ann Tripp wrote to Mrs. Fletcher that she did "indeed expect a trial respecting [their] Deceased Friends papers."

> May the 6. I recd a letter from Mrs. Mor[timer] informing me "she & Mr Benson had read the first experience and thought it should be shortened, which could not be done without copying, that he had desired her to take out of the diary small paragraphs expressive of the state of her mind, & that I must draw up an account of the closing scene: & he would insert it in the Magazines: that he would do all in his power to let me have any of the original papers (she sent him after with a pencil) back again." I wrote my mind pretty freely upon it & have heard nothing since; But I can do nothing but commit the whole to GOD.[21]

Taft claimed in his 1828 sketch of Crosby that she clearly had meant her memoirs for publication. He quotes from them, but his encyclopedic project could scarcely do justice to a three-hundred-page manuscript. It has never been published.[22] Fortunately, Sarah Crosby's prominence and activities are preserved in correspondence, especially that of John Wesley.[23]

Mary Bosanquet Fletcher took precautions to protect her own manuscripts after her death. She had witnessed Joseph Benson's handling of Sarah Crosby's writings, and had encountered his editorial practices firsthand when she approached him about the publication of one of her late husband's manuscripts. From Benson's letters to Fletcher it is clear that he took liberties with the Reverend Fletcher's text on the grounds that he was making it more orthodox.[24] Publication was delayed not only by Benson's "editing" but by his preparation of his own continuation of the Reverend Fletcher's work. Mary Fletcher stood by helplessly during more than a decade of Benson's machinations, having turned the sole copy of her husband's manuscript over to the editor. In order to protect her own memoirs from such abuse, she left them to Mary Tooth, her friend and assistant, with specific instructions regarding their publication. Fletcher correctly anticipated the pressure Benson would put on Tooth to relinquish her manuscripts, and the pledges Tooth had made to Fletcher provided Tooth with a defense against Benson. When Benson began losing patience with the intractable Miss Tooth, he wrote her the following letter.

> I do not in the least doubt your being influenced by integrity & faithfulness, according to your views of the engagement Mrs Fletcher laid you under. Nor am I very desirous of being the Editor of the Manuscripts She has left, or of having any concern in correcting them & preparing them for the press, having more work upon my hands every day than I can well get through. Knowing her very incorrect manner of writing I shd. indeed be sorry if they got out into th world in a state that would not do her credit; but I hope that will not be the case. As to our sending a preacher, or any other person as far as Madeley upon the business of examining these writings, the expense of the journey would be too great to think of our doing a thing of that kind. But could you not venture to send them by coach, or by some of the preachers from your Circuit (coming next July to the Conference here) to Mrs. Mortimer, where I could see them. Certainly I would engage not to alter any thing, unless some mis-spelling, or some grammatical error, without your knowledge & counsel. If this do not meet with your approbation, perhaps, I could prevail on a preacher in whose judgment I trust Dudley, or some other neighbouring circuit, & give them a reading. I hope the Lord will direct you in this, & all things.[25]

From the thinly disguised coercion of this letter, Tooth undoubtedly perceived Benson meant trouble. Tooth held out against Benson, and in a letter dated April 15, 1816, politely informed him that he need not trouble himself further as she had found a more trustworthy clergyman, a Mr. Waddy, who had agreed to see Fletcher's manuscript into print.[26]

Tooth's brief account of Fletcher's final days was one of the first biographies of a woman preacher. She cast it in the form of *A Letter to the Loving and Beloved People of the Parish of Madeley*. The purpose of this "letter," Tooth began by explaining, was to comfort Fletcher's flock at Madeley in their loss, and satisfy the curiosity she assumed they would have had concerning her death. Tooth proceeded to recount Fletcher's last meeting with her Madeley congregation. The Reverend Melville, who was officiating, was called away early to conduct a funeral, leaving Fletcher to finish the service. Fletcher was prepared for this opportunity, and Tooth, as biographer, could reproduce Fletcher's last sermon, her own eulogy. After offering a general prayer for her congregation, Fletcher continued:

> I will speak freely; since I have been preparing this place, these words of our Lord have repeatedly come into mind, "With desire have I desired to eat this passover with you before I suffer." This has caused me sometimes to think, does my Lord intend shortly to remove me to himself? Be that as it may, I have a confidence that this place will be continued to your use for some years to come, and that the Lord will bless you therein. And now I have two petitions to ask you, which I think you will not deny me. My dear friends, my first petition is, that you would consider this day as a fresh convenanting with the Lord to be his without reserve, and that we may with one consent unite in a solemn vow never to draw back. My second request is, that when I am laid silent in the grave, (which, be it sooner or later, most of you will probably see,) I ask you at *that Time* to remember the transaction of this day, and whensoever you pass by this place, grant me a moment's thought. . . . I will tell you what it shall be. On the first sabbath in July, 1788, beneath that roof I covenanted to be the Lord's; then pause a moment, and say, "Thy vows are upon me, O God, I have opened my mouth unto the Lord, and cannot draw back."[27]

Thus, Tooth's letter not only provides a record of her friend's final days, but helps to ensure that Fletcher's vocation and her very words would be "grant[ed] . . . a moment's thought" by posterity.

Perhaps owing to Mary Tooth's tenacity, Mary Bosanquet Fletcher is the best known of the Methodist women preachers.

She has been the subject of three full-length biographies (one of which was read by George Eliot),[28] and figures prominently in various collections of biographical sketches. She is the only Methodist woman to have been included among the church-women in Samuel Burder's *Memoirs of Eminently Pious Women* (1815). Henry Moore's *Life of Mrs. Mary Fletcher* (1818), which reproduced substantial portions of her memoirs, including frank discussion of her ministry, was reprinted twenty times in the nineteenth century. Yet Fletcher's story might have been silenced as was Crosby's had Tooth not found a sympathetic clergyman who would agree to see it into print. For most other women preachers, Taft's *Biographical Sketches of the Lives and Public Ministry of Various Holy Women* (1825, 1828), which includes sketches of seventy-eight women preachers, provides the only surviving record of their activities and gives us a sense of the magnitude of our loss.

The importance of such biographies to their authors' careers is illustrated by the case of Agnes Bulmer (1775–1836). In an obituary notice of October 1840, the *Wesleyan Magazine* remembered Bulmer primarily as the biographer of Elizabeth Ritchie Mortimer. The obituary writer failed to mention Mortimer's prominence as a preacher, but also notes only one other publication of Bulmer's: the fourteen-thousand-line poem *Messiah's Kingdom* (1833). Annie Keeling's chapter on Bulmer in *Eminent Methodist Women* (1899) is one of the few recognitions from the Methodist community of Bulmer's literary and intellectual accomplishments.[29] Keeling, in a chapter entitled "A Christian Poetess," notes *Messiah's Kingdom* as well as Bulmer's contribution to the Methodist hymnbook ("Thou who hast in Zion laid/The true foundation stone"), her three volumes of *Scripture Histories*, her *History of David* and her contributions to the *Wesleyan Methodist Magazine* itself.[30] She also describes Bulmer's interest in philosophy, history, and theology. Given the experience of many early Methodist women, Bulmer might not have been surprised that her reputation depended for so long on the biography of Mortimer.

Like Gaskell's biography of Charlotte Brontë, *The Memoirs of Mrs. Mortimer* provides a key to the biographer's understanding of her own vocation as an author, as well as her anxieties about it. Bulmer, who had married at seventeen, devoted considerable attention in the *Memoirs* to the compatibility of Mortimer's evangelistic vocation with her domestic duties. She argues that the qualities of "wisdom, piety, and prudence,"[31] which had made Elizabeth Ritchie a "ministering angel,"[32] proved suitable for her new role as Mrs. Mortimer. But Bulmer also implicitly sanctions Ritchie's resistance to marriage by reproducing from her journal Ritchie's argument that it was an impediment to the liberty necessary for the pursuit of her evangelistic mission.[33] In the relatively unobtrusive manner of an editor of memoirs, Bulmer could defend the legitimacy of a woman's call to evangelistic—or to literary—vocations.

In 1866, Edith Rowley would proclaim in her biography of Susanna Knapp that

> When as yet a formal agency that should follow the order of the Son of Man, and first seek that it might afterwards save the lost, was unknown; when from highways, and hedges, and streets, and lanes, the poor, and maimed, and halt, and blind were not gathered; and the souls that should have seen the gospel's great light, were left to stumble in the darkness; a company of women, whose hearts God had touched, assembled themselves . . . to devise means for this species of evangelism in the city of Worchester.[34]

But for all the bravado of Rowley's claim, it betrays a defeat for women's voices in the religious sphere. The great philanthropic projects begun by women were, by 1866, largely administered by men. And the women preachers personally responsible for so much early evangelism had been driven from the community which had inspired them. Rowley, belated herself, performs the secondary role of biographer and historian of a diminished tradition rather than prophesying within a vital movement.

Women preachers caused anxiety for men like Bunting and Benson because the source of their power lay at the heart of Methodism. The very teachings that the Methodists strove to revive inspired and justified women's preaching: the importance of personal conversion and public testimony, of studying the Bible to discern God's will, of conforming one's life to scripture rather than the opinions of the world, of applying one's talents to the services of God. Women preachers were orthodox Christians and loyal Methodists with considerable talents who, like Bunting or Benson, had simply answered Wesley's call. Their stance as prophets enabled them to occupy this precarious position, conferring scriptural orthodoxy on what for women was most extraordinary rhetorical power. Such contemporaries as Hannah More and Sarah Trimmer transferred the woman preacher's voice into print and adopted her subversive strategies to penetrate dominant social discourses and become prophets of reform.

Though it provided women preachers' opponents with a deadly weapon, the Methodists' insistence on the authority of scripture must be seen as ultimately beneficial to the heirs of their tradition. By undermining scriptural authority to admit women preachers, the Quakers had reduced preaching to pure charism, robbing the preacher of her role as interpreter of a divinely inspired text. Acceptance under these terms would have proven more costly to women than was an "extraordinary call," or even their exclusion from the Methodist Connexion. While they were preaching, Methodist women were interpreters of scripture, and not merely passive mouthpieces for God's message. The influence of their simple and sincere preaching style, presenting scripture truths in terms of personal experience and in intimate language rather than impersonal abstractions, survived in the dialect of Hannah More's homely tales, the humble exhortations of Tonna's character, Helen Fleetwood, or in the "Bible language" spoken not only by Gaskell's characters, but often most movingly by her narrator. All these voices, in the tradition of the women preachers, are enhanced by the authority of the sacred text. Further, with the voice of a Mother of Israel, the eighteenth-century women preachers had enjoined their congregations to repent not only of those behaviors which prevented them from accepting God but also of those beliefs which prevented women from fulfilling their higher duties as prophets to their nation.

Part Two
The Writers

Introduction

The women writers treated in the second part of this study adopted evangelical discursive conventions and the constructions of author and audience provided by evangelical teaching to meet social and literary crises, which had their most pronounced impact on the groups traditionally drawn to evangelicalism: women and the poor. Hannah More, Charlotte Elizabeth Tonna, Elizabeth Gaskell, and George Eliot each understood those threats differently—indeed sometimes in conflicting ways—their views shaped by different historical circumstances and political agendas. Writing in the wake of the French Revolution, More found in the preaching tradition a culturally sanctioned position as a prophet denouncing atheism and regicide, while at the same time it enabled her to insinuate arguments in favor of women's education and moral superiority and to castigate her betters for their impiety. Conversely, Elizabeth Gaskell, a reform-minded Unitarian, recognized the authority accorded the preacher's role to challenge the politics of social pseudo-sciences, such as political economy. Furthermore, she used evangelical rhetoric to identify herself, as well as her middle-class readers, with the oppressed and outcasts—most notably, fallen women.

What these major writers of nineteenth-century social discourse share is a resistance to intellectual, political, and aesthetic movements that devalued or colonized women's experiences and expressions by confining them to an ostensibly depoliticized domestic sphere. On essentially evangelical grounds, they could insist on the interconnections between all aspects of human experience, bound together as a spiritual whole. English reformers of the Romantic school, especially Thomas Carlyle and S. T. Coleridge, espoused a similar organicism,[1] but saw no contradiction in exiling women to the domestic sphere. Unlike their male counterparts, then, women writers who attacked Utilitarianism and Political Economy as theories which dismissed social relations based on moral obligation in favor of market laws, or sheer expediency, were also defending women's right to any place at all in the public sphere and their own authority as social critics. Likewise, the traditional evangelical assault on authoritarian clerical rule provided these women writers with a rhetoric to condemn any new priesthood— secular or sacred—that barred women's access to moral authority. From More's attacks on the new Parnassus of the French Rationalists, to Tonna's anti-Papist bigotry, to Gaskell's and Eliot's critiques of the legal establishment, one finds a consistent thread of feminist resistance. In diverse ways, they saw their role as prophets calling the wayward proponents of a masculine hegemony back into the fold; to accomplish their readers' repentance.

The preaching tradition of nineteenth-century social discourse by women, as I see it, responds to three broadly defined phenomena: the male hegemony of Romantic aesthetics; the professionalization of "wisdom writing" through such developments as secular "sage discourse" and authoritative social-scientific discourses; and the stratification of English society along gender and class lines exacerbated by the industrial revolution. My analyses of More, Tonna, Gaskell, and George Eliot use the terms of the preaching tradition to account in a gender-conscious way for characteristics long associated with Victorian social-problem fiction in general, specifically realism, apocalyptic prophecy, and social reform modeled on individual spiritual conversion.[2] Furthermore, they interrogate and reassess qualities often noticed in such writing by women, including the paradox of female paternalism, double-voiced narratives, the author's guise as passive medium, and above all, the writing's often vexed feminism.[3]

The gender-exclusive and colonizing tendencies of Romantic aesthetics have been analyzed by Sandra Gilbert, Susan Gubar, Margaret Homans, and Alan Richardson, among others.[4] Constructions of authorship based on male sexuality—literary paternity, oedipal struggles between authors, inspiration located in the female muse or a feminized nature—have long been used to bar women from literary authority. In the early decades of the nineteenth century, male poets of the Romantic school reasserted a phallocentric version of inspiration and metaphors of expression that evangelical discourse, as used by both male and female preachers, had helped to erode. Reading M. H. Abrams's classic study of Romantic poetics, *The Mirror and the Lamp,* with attention to gender produces a catalogue of phallocentric images of literary creation:

> Schlegel in 1801: "The word expression is very strikingly chosen for this: the inner is pressed out as though by a force alien to us."
> Wordsworth in 1802: "poetry is the spontaneous overflow of powerful feelings."
> Byron in 1813: poetry "is the lava of the imagination whose eruption prevents an earthquake."[5]

Sandra Gilbert and Susan Gubar's arresting question, "Is the pen a metaphorical penis?" was not asked in the context of nineteenth-century poetics for nothing.

Wordsworth, Byron, Shelley, and their contemporaries were equally keen to appropriate motherhood, turning against women the evangelical model of inspiration as bearing the Word. The secularized and androcentric version of this model—the passive Aeolian harp, for example—was inaccessible to women writers. Female receptivity to the essentially pagan spirit of "intellectual beauty" or "the deep power of joy" was literalized in an inherently sexual relationship that positioned the woman writer as whore. What is more, any hint of a female creative power—be it feminized Nature, or actual mothers—could simply be elided from the entire creative process, as Wordsworth does in the *Intimations* ode:

> Earth fills her lap with pleasures of her own;
> Yearnings she hath in her own natural kind,
> And, even with something of a Mother's mind,
>   And no unworthy aim,
> The homely Nurse doth all she can

> To make her foster child, her Inmate Man,
>   Forget the glories he hath known,
> And that imperial palace whence he came. (ll. 78–
> 85)

Mary Shelley's *Frankenstein* (1818), written from within the circle of English Romantics, testifies to the assault on female creativity made by a poetics that erased women from procreation. That novel, in which no speaking female character survives and the often feminized monster is racked with masochistic self-hatred, exposes Shelley's firsthand experience of the objectification, colonization, and, ultimately, annihilation of female creativity by the male writers of the Romantic school.

Furthermore, as sensibility both within and outside of evangelicalism had long threatened to do, the *man* of feeling first defined female subjectivity in terms of his own maternal fantasies, and then appropriated it. As my discussion of Hannah More's dramas and early social pamphlets addressed to the ruling classes will illustrate, the effect of this manuever on women writers' authority was immediate, provoking a feminist response from even this otherwise decidedly conservative writer. The construction of authorship and literary vocation developed by women preachers enabled all of these women to posit alternatives to the male-centered aesthetics of their period's dominant literary movement. Likewise, Elizabeth Gaskell and George Eliot, who so admired and drew upon William Wordsworth's poetry, had constantly to revise what Gaskell called his "seeing-beauty" social vision, or, more anxiously, to work free of his influence. Tonna's relentless commitment to realism, echoed in the fiction of Gaskell and Eliot, can be seen as refuting the decadent romanticism of Victorian sentimentality.

The fierce devotion to realism, variously defined by More, Tonna, Gaskell, and George Eliot, also evinces their resistance to the discourse of social science. Indeed, the rise of social science conspired effectively with the cult of sensibility to exclude women writers from social discourse. While the one defined female subjectivity according to women's maternal functions and their allegedly consequent qualities of empathy, emotionalism, and nurturing, the other strove to extricate social analysis from these very "unscientific" influences. Political Economy, an influential form of this pseudo-science, described human society as operating according to ineluctable, amoral laws, "discovered" by means of "objective" scientific methods. Male writers in the Romantic tradition, such as Thomas Carlyle, could rail against utilitarian arguments that soul did not equal stomach, and this cry was taken up by Gaskell and George Eliot. But women writers had a particular stake in this debate, since it was along peculiarly gendered lines that social science constituted reality. Hence, they insisted on the unreality of any system of thought that excluded female experiences and desires. Reality meant more than market principles, and was not even comprised by the male-centered desires of the Romantic "individual," but was made up as well of so-called "redundant women," "fallen women," and the similarly victimized poor, whom these writers construed as central to their feminized social mission as they had been to the evangelical mission.

Male writers of "sage discourse" likewise adopted marginal positions in order to criticize their society's received wisdom. George P. Landow, describing the close ties between Victorian jeremiads and their Old Testament models, distinguishes between "the wisdom speaker or Augustan satirist, both of whom speak and write as if they confidently embody their culture's accepted wisdom, [and] the sage [who] aggressively stands apart from others" like an Old Testament prophet.[6] However, male writers such as Carlyle or Ruskin benefited from their culture's identification of rationality and authority with masculinity, and thereby succeeded in relocating normative standards within their own texts, while female writers adopting the prophetic stance against a patriarchal center risked engaging in self-fulfilling prophecy: that is, they were themselves marginalized. George Eliot's distaste for oracular novels by lady novelists betrays her fear that prophetic fiction by women will be read as the rantings of madwomen. As Alex Owen has poignantly documented in her study of late nineteenth-century spiritualism, women who acted as mediums, or even expressed their beliefs in voices from the spirit world, could in fact be incarcerated as lunatics, and a range of male experts, including surgeons, attorneys, and alienists, would confirm the insanity of their practices.[7]

Yet women writers in the preaching tradition, particularly Hannah More, were powerful contributors to the genres of social criticism before their domination by the likes of Carlyle, whom Landow credits with the invention of sage writing.[8] By demanding recognition for the tradition of female prophets going back to the Old Testament, Charlotte Elizabeth Tonna, publishing in the 1830s as Carlyle was introducing his invention, took up her mentor Hannah More's battle against the efforts of male writers to exclude women from social discourse. If anything, the consolidation of a decidedly male "sage discourse" during the middle decades of the nineteenth century should be seen as a circling of the wagons against the considerable power of female preaching. Or, as Carol Christ puts it, "the way in which the Victorians began to privilege nonfiction prose, sage discourse could become a heroic masculine bulwark set up against a democratized and feminized novel."[9]

It is important to recognize that the adoption of evangelical discursive strategies by More, Tonna, Gaskell, and George Eliot was not an unambiguously progressive choice for women's writing. Although perhaps one of the most successful strategies employed by these writers, it nevertheless brought with it serious handicaps, often noted by its practitioners. For eighteenth-century women preachers, even those who maintained a significant degree of respectability, evangelicalism entailed a radical social position. For their nineteenth-century counterparts, by contrast, this could not be the case: evangelicalism itself was reappropriated by the established church with the founding of Anglican Evangelicalism. Whatever might be said about the political conservatism of the Methodists, joining their ranks entailed a public rejection of the established church and alignment with Dissent. In the wake of the French Revolution, the Anglican Evangelicals sought to accommodate evangelical spiritualism, including its critique of clerical practices, to the state institution of the established church. By so doing, they could vitiate both the religious and political threats of Dissent, at once appropriating some of its most attractive teachings and reviving the specter of Dissent as a revolutionary force. Rather than undermining clerical hierarchy, as Methodists had done, they extended their power by infiltrating the clergy with their adherents.[10] For women writers, this new phase of evangelicalism might preserve them from the fate suffered by Mary Wollstonecraft, vilified in the eighteenth century as a Dissenter, revolutionary, and feminist. However, it meant that a strategy had been put in place whereby appeals to evangelical doctrines could be assimilated into political reaction and patriarchal hierarchy. As a result, women writers' affiliation with evangelicalism became even more vexed.

The period also saw the formulation of "Woman's Mission"—that much-discussed concept by which women's public role was to be thoroughly defined.[11] F. K. Prochaska has argued that the philanthropic activities which characterized "Woman's Mission" afforded women access to the public sphere and, potentially, to political influence. While this is no doubt true to some extent, it must be qualified substantially with skepticism concerning their real power, skepticism such as Harriet Taylor Mill expressed when she referred to philanthropic women as the "sentimental priesthood."[12] Taylor Mill had nothing but contempt for women who accepted the quasi-mystical notion of their own powers of "benevolent influence" and willingly placed that power in the service of society by creating a morally wholesome domestic sphere, adding their names to charity subscription lists and venturing outside the home to participate in strictly organized and generally male-led philanthropic organizations. Like other ideologies of womanhood, this one became a self-fulfilling prophecy, encouraging male leaders of political organizations to exploit women's "benevolent influence" to lend moral credibility to their causes. Furthermore, women were proving to be most effective fund-raisers.[13]

Anglican Evangelicals, such as William Wilberforce and his Clapham Sect, were at the forefront of the effort to employ, and thereby to direct and contain, women's public influence. Wilberforce and Zachary Macaulay of the Clapham Sect, and Bishop Proteus encouraged Hannah More to devote her literary talents to reforming the morals of the upper classes and impressing on the lower their Christian duties. Charlotte Elizabeth Tonna's calling as a writer came from the Dublin

Tract Society, an Anglican organization whose aim was to evangelize and convert Irish Catholics. "Woman's Mission" was hardly confined to any one sect, however. Elizabeth Gaskell, who ran a ragged school as part of her husband's ministry to his Unitarian congregation, claimed to have based incidents in *Mary Barton* on observations of working-class life she must have made while on visits of charity. For a woman to claim "Woman's Mission" as the justification of her public activity was to leave herself vulnerable to appropriation and exploitation. Indeed, Charlotte Brontë resisted writing social-problem fiction for precisely this reason.[14] The writers in the preaching tradition, whose own rhetoric of vocation had been taken over by "Woman's Mission" ideology, were forced to create new and more elaborate literary strategies by which to elude male control of their writing and in order to introduce challenges to male authority.

Always a politically conflicted discourse, evangelicalism could now only be disassociated from its establishment connections when adherents adopted ever more extreme social and theological positions. This is precisely what the courageous women preachers of the Leeds revival did, identifying wholeheartedly with the working class, as Deborah Valenze has argued. However, while such politics appear more unequivocally progressive and admirable to us, they caused the nearly complete marginalization of their adherents. Furthermore, in a climate of frequently hysterical reaction to Continental revolutionary activity and fears of workers' rebellions at home, even the most innocent call to repentance and reform might unleash vicious abuse or legal action. Since it was no longer possible to negotiate the contradictions in evangelicalism between marginality and privilege as eighteenth-century preachers had done, few women writers successfully eluded substantial complicity with ruling-class interests. Consequently, although I would agree that Valenze's subjects are of great historical importance, I do not merely repeat the judgments that originally marginalized these nineteenth-century preachers by noting that their *literary* impact was small.

In addition to the fear of reprisals which forced compromises from many reform writers, women writers' anxieties continued to produce peculiarly sexualized handicaps. Like the women preachers who maintained a stake in preserving the patriarchy wherein they located the source of their authority, More, Tonna, Gaskell, and George Eliot also display varying degrees of dependence on male-dominated social and literary hierarchies. All of these women had more or less debilitating relationships with male mentors, to whom they often sacrificed their egos, literary prestige, and desires, not to mention their money. Each, especially Elizabeth Gaskell, saw the need, as women preachers had done, for female interpretive communities and women's solidarity. But beyond their literal dependence on male authorities, collusion with patriarchy inevitably produced what Rosemary Bodenheimer has termed "female paternalism" in their social-problem writing. Of this group, only Gaskell (who, incidentally, Bodenheimer takes as an example of the female paternalist) seems ever to have imagined social reform that would entail the destruction of paternalistic relationships.

Taking into consideration these contexts for nineteenth-century social discourse, we are faced with the dilemma of simultaneously acknowledging the power and contributions to feminist writing of such undeniably influential literary fore-mothers as More, Tonna, Gaskell, and George Eliot, and of criticizing their politics. In the following chapters I endeavor to fulfill these two goals.

Six

Social Prophet:
Hannah More as Political Writer

Nineteenth-century social-problem writing, with all its propagandistic force, vexed politics, and rich duplicity, evolved
out of literary innovations inseparable from the female preaching tradition. Women writers, most notably Hannah More, often dominated the creation of social narrative by adapting
evangelical rhetorical strategies and conceptions of literary authority, drawing the political conclusions implicit in women
preachers' writings. By the 1790s, while the Methodist women
preachers were exploring—and expounding—the feminist
implications of evangelical teaching, a passionate debate was
going on around them over the relationship of religious to social discourse generally. Writers of social discourse debated
questions of authority and decorum along much the same lines
that were argued among religious writers, recapitulating the
conflicting ideological stances that were enabling women to assume vocal roles in spiritual life. The vital connections between
religious belief, political practice, and literary authority—
more crucial than ever when many English imagined French
atheism as having led inevitably to regicide and anarchy—
provided female writers as ideologically diverse as More and
Mary Wollstonecraft with the means to establish their calling as
social critics, with powerful language to present their critiques,
and with ploys by which they might defend themselves against
their critics.

No writer manipulated the ideology and rhetoric of evangelicalism to shape social discourse more successfully than Hannah
More. Like the women preachers, she identified herself with

patriarchal authority, employing many of the preachers' strategies to attain political influence in a vigorously reactionary period. She too was able to distinguish between various manifestations of patriarchy, resulting in a more complicated—and sometimes contradictory—political response than can be accommodated by the labels "progressive" and "reactionary." Most often, she cast herself as what Rosemarie Bodenheimer, speaking of Victorian novelists, has termed the "female paternalist."[1] Her religious principles enabled More, as a woman, to denounce the tyranny, decadence, and impiety of the ruling classes (for which she was both abused as a radical and praised as a moralist), only to defend a providentially ordained social hierarchy as inviolate. Her influential supporters ranked More as a moralist with no less a man than Dr. Johnson, but she clearly saw her calling as extraordinary, for though she believed that women's education should be reformed to address their rational faculties, yet she concluded of her sex generally that "there is no animal so indebted to subordination for its good behaviour as woman."[2] Her role, like that of women preachers among the Methodist hierarchy, was ambiguous, for the same patriarchal beliefs that made her a powerful evangelist inspired her prophetic rebuke of patriarchal sins. Precisely that ambiguity enabled More's reputation to survive the anti-Jacobin "purges" that anathematized Wollstonecraft, leaving More's conflicted writings as an important model for the next generation of female social writers.

More's place in the development of social-problem fiction has rested principally on the "realistic" *Cheap Repository Tracts*,[3] often because the tracts supply clear precedents for the muckraking depictions of laborers' lives that characterize Victorian social fiction. Removed from the context of her other writings, More's contributions to the crisis delineated by Burke and Paine—namely, her "Village Politics" and the *Cheap Repository Tracts*—have been used to present the author as an unequivocal defender of God, king, and patriarchy against the atheistical, leveling sons of Paine. This selective rendering of More's social writing has served to diminish her importance in several ways: first, by disregarding the originality of her social thought both before and after the 1790s, More's writing can be treated as derivative of male conservatives, such as Burke and

Christian ethics by disregarding paternalistic responsibility. Heroic women, in turn, are responsible for defending a righteous patriarchal ideal against actual, self-interested patriarchs. Critics, including More's biographer, have derided *The Inflexible Captive* (1775), *Percy* (1777), and *The Fatal Falsehood* (1779) as formulaic, wooden productions, despite the fact that the first two drew large, enthusiastic audiences. Aesthetic disputes aside, all three plays are remarkable for their ideological—specifically feminist—tensions, boasting representations of powerful female speakers in the evangelical tradition.

The Inflexible Captive, consisting mainly of a series of debates over the relative importance of public and private virtues, might be seen as More's defense of stoic self-denial and public duty. However, the very terms of this debate, set by the spokesman of public virtue, the Roman hero Marcus Attilius Regulus, are shown to set a false dichotomy. Regulus, the inflexible captive of Carthage, prevails only insofar as he resists the efforts of his friends and family to bargain for his life and instead submits to a gruesome and rather pointless death at the hands of his captors. The play's title, as well as More's later explicit renunciation of tragedy as glorifying anti-Christian virtues, here espoused by Regulus, shifts the play's focus to the eloquent case that Regulus's daughter, Attilia, makes for so-called private duties. Attilia, whose position is dismissed by her father as feminine sentimentality, argues that proper virtue should consist in the coincidence of obligations to family and to the state, claiming that no notion of virtue can violate "natural" obligations to friends and kin. For a woman to betray her father, who is a patriarch of her society as well, by failing to prevent his execution would be barbarous, while Regulus, by seeking such a death, fails to acknowledge the claims of his dependents against his egotistical desire for honor. Attilia pleads with the Consul Manlius, urging that her desires should likewise be those of the state:

> If ever pity's sweet emotions touch'd thee,—
> If ever gentle love assail'd thy breast,—
> If ever virtuous friendship fir'd thy soul;—
> By the dear name of husband, and of parent—
> By all the soft, yet powerful ties of nature;

> If e'er thy lisping infants charm'd thine ear,
> And waken'd all the father in thy soul—
> If e'er thou hop'st to have thy latter days,
> Blest by their love and sweeten'd by their duty—
> Oh! hear a kneeling weeping wretched daughter,
> Who begs, intreats, implores a father's life—
> Nor *her's* alone—but *Rome's*—his *country's* father.
>
> (*IC*, act IV)

Attilia's argument rests on *men's* status as relative creatures as a foundation for social relations. More calls on scriptural authority to sanction this view of an ideal patriarchy, alluding to the fourth commandment promise that obedient children will be blessed with long life ("If e'er thou hop'st to have thy latter days . . . ").

Constancy to Regulus's version of filial duty demands that Attilia obey him, even in his wish to meet a heroic death; therefore, she must accede to the play's tragic end. However, More denies his claims to heroism by characterizing them as a peculiarly pagan form of madness, combining masculine egotism with the fatalism of classical tragedy, which contaminates his entire society. In the voice of the Carthaginian slave woman, Barce—whose privileged judgment stems from her marginality—More condemns Regulus's absurd inflexibility:

> This love of glory's the disease of Rome;
> It makes her mad, it is a wild delirium,
> An universal and contagious frenzy;
> It preys on all, it spares nor sex nor age:
> The Consul envies Regulus his chains—
> He, not less mad, contemns his life and freedom—
> The daughter glories in the father's ruin . . .
> This may be virtue; but I thank the Gods,
> That Barce's soul is not a Roman soul.
>
> (*IC*, act V)

As Barce's speech makes clear, the play's tragedy stems from the suppression of values identified with marginalized women, and consistent with Christian ethics. Only Barce escapes the phallocentric ideology promulgated by Regulus, which infects the other characters, including Attilia, and leads them to sacri-

> I murdered mine! With impious pride I snatch'd
> The bolt of vengeance from the hand of heav'n.
> My punishment is great—but Oh! 'tis just.
> My soul submissive bows. A righteous god
> Has made my crime become my chastisement.
>
> (*P*, act V)

Introducing a higher power, the hand of God, into this scene obviously modeled on Lear's mourning for Cordelia, reveals that Elwina alone is insufficient as evangelist. In fact, More suggests that the divine author requires the daughter's sacrifice to fulfill his "plot": the father is redeemed by the death of his own loving child.

More attempted to exorcise her fear of this demand for female martyrdom with her *Sacred Dramas*. Published in 1782, they were originally undertaken as pedagogical tools to teach her charges biblical history by enacting such events as the discovery of Moses in the bulrushes. She termed these plays a "bold experiment," enabling playwright and actresses to assume heroic roles and employ powerful biblical language. Each play treats the empowerment of a marginal character through divine assistance. Most interesting in terms of More's development as social prophet is her play *Daniel*. More takes her subject from the book of Daniel, chapter 6, where Daniel's rivals are jealous of his influence over King Darius and plot to bring about the prophet's execution, an incident highlighting conflicts between the prophet's spiritual authority and the law of the state. Daniel's enemies trick the benevolent king into signing an edict which, by forbidding petitions made to any power besides the king, would force Daniel to abandon communication with God in daily prayer: his access to the authoritative discourse. They seek thereby to erode Daniel's own authority as a prophet. Daniel refuses to be silenced, and the king is forced by his own edict to throw his favorite to the lions.

Faced with death, More's Daniel names God, defender of the weak and origin of all temporal power, as the source of his strength. "I'll teach thee to be bold," Daniel tells his friend, the young nobleman Araspes,

> Tho' sword I never drew! Fear not, Araspes,
> The feeble vengeance of a mortal man,

Whose breath is in his nostrils; for wherein
Is he to be accounted of? but fear
The awaken'd vengeance of the living Lord;
He who can plunge the everlasting soul
In infinite perdition![6]

This advice recalls Bosanquet's to single women, whom she encourages to be brave. God will sustain a righteous cause against its enemies, Daniel counsels, and the prophet who remains steadfast to the truth has nothing to fear from lions—or critics. The martial imagery of this passage reveals the prophet's refusal to use his power as a weapon of aggression. He need not draw a sword and enter into battle on his own behalf, but simply wait patiently to be rescued. Prophecy is God's weapon. Furthermore, persecution becomes an occasion for the manifestation of God's power in defending his prophet. Daniel survives, and the people acknowledge him second only to Darius, the king.

As it is delineated in this play, the relation of the prophet to the monarch as instruments of God's power, and of both to the law, describes More's own position as a social critic. The prophet's enemy is the secular law as manipulated by his enemies; not the divinely sanctioned patriarchy, but those who would abuse it. Subject to his own laws, Darius, the temporal authority, becomes powerless to save Daniel, and Daniel declares that his "allegiance is to the King of kings," who empowers him. More does not seek political power for herself because as a prophet, announcing the truth which temporal authority must be content to administer, her power would actually be superior. Those who would deny her power are like Daniel's rivals, enemies of the monarchy, the people, and most important, of God.

However, the relationship of *prophetess* to the "king," was complicated by increasingly rigid gender differentiation. Wesley had represented benevolent temporal authority (the king) for the women preachers, and the Anglican Evangelicals who called on More's literary talents served an analogous function. The Anglican divine Dr. Horne urged More to evangelize "the great and gay," reminding her that "Providence has led you to associate with them, as it raised Esther of old to the

cepted; nor will the deficiencies of the composition
be allowed to defeat the honesty of the intention.[11]

The insecurity of the female prophet's position is clear in this
passage. Whereas she could imagine the male prophet as transcending the prejudices of his audience, as a woman writer she
seeks a dialogue with her readers, particularly other women.
In so doing, she ran the risk of being thrown to the lions, and
Wilberforce, like Darius, would be powerless to save her.

Nevertheless, the potential inherent in evangelicalism as espoused by either sex to transcend temporal authority is evident
in these essays. More's strategy in evangelizing the upper ranks
is to appeal to their self-interest by pointing out the reciprocity
between religion and politics. But then she goes on to characterize religious behavior in the curiously subversive manner
distinctive of evangelicalism. In "Thoughts on the Manners of
the Great" More writes:

> But though the passive and self-denying virtues are
> not high in the esteem of mere good sort of people,
> yet they are peculiarly the evangelical virtues. The
> world extolls brilliant actions; the Gospel enjoins
> good habits and right motives; it seldom inculcates
> those splendid deeds which make heroes, or teaches
> those lofty sentiments which constitute philoso-
> phers; but it enjoins the harder task of renouncing
> self, of living uncorrupted in the world, of subduing
> besetting sins, and of "not thinking of ourselves
> more highly than we ought." The *acquisition* of glory
> was the precept of other religions, the *contempt* of it
> is the perfection of Christianity.[12]

Evangelicalism redefines heroism in such a way as to disrupt
gender categories, making possible the Helen Fleetwoods,
Margaret Hales, and Dinah Morrises of the Victorian novelists,
as it had empowered women preachers. As this passage makes
clear, evangelicalism could transform traditional power structures by valuing passivity and self-abnegation over "heroic"
qualities which encourage aggression and domination. Undeniably, this transformation was driven in part by the class and
gender interests striving to reconfigure social relations along

the lines of a rigidly structured domestic model. In the model, women might be compensated for their passivity and self-abnegation by assuming authority to regulate social and sexual behavior in the home. Nevertheless, the healthy "contempt" of glory expressed in this passage demystifies an exalted patriarchy and enables women to mount a critique of ruling-class practices, trusting in their own worth rather than in any judgment according to "wordly" standards. Though More herself may not have been conscious of the feminist implications of this philosophy, later women writers including Elizabeth Gaskell and George Eliot certainly would be, and they could construct their arguments on this evangelical base regardless of their own religious convictions.

Recognition of a prophetic calling came as a mixed blessing to More because it imposed duties on her which at first limited her voice and her audience. The bishop of London requested that More produce a popularization of Burke's arguments in *Reflections* to counteract the effects of Paine's *Rights of Man* on the lower classes.[13] "Village Politics" (1793) translates Burke's prose into an "entertaining" and somewhat debased variation on the dialogue form that was a favorite evangelistic technique for women preachers. Despite the potential of such a project to reduce More from a prophet to a national governess, she did her best to turn its limitations to her advantage. More's experiments with dialogue opened new possibilities for evangelical women writers. A narrated dialogue, like its real-life counterpart, arrives at its conclusion through a dialectical process, and requires no privileged voice, no hierarchical relation between speaker and listener. Though there is no mystery for any but the most naive reader as to the relative moral authority of the characters in "Village Politics," Jack Anvil, the anti-Jacobin blacksmith, does not enjoy a privileged status relative to Tom Hood, the village mason and reader of Paine. They speak the same dialect, presumably have received the same level of education, and occupy equivalent positions in society. When Hood converts to Anvil's way of thinking, it is meant to be the result of the moral and logical superiority of the blacksmith's position, revealed in a dialectical discourse whose participants had equal chance to present their arguments.

Tom quotes a list of terms he has learned from a radical

friend (e.g., "organization," "equalization," "fraternization"),
and though he does not know their meaning, is convinced that
"he never shall be happy till all these fine things are brought
over to England."[14]

> *Jack.* What! into this Christian country, Tom?
> Why, dost thou know they have no *Sabbath* in
> France? . . .
> *Tom.* And dost thou believe they are as cruel as
> some folks pretend?
> *Jack.* I am sure they are, and I think I know the
> reason. We Christians set a high value on life, be-
> cause we know that every fellow-creature has an im-
> mortal soul: a soul to be saved or lost, Tom—
> Whoever believes that, is a little cautious how he
> sends a soul unprepared to his grand account. But
> he who believes a man is no better than a dog, will
> make no more scruple of killing one than the other.
> *Tom.* And dost thou think our rights of man will
> lead to all this wickedness?
> *Jack.* As sure as eggs are eggs.
> *Tom.* I begin to think we are better off as we are.[15]

The fiction of such a dialogue is that conversion occurs as a
matter of free assent to a proposition of obvious merit. Its author, who seems to be absent from this process, does not appear to possess any exceptional authority, for authority in
dialectic can finally be attributed not to speakers, but to discourse. The dialogue's conclusion thus seems to transcend its
participants. This technique would eventually bring More to
appreciate marginalized social positions for their strategic
worth as well as for the critical insight they afforded into dominant cultural practices.

"Village Politics" pleased a powerful, elite audience as well as
the class of readers for which it was explicitly intended.[16] In
fact, rumors circulated that More's work was being subsidized
by the government.[17] This project secured her reputation as a
political propagandist, and as late as 1888, Charlotte Yonge, in
her biography of More, characterized the author of "Village
Politics" as "the Britomart of Mendip," who, "against [the] arguments of Sansfoy," "couched her lance, in a pamphlet whose

proceeds were devoted to the support of the seven thousand emigrant clergy."[18] Despite the pamphlet's success, however, More expressed some disgust both at the task she had been called to do, and at the idiom required to execute it. Writing to her friend Mrs. Boscawen in 1793, she claimed to have written the pamphlet "against my will and judgement" in a style "as vulgar as heart could wish; but it is only destined for the most vulgar class of readers."[19] More had yet to discover the power available to her in marginal "vulgar" language, and therefore "Village Politics" only managed to frustrate an author who longed to draw her rhetorical sword.

The opportunity to do so presented itself in the English furor touched off by proclamations of atheism in France. Like the Old Testament prophetess Deborah, who had to lead the cowardly general Barak into battle, More felt compelled to respond because her own bishops had neglected to do so. In this she echoes Susanna Wesley's or Grace Bennet's justifications of their missions. With the support of her Evangelical friends, More wrote *Remarks on the Speech of M. Dupont* (1792). In that work one finds further evidence that her evangelicalism helped More to recognize the threat that a non-Christian authoritative discourse posed not only to political and religious stability, but to the fledgling public voices of women.

In terms revealing the connections between religious and literary categories she attacked Dupont for attempting to reinstate pagan values:

> It is the same over-ruling vanity which operates in their politics, and in their religion . . . which makes [Kersaint] menace to outstrip the most extravagant hero of romance. . . .
>
> It is the same vanity . . . which leads Dupont and Manuel to undertake in their orations to abolish the Sabbath, to exterminate the priesthood, to erect a pantheon for the world, to restore the Peripatetic philosophy, and in short to revive every thing of ancient Greece, except the pure taste, the profound wisdom, the love of virtue, the veneration of the laws, and the high degree of reverence which even virtuous Pagans professed for the Diety.[20]

That is, the French revolutionaries sought to revive everything except those aspects of pagan philosophy which were consistent with the transcendent values appealed to by women to sanction their speech. More exposes Dupont's and Kersaint's desire to dominate, not liberate—to be heroes, not saviors.

More harbored no illusions about who would inhabit the new pantheon. In his speech to the National Convention, translated and published with More's remarks, Dupont prophesied thus:

> Let me then represent to you the times, that are fast approaching, when our philosophers, whose names are celebrated throughout Europe, PETION, SYEYES, CONDORCET, and others—surrounded in our Pantheon, as the Greek philosophers were at Athens, with a crowd of disciples coming from all parts of Europe, walking like the Peripatetics, and teaching— this man, the system of the universe, and developing the progress of all human knowledge.[21]

More perceived in the triumph of atheistic rationalism the hegemony of the male voice. It would reassert a language inaccessible to women. In 1835, Charlotte Elizabeth Tonna could look back and claim that all of More's prophecies had come true.[22]

According to More, Christianity was liberating by contrast:

> In vain we look around us to discover the ravages of religious tyranny, or the triumphs of priestcraft or superstition. Who attempts to impose any yoke upon our reason? Who seeks to put any blind on the eyes of the most illiterate? Who fetters the judgment or enslaves the conscience of the meanest of our Protestant brethren? Nay, such is the power of pure Christianity, that genuine Christianity which is exhibited in our liturgy to enlighten the understanding, as well as to reform the heart. . . .[23]

Their clear anti-Jacobin intent aside, More's questions evoke the same evangelical principles that had liberated women's voices. The pantheon, by contrast, appeared an impenetrable bastion of male authority, where women could not appeal to a common allegiance to a transcendent authority in order to gain an audience for their speech.

Typical of the qualified approval with which women preachers had to content themselves, More's pamphlet won her the epithet "Bishop in Petticoats," a title at once complimentary and dismissive. But ambiguous power was to be preferred to silence. More was destined to serve the evangelical cause not as a theologian or a philosopher, but as a writer of popular fiction. Her *Cheap Repository Tracts,* begun in 1795 at the behest of Wilberforce and other members of the Clapham sect, were among the most politically influential writings of the period, even though they were aimed at a barely literate audience with unsophisticated tastes and limited interests. More brought all her skills as dramatist to bear on the task of creating lively, entertaining tales, ballads, and dialogues that would insinuate the anti-Jacobin philosophies into the working-class consciousness. Thanks to More's study of popular publications, including those produced by the Jacobins, as well as the shrewd marketing strategies of the project's sponsors, *Cheap Repository Tracts* reached virtually every laborer's home.[24] But of even greater significance was More's discovery of the lower-class voice as a vehicle for converting her peers.

Though the lower orders constituted the primary audience for the *Cheap Repository Tracts,* the nature of More's political message reflects her awareness of a dual audience. Many of the tracts were purchased by the upper and middle classes to be distributed *gratis* among workers. But these gentle people undoubtedly read the tracts themselves, and among the one hundred and fourteen tracts published between 1795 and 1798 were a number in which More used a combination of colloquial, or "vulgar," language and scriptural language to address herself to her peers.

In the most popular of the tracts, "The Shepherd of Salisbury Plain," More presents the titular character and his family through the experience of a middle-class observer, Mr. Johnson. However, in dialogues with Johnson, the shepherd reveals the values, beliefs, and even tastes he shares in common with the higher ranks through his use of "Bible language." The story opens with the narrator's description of Johnson contemplating the beauty of his rural surroundings. Psalm 19 comes to Johnson's mind, the narrator tells us, but he does not quote it. Instead when Johnson first meets the shepherd and

to an habitual interior restraint, an early government of the affections, and a course of self-controul over those tyrannizing inclinations, which have so natural a tendency to enslave the human heart."[30]

Furthermore, some of More's calls to repentance are directed squarely at a male audience. One can well imagine the effect she intended the following to have on a male reader interested in the education of his daughters:

> Strong truths, whenever such happen to be addressed to [women], are either diluted with flattery, or kept back in part, or softened to their taste; or if the ladies express a wish for information on any point, they are put off with a compliment instead of a reason. They are reminded of their beauty when they are seeking to inform their understanding, and are considered as beings who must be contented to behold every thing through a false medium, and are not expected to see and to judge of things as they really exist.[31]

This exhortation cannot be addressed to women, only to men capable of conveying "strong truths" to them.[32] It proceeds logically from Law's and Wesley's writings on women's education. Though she does not argue overtly for a public role for women, More repeatedly demands that women be allowed to exercise their intellects through rigorous conversation. Denied access to public education where men's intellectual and verbal skills were honed in discussion, women lacked immediate experience of the authoritative discourses they might read. But if there were a domestic academy as there were already domestic ministries, women might learn to speak the empowering languages of history, philosophy, or politics, as they had learned to speak in the voices of prophets.

This new verbal power would not constitute a threat to any divinely sanctioned patriarchy, one in which the strong defended the weak, for truth should be of a piece:

> Even the news of the day, in such an eventful period as the present, may lead [sic] frequent occasions to a woman of principle to declare, without parade, her

faith in a moral Governor of the world; her trust in particular Providence; her belief in the Divine Omnipotence; her confidence in the power of God, in educing good from evil, in his employing wicked nations, not as favourites but instruments . . . in short, some intimation that she is not ashamed to declare that her mind is under the influence of Christian faith; that she is steadily governed by an unalterable principle, of which no authority is too great to make her ashamed, which no occasion is too trivial to call into exercise.[33]

This is essentially an evangelical argument, justifying woman's education and her participation in social discourse on the grounds that the call to witness to God's providence and against the atheist threat requires this participation. Such a strategy is designed to enlist the entire anti-Jacobin movement on More's side.

As if she had tempted fate with this subversion, More was about to experience a violent attack on her public voice, ironically provoked by her activities as national governess. Shortly after the publication of *Strictures* came an episode in More's life which rivaled the persecution of the Old Testament prophets, and revealed once again the terrifying vulnerability of a woman in public life. Ostensibly, it was not brought on by any of More's writings but by her work as an educator of the poor at Blagdon school. Yet the attack on More savors of the misogynistic attacks on vocal women as diverse in their messages as Mary Bosanquet and Mary Wollstonecraft. Significantly, More's evangelicalism was taken to be her great sin, the same teaching that informed her writing.

In 1795, More had opened a school at Blagdon in answer to a plea from the town's curate, Mr. Bere. Bere feared the riotous people of his parish, but, even more so, he seemed to have been threatened by the possibility that Jacobin reformers might educate them in the rights of man before More could educate them in their Christian duty towards him and his brethren. The school was a classic instance of anti-Jacobin female charity. Nevertheless, when the schoolmaster, Mr. Younge, was accused of Methodistical practices in 1798, charges of Jacobinism were leveled at the school's foundress, Hannah More. Anti-Jacobin sentiment, which inspired More herself, rose in this instance to hysteria. Younge's evangelical prayers and Bible reading with his students meant Methodism; Methodism implied subversion of the established church; dissent from the established church was indistinguishable from political dissent; therefore, Younge's patroness, a staunch defender of church and crown, must be denounced as both a Methodist and a Jacobin. This absurd charge was registered first by Bere himself and, before the controversy died down in 1802, had traveled all the way to the *Anti-Jacobin Review,* where attacking Hannah More became a favorite sport in the first three years of the century.[34]

As was so often the case when women were the objects of such scandal, the abuse More endured was vicious, and unnecessarily personal. Edward Spencer, in his pamphlet entitled "Truth respecting Miss H. More's Meeting Houses, and the Conduct of her Followers" (1802), claimed that More "had not kept her mind in temperance, sobriety, and chastity" as a young woman.[35] The misogyny of Spencer's accusation against the woman he sneeringly referred to as the "She-Bishop," recalls the anxiety caused to women preachers by insinuations that their desire to speak publicly—to penetrate an authoritative discourse—indicated sexual immodesty. More's fears, expressed in the preface to the second edition of "Manners of the Great," had been realized.

Like her character Daniel, More refrained from speaking publicly on her own behalf, trusting to the God of moral and political authority to defend her as he had the prophets of old. In 1802, she wrote to Wilberforce:

> I resolve not to defend myself, let them bring what charges they will. If it please God to put an end to my little (how little) usefullness, I hope to be enabled to submit to his will, not only to submit because I cannot help it, but to acquiesce in it, because it is holy, just, and good. B[ere]'s threats of a pamphlet were suspended by a fit of the gout, but Shaw was at work with him, and he had emissaries in all the villages, who were sent to pick up any stories they could against me; his object being to destroy

my remaining schools. I had hoped to mollify him
by silence; far from it; he has ventured ten times
greater lengths from the certainty of not being con-
tradicted.[36]

More's faith in God's will is impressive. She recognized that
Bere was baiting her, and would not compromise her evangelistic mission and debase her literary powers by engaging in polemics. Publicly she maintained a stance of patient waiting for
vindication by her God.

Privately she turned to God's servant, namely, the bishop of
Bath and Wells, and denied to Bishop Beadon all the charges
brought against her. The bishop vindicated More, but her diary reveals that she was scarred by the years of abuse. On her
birthday, February 2, 1803, More, aged fifty-eight, wrote:

> My birth-day! How little was my prospect this day
> twelvemonth, that I should live to see it. I would
> enumerate some of the mercies of the past year . . .
> restored to a serene and resigned state of mind—
> able to thank God, not only for amended health and
> spirits, for the many comforts and alleviations of my
> long and heavy trial, but enabled to thank him for
> the trial itself—it has shown me more of the world,
> more of its corruptions, more of my own heart,
> more of the instability of human opinion; it has
> weaned me from many attachments which were too
> strong to be right.[37]

The "attachments" this trial had broken seemed to have sharp-
ened More's recognition that she could not be of true service to
any patriarchal authority short of God himself. Indeed, always
one to disparage her own literary talents publicly, More came
to do so more vehemently while privately responding to criticism with greater detachment and equanimity. The result was
a daring literary experiment for More: *Coelebs in Search of a
Wife.*

Attempting an Evangelical Novel: Coelebs in Search of a Wife

No evangelical woman writer of Hannah More's political sta-
ture had previously employed the novel as a means of serious

instruction and edification. From our perspective, *Coelebs* may seem a clear example of what Nancy Armstrong describes as "domestic fiction"; that is, part of a basically disciplinary genre, working to produce a concept of feminine virtues advantageous to the interests of bourgeois dominance. It could be said that More had served such interests throughout her career. But for an evangelical writer of the early nineteenth century the decision to address these goals in a novel would be fraught with ideological and literary difficulties. Fiction was a necessary evil when attempting to influence the vulgar, or children. But evangelical opinion held that it could only corrupt a polite—and female—readership. Because the novel encourages a "dangerous" play of the imagination, writers from More to Wollstonecraft banned it from women's reading. Indeed, novelistic discourse proved to be ideologically disruptive; the multivocality of the novel would render the contradictions apparent in More's earlier works in a manner more resistant to authoritarian closure. Why, then, did More attempt a novel?

The "instability of human opinion" meant that any audience was potentially as alien, and could be as hostile, to a woman's voice as any other. There was no guarantee that her fellow Anglican Evangelicals, or women, would be more sympathetic to the outpourings of her soul the way Bosanquet had imagined an audience of single Methodist women might be. Consequently, the subtle polemical potential of fiction, with which More had become acquainted in writing the *Cheap Repository Tracts,* was needed in order to address an audience of equals and superiors on matters religious, political, and feminist. The only alternative to fiction at this point might have been silence.

But of even wider significance than concerns about audience was the nature of the genres available to her. Those nonfiction genres which More had employed excluded marginal voices, even when the author argued on women's behalf. The writer of the moral essay adopted the voice of the moral authority, still an exceptional mode of expression for a woman. Distinct from the growing authority of women as experts in domestic piety, evidenced in the profusion of female-authored conduct books, the moral essayist claimed extensive knowledge of the world, a quasi-mystical insight into the workings of Nature or Providence, and the cultural wherewithal to enforce his views. In this respect, More's calling as a moral essayist was extraordinary in a very ordinary sense. More had to look back to her play *The Search for Happiness* to find representations of intelligent women speaking in an authoritative manner, if not in realistic language, at least in a plausible, conversational context. But her Evangelical connections precluded drama. More's search was for a genre that would enable her to represent woman's voice realistically in the context of enlightened conversation, as she had imagined in *Strictures*.

The novel was already a feminized genre, able to represent a new range of women's voices, and that, perhaps more than any evidence of its domesticating powers, may have appealed to More much as it had to Wollstonecraft, who had likewise written disparagingly of the novel. However, Wollstonecraft's fiction had openly challenged the domestic ideology that informed many novels of the time, and later her reputation suffered accordingly. Her appeals to transcendent authority through the "Bible language" of her female characters had been lost in the furor over her radical politics and unconventional private life. She did not attain the prophet's role. Eventually she was associated with a philosophical movement intent on undermining the very transcendent divine authority to which women could appeal. During the first half of the nineteenth century, while Wollstonecraft's writings languished along with her reputation, the more complicitous *Coelebs* persevered. Nevertheless, by uniting evangelicalism and feminism in fiction, *Coelebs* supplied an essential link in the history of women's public voice as it came down to the Victorians.

The novel, published anonymously, is narrated in the first person by a male character under the assumed name "Coelebs." Its author seems to absent herself from the novel by a series of disguises, speaks only as a ventriloquist, and presents her most interesting points by indirection. Thanks to this caginess, *Coelebs* is fascinating as the first major effort to combine the forces of two media so volatile as the evangelical idiom and the novel on behalf of Christian feminism and women's public voice.

Coelebs is a pious, well-bred young man on a quest for a wife of equal merit. More takes this opportunity to excoriate the gamut of female vanity. Significantly, however, women who fail to adhere to evangelical standards of behavior are shown to betray their own voices. Foolish women simply undermine themselves by illogic, but more interesting is More's attack on the bluestocking, Madame Sparkes. In her allegiance to classical philosophy, Madame Sparkes ignores the debt which she, as an educated woman, owes to the "modern English" (i.e., Protestant) philosophy she rejects. Not the pagan world, but the Protestant one recognizes an imperative to value woman's intellect. The novel suggests that without the evangelical imperative articulated by such people as William Law and John Wesley, Madame Sparkes would not know of classical philosophy, much less have the opportunity to discuss it with men. More casts the argument in such a way as to make it appear to be yet another attack on pagan France on behalf of Christian England. Yet it is applicable to the relation of women to Christianity as well. Madame Sparkes's disputant, Mr. Flam, reminds her that the French, like the heroes of the ancient world "freed [the people] from mild masters to make them their own slaves," "*they* [the French] pull down the prosperous" while "*we* [the English] raise the weak" (*CW,* 12: 195). The politics of this passage are questionable. Nevertheless, there is truth in the contention that an authority that can be appropriated by the marginalized is to be preferred to anarchy, where power is a matter of brute force. A literary tradition appealing to religious criteria to define "instruction" is preferable to one that silences all voices which fail to "delight" the dominant male tastes.

In *Coelebs,* More thus presents Christian patriarchy as the most likely of the currently available social structures to foster women's voices. Granted, we may find Coelebs, the representation of the Christian hero, a boring prig. But More's point is that such a man will make a woman a far better husband than one modeled on the heroes of pagan patriarchal epics or atheistical romances. As a Christian, Coelebs is ultimately subject to the same authority as his wife. Lord Staunton, a pale version of Richardson's Lovelace, suffers rejection by Lucilla Stanley due to his irreligiousness, and Lucilla's parents approve her decision. The qualities Staunton desires in a wife range from sexual to aesthetic to financial. Coelebs, on the other hand, requires of a wife submission, but also knowledge of scripture and the ability to converse sensibly on matters of morals and piety. He falls in love with Lucilla's wise and eloquent conversation. Indeed, sometimes gently catechizing her lover Coelebs, Lucilla occasionally comes off as the superior, albeit unselfconscious, moralist.

An apparently trivial conversation on gardening becomes an occasion for suggesting a hidden, inner life of which men, too concerned with surfaces, are unaware. Coelebs remarks on the barren appearance of the garden in winter:

> "There is little pleasure in contemplating vegetation in its torpid state, in surveying
> 'The naked shoots, barren as lances,'
> as Cowper describes the winter shrubbery."
> "The pleasure is in the preparation," replied she.
> "When all appears dead and torpid to you idle spectators, all is secretly at work." (*CW*, 12: 111)

The metaphoric subtext of this passage shows the importance of a genre—and a patriarchy—which enable the female voice to coexist with the male voice, if at first only in this severely limited way. Lucilla corrects Coelebs for privileging a time when the phallus-like "lances" are not barren but in their glory. Regardless of their covering, lances are lances—symbols of power and domination. She would convert him to an appreciation of the potential hidden in the ground. More would associate this quality with "those meek and passive virtues which we all agreed were peculiarly Christian and peculiarly feminine" (*CW*, 12: 186), as Coelebs comments earlier in the novel. Lucilla gives no prophetic speeches, but the moral authority of her voice is never undermined, her eloquence always admired.

The patriarchy of which Coelebs is a part allows this voice to penetrate its authority. As the father of the bride-to-be writes of his daughter,

> We accustomed her to reflect that she was an intellectual creature; that she was a Christian.—That to an intellectual being, diversions must always be subordinate to the exercise of the mental faculties; that to the immortal being, born to higher hopes than enjoyments, the exercise of the mental faculties

must be subordinate to religious duties. (*CW*, 12:
421)

In other words, Lucilla Stanley, destined to be Coelebs's wife,
possesses all those qualities which empowered the original
women preachers and Hannah More herself. Not only does
she enjoy a facility at discourse acquired through the exercise
of her intellect, but her vital religion also places in her hands
the transcendent authority of religious duties. These duties
transcend the confining "natural duties" of wife and mother,
and can overrule them.

Unlike the Methodist women preachers, More stops short of
challenging the family structure. The political climate was far
too unsettled for her to do so, and even Wollstonecraft did not
take that tack. Nevertheless, she wished to transform the family intellectually as evangelicalism had done spiritually. Mr.
Stanley continues,

> It would be cruel to condemn a creature to a retired
> life without qualifying her for retirement; next to
> religion, nothing can possibly do this but mental
> cultivation in women who are above the exercise of
> vulgar employments. . . . Now the woman who de-
> rives her principles from the Bible, and her amuse-
> ments from intellectual sources, will not pant for
> *beholders*.
>
> She lives on her own stock. Her resources are
> within herself. She possesses the truest indepen-
> dence. She does not wait for the opinion of the
> world, to know if she is right; nor for the applause of
> the world, to know if she is happy. (*CW*, 12: 424)

I do not mean to claim that this passage represents an unambiguously feminist argument. Clearly that is far from the case.
What should be acknowledged is the significant degree to
which evangelicalism enabled a women writer, even in a highly
reactionary period, to encourage the intellectual and verbal
empowerment of women without being ostracized. From behind her elaborate disguises we hear Hannah More's voice
preaching women's self-reliance and independence from temporal authority, based on intellectual mastery and sanctioned
by transcendent authority.

Though More's preachment may seem timid by our standards, the abuse heaped on More after the identity of *Coeleb*'s author came to light suggests the moral courage required to deliver this prophetic message. Her friends refused to believe that such a novel could have been written by a woman, much less one of More's pious nature. Charmile Grant wrote to Mrs. Thornton that they were of the same mind concerning the author: that he was doubtless "vain, coarse and somewhat presumptuous. A report reached us that it was written by Mrs. H. More, which till we have it from herself, or from you, I will not believe."[38] When the *Christian Observer,* unaware of the author's identity, regretted *Coelebs*'s "want of taste and strict moral delicacy," More exploded with indignation. The Evangelicals were denying their own heritage. Faulted by the Evangelicals' magazine for preaching their doctrine, More defended herself in an angry letter to Macaulay.

When the secular press got hold of the novel, More had every right to feel herself to be the persecuted prophet. Even more than the criticism from Evangelical quarters, the attacks in the *London Review* and *Edinburgh Magazine* declare their misogynistic inspiration. These writers fasten on behaviors More recommends to empower women, not only spiritually and intellectually, but sexually. They are unrestrained in their ridicule of domestic piety, religious conversation between the sexes, and modest female dress.[39] Despite William Pepys's encouraging remark in a letter to More that he had "not met with such writing as I can produce in Coelebs, since the days of Burke, unless it be from your own works,"[40] More's career as a novelist was at an end.

In the context of the novels of Fanny Burney, Jane Austen, or Maria Edgeworth, the only thing that might be considered exceptional about *Coelebs in Search of a Wife* is that a work of such modest literary merit received so much attention. However, if we recall the indebtedness of the female evangelical novelists who followed in More's footsteps, the appropriation of the novel by a woman preacher is profoundly significant. Authorizing the voice of such a novelist is the supreme authority of God, transcending politics, sects, and gender. *Coelebs,* and novels like it, undoubtedly contributed to efforts to domesticate women's writing. Nevertheless, *Coelebs* also shows that a novelistic representation of evangelical domestic piety retained opposition to male domination. In the following decades, when domestic ideology was to be proffered as a panacea for working-class restiveness, aristocratic decadence, and, above all, feminist discontent, women writers became adept at turning the domestic novel into a vehicle of social criticism, assuming the role of prophets to call their readers to repentance.

Seven

Preaching Fiction: The Contribution of Charlotte Elizabeth Tonna

Charlotte Elizabeth Tonna (1790–1846) was intensely conscious of her female precursors in the tradition of evangelical social writing—particularly Hannah More—and of her obligation to secure a place for women's voices in social discourse. She adapted evangelical and novelistic strategies to answer the discursive threat of social science, which could naturalize according to market laws the human suffering she sought to expose and robbed her of the moral authority to protest. Her evangelical mission consisted in creating a mode of realistic fiction that conveyed the graphic material of parliamentary blue book reports on laboring conditions to a reading public of her peers, exhorting them, as More had done, to repent of immoral social and economic practices. Indeed, Tonna saw Hannah More as her mentor, rather than any male writer, and construed the failure of male writers to act as social prophets as constituting her own extraordinary call. The fruits of that call were passed on to Victorian writers as the early models of social realism.

Though the prophetic role enabled Tonna to justify her social-problem writing, it exacted a high price from a woman writer because it demanded she defend the Christian patriarchy that authorized her own voice. For Tonna, as an Anglican Evangelical during a period of paranoid defensiveness regarding church and monarch, her position was especially fraught with difficulties. She had to underscore every claim she made for her "extraordinary call" with assurances that it was indeed an exception, that she was not challenging the traditional role of women in the patriarchy. At some points in her polemical writing, Tonna's desire to serve two masters—the God who calls her to rebuke temporal authority and the patriarchy that sustains and controls her—has absurd consequences; her argument becomes a series of sallies and retreats. Furthermore, the extraordinary call to prophesy forced Tonna into a perpetual crisis mentality. If women were called to prophesy only in extraordinary circumstances, then Tonna needed to characterize every social problem she wished to discuss as a social crisis in order to justify her treatment of it. Quite early in her career, Tonna became an adherent of millennialism, thereby providing herself with an endless supply of emergencies leading up to one massive, biblically sanctioned cataclysm. Such a worldview cried out for a prophet.

Ultimately, fiction provided Tonna with a means of surviving, and even exploiting, these contradictions and demands. The novel could encompass both secular and sacred scripture, blue book and Bible. However, it would also admit the voices of the marginalized, their stories, in the way that facts and figures did not. The novel could appropriate from scripture the same transcendent moral authority that the preachers enjoyed, but it could also enable Tonna to reach the audience denied to women preachers of her time. Finally, it could elicit the desired response—repentance—without employing the sorts of authoritarian arguments Tonna wished to avoid. By appealing to imaginative "sympathies," it would evoke a confession, a willing assent.

In retrospect it may seem obvious that the best genre for presenting the wrongs of women or the exploitation of factory workers would be the novel, but for early nineteenth-century Evangelicals, still deeply suspicious of fiction, this remained a risky strategy. Yet evangelical teaching itself held the key to this difficulty. Just as women preachers had avoided rhetorical flourishes in their language in order to deliver a divine message unadulterated by human vanity, so Tonna tried in her fiction to eschew conventions of the lending-library romances and present as much as possible a realistic, unsentimental picture of her subject matter. The result was fiction that was sometimes aesthetically flawed but of unprecedented veracity and significant propagandistic power.

Answering the Call

The daughter of a Norwich clergyman, Charlotte Elizabeth was encouraged to have confidence in her ability to appropriate the privileged language of scripture. From Tonna's description of her childhood in her *Personal Recollections* (1841), one would guess that her father had read More's *Strictures*. He encouraged her participation in family discussions of current events, to which she credited her lifelong interest in politics, reflected in her writings.[1] A plan for young ladies' bible classes which she put forward in the pages of *The Christian Lady's Magazine* may have been patterned on Tonna's own religious education. In that plan she stressed the importance of individual scriptural interpretation, recommending that each student be required to "give her opinion" on a common biblical text, as well as "proofs in support of it from all parts of the scriptures."[2]

Tonna's education, like that of her predecessors in the preaching tradition, emphasized literature. Rendered deaf by an illness at age ten, Tonna turned to literature for adventure and companionship and from her reading of Shakespeare developed what she later called a "dangerous" taste for romance.[3] Though Shakespeare may have influenced her literary imagination, her religious convictions seem never to have been seriously endangered by exposure to such frivolous reading, defended as they were by a thorough knowledge of scripture and pious habits. Instead, her Evangelicalism shaped both her literary techniques and her goals as a fiction writer.

Like that of many women preachers, Tonna's call to authorship coincided with a break from temporal patriarchal authority. She wrote little of her adolescence or her courtship and marriage to a man remembered only as Captain Phelan. The marriage was disastrous: Phelan took his wife to his family estate outside Dublin, stranded her there alone for long periods of time, and treated her violently when he was present. Perhaps the best thing that can be said for Tonna's first husband is that he was indirectly responsible for her writing career. Tonna herself claimed that marriage had saved her from the temptation of seeking fame and fortune as a fiction writer; however, her solitary life in Ireland was devoted to collecting, transcribing, and writing "documentary materials" for lawyers engaged in representing her husband in a lawsuit over some land. Doubtless this experience aided her when she began writing political and economic analyses. As a more immediate consequence, she acquired a reputation as a "literary recluse," inspiring a female acquaintance to send her the packet of religious tracts published by the Dublin Tract Society that would launch her career as a writer.[4]

Having recently had a conversion experience, which for an already devout Anglican Evangelical meant a heightened sense of vocation, Tonna was convinced that the tracts were a sign that God was calling her to a vocation as a religious writer. On the night after the tracts arrived, Tonna began her first contribution to the society's efforts, and by morning had completed a didactic story which she promptly sent off to Dublin. This, Tonna wrote, was "the commencement of my literary labours in the Lord's cause."[5] Approving of her first submission, the Dublin Tract Society hired Tonna to write for them. Her tracts were well received by the society, and her efforts sufficiently lucrative to attract the attention of her wastrel husband. Fearful that he would sue her for her earnings, "Mrs. Phelan" legally and symbolically broke from his control by publishing under her Christian name, "Charlotte Elizabeth." In 1824 she separated from her husband and returned to England to live with her brother at Clifton, in close proximity to Hannah More at Cowslip Green.

As the result of her newfound evangelical vocation, Tonna had thrown off her husband's authority and taken as her mentor Hannah More, the most influential evangelical writer of the day. Clearly Tonna understood More's claims to the prophet's role and not only considered them just but personally inspiring. She visited More on several occasions, and in recounting those visits in her *Recollections* compared More to the Old Testament figures of Deborah, Jeremiah, and Ezekiel.[6] The connection between More's *Cheap Repository Tracts* and Tonna's work for the Dublin Tract Society is more than superficial, as both had as their implicit goal to combat the threat of a patriarchal structure hostile to women's speech. Certainly, the society's mission, to convert Irish Catholics to the Church of England, appealed to Tonna's vehement allegiance to the church and country she had left behind in following her husband to Ireland. However, the Roman Catholic church had special significance for Tonna as a woman. Like the French revolutionary government in the mind of Hannah More, the Catholic church represented for Tonna everything that excluded women from power: most important, it appeared to restrict access to scripture—the evangelical Protestant's ultimate source of power—to the ordained clergy.

In her response to the Catholic Emancipation Bill of 1829, Tonna made clear that she equated Catholicism with a male monopoly on moral and linguistic power. "Why," asked Tonna in her memoirs, "had I not been taught in early life that a fellow mortal held in his hands the power of saving or destroying my soul, and then commanded by that irresistable authority to abstain from looking into the word of God?"

> Because I was the subject of a Protestant country, basking in the sunshine of its spiritual lights, and sheltered by the enactments of a state that owned no earthly power superior to its own.[7]

Under the protection of the Protestant patriarchy, particularly in its current evangelical phase, women like Tonna had flourished, and she had no intention of standing idly by while that power base was threatened. "'But suppose a woman feels herself called on to take a personal interest in public affairs, what can she do, without stepping out of her proper sphere, and intruding into the province of the superior sex?'"[8] Tonna answered her own rhetorical question thus:

> I am going to tell you what a woman may do; for it may surely be said "Where there's a will, there's a way." When we set our hearts upon any thing, we are tolerably enterprising and persevering too, in its attainment; and this natural love of pleasing ourselves may be turned to a very good account.[9]

What Tonna did do to defend her self-interest was to circulate a petition against the Catholic Emancipation Bill, contact friends to oppose it, and devote special attention to it in her family's prayers. In this political activity, Tonna saw herself acting as a prophet: "I have staid [sic] up nearly all night, making, like Daniel, with tears, my supplications unto the Lord that he would pardon the sin of our princes and rulers, and have mercy on my people."[10] Her tears were to no avail, the bill passing on April 13, 1829; but even in her defeat Tonna remained confident of God's support. "For all this," she wrote of her political efforts, "and for the deep despondency that oppressed me then, I was rebuked, of course, by man; but God never rebuked me for it."[11]

Tonna articulated her own criteria for access to a public discourse when she, like More, acted as an editor. Tonna became editor of *The Christian Lady's Magazine* in 1834. She edited the *Protestant Annual* in 1840, and took up the editorship of the *Protestant Magazine* in 1841. Tonna led this magazine, and *The Christian Lady's Magazine*, until her death. As editor, Tonna had far greater control of her material than women who were at the mercy of male editors, and yet it is clear that Tonna went out of her way to assure the magazines' male publishers of her loyalty to their common Evangelical goals. Of course, within the context of the Evangelical patriarchy, Tonna had room to maneuver, and the periodicals she edited are filled with shrewdly feminized discussions of social reform.

Tonna's Preface to the first number of *The Christian Lady's Magazine* (January 1834) illustrates the editor's strategy. The magazine will avoid controversy, the editor promises, not wishing to offend any reader. Nevertheless,

> we too have our private opinions on such matters; and we do not hold ourselves pledged not to advance them, on a fitting occasion—nor to keep our pages always closed against correspondents who may bring them forward: but our present impression is, that we can go on as well, or better, without their introduction.[12]

What splendid prevarication! Tonna's brief remarks capture the essence of the evasions by which women eluded patriarchal control of social discourse. Women agree to sit in silence, to keep their "private opinions," until an extraordinary call comes—from God—to speak out. In the meantime, they might share their thoughts with one another in the "private" form of the letter. Apparently it makes little difference that Tonna speaks of letters to a magazine editor. But, of course, women are most interested in "practical" rather than theoretical matters anyway, Tonna innocently writes, hence the magazine will be especially pleased to receive "articles on subjects deeply practical, affecting our Christian ladies in their various and important domestic relationships."[13] Contributors to this department were advised to use "brevity and scriptural simplicity."[14] Doubtless the many articles on politics, factory reform, rehabilitation of prostitutes, charity, women writers, and great women of the Bible, "affected Christian ladies" quite profoundly. And, thanks to their "scriptural simplicity," they might carry divine authority.

Two major features of *The Christian Lady's Magazine* illustrate Tonna's ability as an editor and writer to introduce issues outside the strictly defined sphere of women's expertise. One entitled "Politics" ran regularly in the first two years; the other, "Female Biography of Scripture," commenced in 1839 and ran frequently, though at rather unpredictable intervals, through July 1843. Apparently, Tonna did not consider that she was violating her vow to avoid fiction when she cast her "Politics" column in the form of a dialogue between a well-educated young woman and her curmudgeonly uncle. The series begins quite self-consciously, with the uncle's discovery of his niece penning the word "Politics" at the top of her paper.

> "POLITICS!" exclaimed my uncle, who very unexpectedly popped his head over my shoulder, just as I had traced, in well rounded capitals, the imposing word which tops this page; "what in the world have you to do with politics?"
>
> This plain question, propounded in a tone of mirthful surprise, somewhat discomposed me; casting an air, almost of the ludicrous over the conscious self-importance with which I had been invested but a moment before. However, I mustered courage, and confidently replied, "A great deal, uncle: I have undertaken to conduct the political department in the new Lady's Magazine."

> "Humph! Lady's Magazine—the political depart-
> ment in a Lady's Magazine—humph!"
> You must know reader, that my uncle's "humph!"
> has something peculiarly annihilating in it. I can re-
> tort his raillery, avert his arguments, cavil at his
> conclusions,—but his "humph!" is unanswerable.[15]

The annihilating quality of the "humph" describes the silencing, exclusionary nature of a privileged discourse which need
not enter into dialogue with the marginal even to inform them
of their marginality. The uncle follows up his "humph" with a
chuckle, while the writer "silently awaited some remark that
could be replied to."[16]

> "Why don't you go on?" [the uncle asks.]
> "How can I, uncle, while you stand peeping over
> me, prepared to laugh at my humble attempts."[17]

Tonna's female character expresses the same frustration which
must have filled the heckled women preachers. The niece asks
her uncle what he finds so amusing about her reporting "important public events for the consideration of her own sex,"
and he responds significantly that "it is the fashion of the age
for women to leave their assigned sphere, setting themselves
up for political agitators, political economists, and what not."
But the niece assures her uncle that this is not her intention,
and "pull[s] the kind-hearted gentleman into" a chair at her
side, thereby drawing him into collusion.

With the strategic manipulation of this passage, Tonna likewise pulls her critics into league with her. She has disassociated
herself from female political writers (especially the political
economist Harriet Martineau), who claim no spiritual sanction
for their writing, and therefore can be easily dismissed as social
critics by a skeptical "humph." The niece appropriates her
uncle's voice, calling on him to assist her narration of the major
political events of the year. Together they treat the Child Labor
Bill, industrial riots, women's education, the Irish troubles,
election results, and a host of other topics generally considered
to be outside woman's sphere.

The uncle figure provides patriarchal sanction, indeed defense, of Charlotte Elizabeth's project. Through his character, she expresses her desire that these columns will find their way to the seat of temporal power, the Parliament, and influence political decisions. He also helps her to encourage middle-class female readers to repent of their silent complicity in social injustice, and to voice their righteous indignation. In the magazine's second number, the uncle fervently hopes that their audience will come to include legislators, and describes the periodical's potential influence in terms clearly evangelical. The "Politics" column will contribute to social discourse, in the uncle's words, by "touching some kind hearts, the opening of some eloquent lips, on behalf of those who are perishing for a lack of a little zeal on our parts."[18] The purpose expressed is dual, reflecting a dual audience. "Touching the kind hearts" of those with political power is sufficient to assist the perishing; but to those without political power, including women, an evangelical call to prophesy must be issued: open your "eloquent lips" if you can make no other contribution.

In addition to this evangelical role, the uncle also reports information considered too disturbing or delicate to be narrated by a woman. He conveys to women the "strong truths" More spoke of in *Strictures*. Through his voice Tonna sets before her readers, in unsentimental detail, the atrocities of factory life as she found them described in Parliamentary blue books. For example, apropos of a discussion of Sadler's Bill requiring the fencing of machinery, the uncle relates the following story from a child labor report:

> On Thursday week, as a youth named Thomas Rhodes, fifteen years of age, was employed as a feeder of woolen engines at Mr. S——'s factory, Rochdale, one of the straps belonging to the engine came off; and while he was attempting to put it on the drum, the strap gathered round his ancle, and carried him up. He screamed out, and two men went to his assistance, but without effect; the poor boy was taken round the drum, and as there were only about ten inches between the top of the drum and the ceiling, his head and legs were torn from his body, and his intestines were scattered about the room.[19]

"Spare me more," the niece responds, "but not the manager's abuse of power." Even out of context this story retains its gruesome power, and not many people could be expected to read it with detachment. Tonna's commitment to realism, evinced here, comes from her evangelical heritage, requiring that she deliver her message without adornment. Sanctioned by her notions of evangelical duty, Tonna engages in an example of the sort of unflinching muckraking journalism associated with the writers of Naturalism at the end of the century.

The niece's role, meanwhile, is to address women's particular interests, not only pointing out to women their duty to inform themselves on current events and to respond to calls for charity, but also urging a male audience to acknowledge both its duty towards women and its need to rely on female influence in the social sphere. Ruskin's claims in "Queens' Gardens" (1865) pale by comparison with some of Tonna's more extravagant proposals for a sort of *mütterpolitick*.

> To woman, a modest and contracted sphere is appointed: but the home wherein her station is found, is the centre of that attraction, which, by its universal influence, diverging unseen to the remotest corners of the earth, binds distant empires together, and harmonizes what would otherwise prove a chaos of ever-jarring elements. Look at man in his uncivilized state, where woman fills but the office of a despised drudge, —or where she manifests the fiercer passion of unsubdued nature in its utter alienation from God. You will find him bent on violence and spoil; going forth to the slaughter of his fellow-man, with the reckless spirit of devastation; his hand against every one, and content that every hand should be against him. It is when man has recovered, under the mild beam of gospel truth, somewhat of the original blessing which constituted woman "an help meet for him,"—it is when his home becomes the abode of gentle sympathy and intellectual companionship, and spiritual communion, that man begins to feel he has somewhat worth fencing around than shield and spear. And thus, in its most secret, most unconscious exercise,

> does the talent of female influence form the basis of
> even all commercial intercourse among the nations
> of the earth.[20]

Tonna constructs this argument to serve two goals. On the one
hand, it characterizes woman's influence conventionally as
mysterious and passive, and wholly confined to the domestic
sphere. On the other, it calls on scripture to justify placing that
sphere at the very center of civilization, and demands that
women be adequately educated to fulfill their role as cultural
leaders. Female virtues are the criteria by which all else in the
culture, including political and economic dealings, must be
judged. If one is looking for evidence of evangelicalism leading
to the femininization of culture, this is a striking example.

Like her preaching foremothers, Tonna can imagine circumstances in which women's influence would be direct, her
domestic ministry called out of the home and into her society.
In the uncle's voice, she confronts the Pauline injunction
against such behavior, and formulates a version of Wesley's
"extraordinary call" which could justify women's entry into a
range of professions. "Women are exhorted to be keepers of
the home," the uncle remarks,

> prohibited from assuming to teach, or usurp au-
> thority over the man; but this in nowise interferes
> with their privilege, and bounden duty, of instruct-
> ing their own households—their servants, and the
> poor around them. Ladies are not called on to study
> medicine, with a view to general practice; but when
> some violent epidemic rages, devastating the land,
> who would object to making them so far acquainted
> with its nature, its tendency, and the most effectual
> mode of applying a cure, as to arm them with heal-
> ing powers for the general benefit? I always wish to
> draw a line very distinctly between the acknowl-
> edged, the universal duties of Christian Ladies, and
> those additional calls which they must be prepared
> to meet in particular emergencies.[21]

Once again, Tonna is careful to toe a patriarchal line, while
making substantial inroads into its power. By analogy, "particular emergencies" may include threats to the government or the

church, as well as to the national health, thereby justifying women's entry into those spheres.

The strongest statement of the conditions warranting women's extraordinary call comes from the niece. As she comments when discussing the agitation by the Irish M.P.s:

> When all goes smoothly, and the good ship is gliding over tranquil waters, before a favouring breeze, once can hardly expect the female passengers to concern themselves much about the working of the vessel: but when stormy winds arise, when the sky darkens above, and the depths heave below, and the breakers are heard, with "sullen roar" struggling amid rocks to leeward, it becomes no matter of surprise, if even the ladies look out with inquisitive anxiety, and ask whether the man at the wheel is capable of steering through a dangerous track; whether the crew are ready-handed, true-hearted and firm, and if the captain has his charts unrolled, his mind collected, his—Here I was fain to leave off.[22]

Tonna's analogy, like More's in her preface to *Strictures*, claims for women complete access to social discourse—in extraordinary circumstances. All that is necessary then is to convince an audience of the gravity of their problems to justify women's activities as social critics.

A few months after she wrote this justification of women's social-problem writing, Tonna defended her mentor against a woman who had written a letter to the editor of the *Christian Lady's Magazine* critical of Hannah More and other women who thrust themselves into the role of social prophet. In discussing More, Tonna was also justifying her own prophetic mission.

> OBSERVING the honoured and revered name of Hannah More introduced in a paper published in the last Christian Lady's Magazine . . . as making one of the "female host, who having thrown aside the scissors and the bodkin, brandished the goose-quill with an energy and perseverance truly admirable," I would remind the writer, *who speaks thus in scorn*, that Hannah More has, *indeed*, brandished the

goose-quill, and that the effect of that brandishing has been instrumental (through the mercy of God) in awakening the souls of many to a deep sense of their helpless, sinful state by nature; yes, many, who have since, perhaps, been led to carry doctrine higher than their first Instructress, still acknowledge, with affectionate gratitude, that piercing convictions of sin were awakened in their minds through her instrumentality.

Tonna speaks of the goose-quill in terms clearly indicating that the evangelical woman writer is God's champion, defending the faith with pen instead of sword. Called by God in time of crisis, a woman must answer or be guilty of sin. Male mentors, like Wilberforce, should not be confused with Barak, who asks Deborah to accompany him against the Canaanites because he is afraid to go alone. Instead, they too are merely acting as God's instruments, calling women to participate in the social discourse, which unlike the battlefield, is within woman's sphere. In acknowledging her debt to More as the first of the female prophets, Tonna also claims to have surpassed her mentor, not of her own volition, but because she has "been led to carry doctrine higher than [her] first Instructress." Led, that is, by God.

When Tonna begins her "Female Biography of Scripture" series three years later, she will treat Deborah and Esther again and again, not as appropriate role models for all women, but as extraordinary examples of women called by God to lead their communities. Tonna makes this clear in her introduction to her first sketch of Deborah.

> I do not, however, intend to hold up Jael as a pattern to the "Christian Ladies" who read this Magazine, nor yet Deborah herself, *literally taken*. I do not wish to see them going forth with our armies, advising our Wellingtons, nor nailing to the floor the head of a Mehemet Ali of the Grand Signor. No: and for this valid reason, that they are not divinely inspired nor divinely commissioned; they are not prophetesses, like Deborah, nor indeed can such

peculiar inspirations be expected in these days of "open vision" and gospel light.[23]

If not "literally," does she mean her readers should take Deborah as a role model "spiritually"? After all, it was not Deborah, but Jael, who nailed Sisera's head to the floor. And were "peculiar inspirations" so unlikely in these latter days? Deborah in fact proves that women can serve as instruments of the word of God.

> To her all the children of Israel came for judgment; that is, for advice in their disputes, and for instruction as to the Mosaic law, and other religious matters. How strange, say some, that such an honour should be put on a woman! True; and under the Christian dispensation, women are appointed to "keep silence," in public, and to "ask" for information "at home;" yet Deborah and other prophetesses are proofs that there is nothing in the *nature* of woman to render her incapable of the highest and noblest public duties. It is part of the original denunciation upon her, that she must be in subjection; nevertheless, God has often been pleased to vindicate the character and powers of those whom man too frequently chooses to view as an inferior class of beings, and he has vouchsafed that deliverance by the hand of woman which He has denied to those who call themselves "the *superior* sex."[24]

The carefully balanced qualifications of this passage reveal Tonna's anxiety over her own increasing power as a social prophet, and the threat she unwillingly poses to the patriarchy that sponsors her. Her hostility to other female prophets, like Wollstonecraft and Martineau, stems from her fear that they will cut the ground out from under all of them by challenging the divine authority which she regards as the only validation of women's speech that her culture will recognize.

Helen Fleetwood: *Fiction and the Prophet*

The pioneering novel of social evangelism, *Helen Fleetwood*, was written by an author deeply suspicious of fiction. Furthermore, it was serialized in the very *Christian Lady's Magazine* from which Tonna had promised to exclude fiction. Tonna was not being hypocritical. For her, fiction meant the lending-library romances. She opposed useless books that distracted readers from the Bible and other edifying and informative texts, and only served to dissipate their intellectual powers. Readers seduced by the impotent language of romance would never learn the languages which would effect social change. With *Helen Fleetwood* she was creating something new: a political sermon in novel form, convicting its audience of the sins of economic exploitation and dereliction of duty. Tonna is the prophet of reality, proclaiming an unadulterated vision of factory conditions as reported in the blue books. Taking on herself the role of a prophet in the Dives and Lazarus parable, she is the evangelist of reform, seeking her reader's conversion to a new sense of responsibility for their working-class brothers as sisters. The novel provided her with strategies for effecting these goals.

As narrator, Tonna assumes the role of prophet in her own retelling of the Dives and Lazarus parable. In the original (Luke 16:19–31), the rich man Dives ignores the pathetic beggar Lazarus, who lies at his gate. Both men die, and Lazarus is taken to Abraham's bosom while Dives is consigned to eternal torment. When Dives begs Abraham to send Lazarus to warn his brothers to repent of their selfishness, the patriarch responds, "they have Moses and the prophets; let them hear them . . . if they hear not Moses and the prophets, neither will they be persuaded, though one rose from the dead" (Luke 16:29, 31). If Tonna's wealthy readers fail to recognize Lazarus at their doorsteps, ignorance cannot be their excuse.

Tonna presents the Lazaruses of the factory system with unflinching realism. Her story is not filtered through a polite perspective but attempts to identify with the point of view of the exploited. Furthermore, many of the novel's Lazarus figures are female. The principal characters are the Green family: four orphaned children, their grandmother, and their orphaned cousin, Helen. The children's orphaned state testifies to the ultimate unreliability of temporal patriarchy. Representatives of patriarchal authority, when they are not positively evil, like the factory foremen and owners, are benevolent but ineffective, like the clergyman, Mr. Barlow.

Mrs. Green assumes responsibility for her family's spiritual
and bodily welfare. As a spiritual leader, this poor, devout
widow is exemplary. Not only does she diligently perform her
evangelical duties within her home, acting as her grand-
children's and niece's spiritual guide, but she also evangelizes
effectively among other poor families as well. However, the
family's matriarch is no match for the heartless world ruled by
the laws of political economy rather than Christian charity. To
save them from the workhouse, the parish clergyman, Mr.
Barlow, naïvely suggests that Mrs. Green move to the nearest
mill town where the children can find work in the factory. They
are walking into the lions' den.

Mrs. Green is triply handicapped in her attempts to provide
for her family economically—by her gender, her class, and her
religion—for those who control the factory system do not acknowledge the same master she does. The children soon begin
to show the ill effects of the factory on both body and spirit.
Females in this story prove to be particularly vulnerable to the
horrors of factory life. When they succumb to the immorality
encouraged by their dehumanizing environment, the consequences of pregnancy or prostitution became disastrous. Yet
when Helen refuses to condone their vices, her fellow workers
abuse her for her evangelistic spirit. Her sinking state prompts
Mrs. Green to speak on Helen's behalf. The grandmother goes
to the foreman to inform him of the immoral conditions of the
factory, but she is dismissed as a troublesome crank. Like the
importunate widow, she takes her cause to the millowner. "Mr.
Z." listens patiently to Mrs. Green's petition, until he notices
that his daughter Amelia is listening as well, and casting com-
passionate looks at the speaker. At that, he sends Amelia from
the room, and angrily reprimands Mrs. Green "for introducing such improper subjects in the presence of a young lady,
whose ears ought not to have been assailed by discourse so unfit
for a delicate mind" (*HF*, p. 560).

The patriarchy, as represented by Mr. Z., would make all the
women of his class like Dives by the imposition of exaggerated
notions of female delicacy. While they are prevented by this enforced ignorance from performing their Christian duty, their
working-class sisters must be subjected to degradation. A
shocked Mrs. Green replies to the millowner:

"Oh, sir, though of very humble rank, my poor
Helen is modest and delicate as you yourself can desire a female to be; and she is abashed to hear and to
see in their worst forms, all the evil things that I
spoke of, and others that I would not even mention
before the young lady. Let this move your compassion for her." But Mr. Z. had worked himself into a
passion, for propriety's sake. (*HF*, p. 560)

"Propriety" serves to exclude disruptive voices. Like Dives, the
millowner cannot be troubled with knowledge of his ability
to alleviate human suffering, but hides behind hypocritical
speeches about female delicacy to insure his own uninter-
rupted comfort.

Women must break this silence. As Mrs. Green is being
shown out of the millowner's house, Amelia comes up to her
with an offer of money. Through Mrs. Green, Tonna informs
her polite female readers that "'it is not money that I want: but
if you could win your father's protection for my poor girls, how
thankful I should be'" (*HF*, p. 560). Influence over men, not
pin money from them, constitutes women's power.

This incident clearly illustrates the imperative to introduce
gender into social discourse. So long as the power to represent
social conditions is controlled by a few powerful men, it will be
impossible to speak on behalf of abused females to the women
who could help them. A social discourse that naturalizes hierarchies of class and gender as "facts" inherently excludes subversive voices. If this were not the case, then the parliamentary
investigations on which Tonna based her own story would have
had a prophetic effect, and the lot of all factory workers, male
and female, would have improved without the need for female
social-problem novelists to espouse their cause. But few signs
of a Dives repenting could be seen either in the fictional world
Tonna creates or in the social actuality of the 1840s.

The inherent exclusivity of an authoritarian, male-dominated social discourse is presented in the novel's trial scene.
Helen Fleetwood is attacked in the factory for defending a
younger Irish girl from the abuse of the other workers. When
the overlooker intervenes to break up the scuffle, he takes this
chance to punish Helen for her subversive influence, and

strikes her cruelly. Mr. Barlow, the rector, visits the Greens and discovers Helen's injury. His indignation against the factory system aroused, he insists the they seek justice through the legal system. Barlow reports the incident to a factory inspector, appointed by Parliament to investigate such abuses, and a hearing is scheduled. However, despite the support of a clergyman and an inspector, Helen cannot overcome the system of social structures erected against her. Her powerlessness is manifested in the ineffectualness of her testimony and that of the other girls who testify on her behalf.

The magistrate questions Mary Green first, but when she tries to explain the history of Katy's persecution that led up to her action, he interrupts with a warning that confine herself to the "facts" of the case. The rules of this investigation allow more freedoms to the accused than to the victim, permitting the overlooker John Roy to question Mary, but not the victim her oppressor. He does his best to confuse and contradict Mary, and because she proves his verbal equal, the magistrate dismisses her as "saucy." Next, Katy herself is called to testify. The magistrate attributes her innocent use of Bible language to the wholesome influence of the factory rather than to widow Green who taught it to her. The overlooker manages to provoke Katy by maligning Mary's character, and the court laughs at her stereotypical Irish temper. When the magistrate demands a translation of her ejaculation in Irish, she gladly responds,

> "It was the verse of a psalm that my father used to say out of the Irish Bible when Helen Fleetwood's character was to be taken away. The English is 'The lying lips shall be put to silence that cruelly, disdainfully, and spitefully speak against the righteous.'"
> (*HF*, p. 588)

"'Are we to have no decent witnesses. . . ? '" the magistrate inquires. Marginalized by race, class, and sex, Katy has become incomprehensible in the legal discourse, as her Irish speech illustrates. However, as Paul writes in Galatians, she is the overlooker's and magistrate's equal in Christ, and her Bible language carries divine authority.

Helen Fleetwood testifies last. Her emaciated condition makes her appear "almost heavenly," thinks her cousin Richard, and she "modestly, but clearly and distinctly" delivers her testimony. She is indeed the most effective prophet. One magistrate acknowledges that she has established Mary's innocence, and the overlooker's attempt to discredit Helen backfires. He hopes that by revealing her dependence on the Green's he will reveal her selfish motives in defending Mary. But thanks to her reliance on God, Helen enjoys a radical independence. "'If by any dispensation of God'" Helen tells the court,

> "I was deprived of my best and only friends on earth, I have still one to go to who has said, "Him that cometh unto me I will in no wise cast out."
>
> "That is to say, I suppose, you would turn preacher" [Roy retorts.]
>
> Here a murmur of "shame!" was distinctly heard; and one of the gentlemen on the bench said, rather warmly, "Enough of this; it will not shake the clear testimony of the young person before us." (*HF*, p. 589)

Though the magistrates recognize the authority of Helen's language, the limitations of the legal discourse prevent them from responding to it. They will not undergo the radical change of heart, replacing the law with the spirit; they will not repent. Like Darius in More's treatment of Daniel's story, they will throw their prophets to the lions.

In order for social discourse to represent the gender- and class-based causes of such injustice, Tonna implies, the woman preacher's voice must play a role. It must penetrate the system's defenses by appealing to the same transcendent authority that sanctions the temporal authority of social institutions. Helen's demeanor, language, and rhetorical strategy unambiguously identify her with the tradition of the woman preacher, and her witness is genuinely heard. But it does not effect a genuine repentance. Roy is made to pay a small fine, and the girls' persecution at the factory continues. The factory system claims its victims as always: Mrs. Green goes to the workhouse, and Helen Fleetwood dies.

What is needed beyond the preaching voice to feminize the social discourse and secure the reader's repentance may be the novel itself. The first installment of *Helen Fleetwood* appeared in the same number of *The Christian Lady's Magazine* as the sketch of Deborah in its series "Female Biography of Scripture." The society that could acquiesce in the atrocities described in *Helen Fleetwood* is clearly in need of a prophetess. Tonna provides several in the novel, including Helen Fleetwood and Mrs. Green. However, within the novel their testimony goes unheeded by the upper classes. They are all effective preachers of the good news to their own class, but it is up to the novelist herself to bring her readers to repentance.

The possibilities of narrative technique in the novel are perfectly suited to the woman preacher's goals. Unlike the discourses employed by her characters or her sources, Tonna's own discourse—the novel—need not be monolithic or exclusionary. The sermon or the blue book imposes a hierarchical relation on the author and reader. By writing in these genres an author assumes an authoritative role, and his readers a silent, passive one. This relationship is incompatible with both evangelical and feminist goals because they require that "readers" be empowered to speak. Converts must confess their sins and witness to God's grace; women must respond to writing with words of their own. The fiction, at least, of the novel is that it creates a dialogue between writer and reader. The good novelist "shows" rather than "tells," to borrow Gaskell's language. That is, like the women preachers, or Hannah More's character Jack Anvil, the novelist merely serves as the unadulterating medium of spiritual truth. The reader is free to respond with a hard heart, or with a heartfelt repentance. The novelist, therefore, coming closest to the prophet in creating scripture rather than commenting on it, recapitulates the relationship of evangelist to convert, of Jesus to the Samaritan woman or Jonah to the Ninevites.

This is the same effect More had attempted to create through *Coelebs*. But the first-person narrator of that novel stands in relation to the reader as would a preacher or moralist. His opinions are virtually synonymous with the author's, and therefore his authority must be upheld. The mild irony implicit in a number of Coelebs's conversations with Lucilla merely confirm his superiority when he readily accepts her slight improvements in his otherwise perfect worldview. That novel lacks the more subtle dynamic possible between a third-person narrator, the presenter of some truth in which the narrator is not immediately involved, and a reader. This is the crucial contribution Tonna makes to the woman preacher's voice, discovering the narrative technique that brings it into the literary mainstream on behalf of women.

By encouraging a dialogic relationship of novelist to reader, Tonna seeks to restore the woman preacher's power to issue a call to evangelize to other women. Despite her rhetoric about the proper female sphere, it was obvious that a point of crisis had been reached in which women not only must prophesy, but must act on one another's behalf: the Baraks of Tonna's world lacked the courage and imagination necessary to rectify the "wrongs of woman." She may not wholly abandon the notion of an "extraordinary call," but she expands its limits considerably. The only way to get this call past the patriarchal censor—the Mr. Z.'s—is by presenting her evangelistic message in a genre notorious as frivolous entertainment. Once she reachers her female audience, her tale serves to educate them and enlist them as sister evangelists in the mission to the patriarchy. The strategy for converting a male audience is to appeal to the authorities—church and government—which legitimize their power. But experience, within the novel and without, proves that a single voice crying in the wilderness may not be enough. That women must recognize their obligation to their sisters over that to any patriarchal institution.

Perils of the Prophet

In 1841 Charlotte Elizabeth published *Helen Fleetwood* in novel form, published her *Personal Recollections*, and married the secretary of the Royal United Institution, Lewis Hippolytus Tonna. She was fifty-one. It was as if Tonna felt compelled to accomplish the hallmarks of the career of a woman preacher within a single year. Both her novel and her memoirs left a permanent record of her activities, including their subversive qualities, which an "official," male-authored account would have censored. At the same time her marriage to a man who supported her literary efforts provided Tonna with a patriarchally sanctioned role free of the "natural duties" of mother, if not wife. This coincidence is striking. Having become "public property" by her authorship, she wished to prevent biographers, critics, or historians from misreading her life. As the experiences of More and the preachers indicate, Tonna's concerns were legitimate. Borrowing evangelical doctrine on scripture interpretation, Tonna claimed that her life could be understood properly only by those who "read" it "spiritually." "Writers who are themselves wholly unenlightened by spiritual knowledge," Tonna wrote, "and uninfluenced by spiritual feeling, will take up as a good speculation, what must to them be a mystery, and wrong the subject of their memorial while they injure the cause in which he laboured."[25] Tonna wished to take control of the text of her own life, to prevent its misconstrual by those who failed to appreciate or wished to suppress the subversive aspects of her writing. Even her husband's *Memoir of Charlotte Elizabeth* manages to mute her powerful voice by applying the conventions of sentimental biography to her life. He gives equal attention to her political writings, her pets, her gardening, and her piety.[26] Well aware of the power of male-authored texts to distort or silence women's voices, Tonna would publish her own story.

These strategies, personal and literary, worked brilliantly, and in the following year the Christian Influence Society approached Tonna to write an extensive polemical work on the condition of the English working class. Tonna was solicited not only for her rhetorical power but for her expertise in matters of labor, economics, and politics. Despite Tonna's skepticism, the Christian Influence Society expected that *The Perils of the Nation: An Appeal to the Legislature, the Clergy, and the Higher and Middle Classes* would convince its audience of the necessity of humanitarian social reform. To that end, they supplied her with all the documentary evidence necessary to achieve command of her subject matter, from parliamentary reports to private investigations.[27] The doors to the inner sanctum of privileged language had been flung open to receive her.

Perils is an excellent example of social evangelism, that genre born of the union of religious and political goals. It musters the forces of several authoritative discourses: those of religion, literature, science, and history. At the same time, Tonna uses scripture to deconstruct those narratives upholding authoritarian hierarchies. Not surprisingly, *Perils* was published anonymously and Tonna refers to herself with masculine pronouns. She explains that society must undergo a radical conversion from the prejudices which allow the powerful to deny their equality with the oppressed. "One taste of the pure delight of charity," Tonna writes,

> resulting from a deed of self-denying charity, having reference less to an individual case than to an oppressed class, would give a new turn to our thoughts, feelings, and pursuits; we should find indeed that
> The proper study of mankind is man,
> but not as an abstract science, aiming to make acquaintance with a series of physical and intellectual phenomena, nor even the higher range of spiritual investigations; but a practical studying of the best means by which at once to elevate the national character, and ensure the national stability, by such a following out of the greatest-happiness-system as Jeremy Bentham never dreamed of. (*Perils*, pp. 99–100)

From the language of this passage—"physical and intellectual phenomena," "spiritual investigations," the quotation from Pope's *Essay on Man*—it is clear that Tonna is adept at manipulating privileged languages, and does not reject them out of a sense of her own inadequacy. Instead, she insists that her readers view the lives of the working class in the context of Christian duty, statistical evidence, historical consequence, etc., and recognize the priority of Christian duty.

One of the immediate goals of Tonna's writing is the passage of the Ten Hours Bill, and her discussion of factory working hours illustrates her facility at combining these discourses. Tonna begins her chapter on the "Manufacturing Poor" with a summary of investigations brought before the House of Commons.[28] Citing these reports, she describes with scientific detachment the fact that children are expected to work twelve-hour days, and that there exists no limit on adults' work hours. Suddenly she places these statistics in a biblical context, shrewdly concluding her paragraph with the observation that these working conditions are "aggravated by man's refusal to be his brother's keeper."[29] God is not such a merciless taskmaster. He

> looks down from heaven upon the children of men, whose frame he well knows, and whom he never willingly afflicts or grieves; each one of whom he sent into the world naked and helpless, and each one of whom in nakedness and helplessness must stand before him at the great day. (*Perils*, p. 20)

Tonna fills this passage with Bible language, paraphrasing Lamentations 3:33 ("For he doth not afflict willingly nor grieve the children of men"); Job 1:21 ("Naked I came out of my mother's womb, and naked shall I return thither"); and Romans 14:10 ("we shall all stand before the judgment seat of Christ"). Scripture, not the author, condemns the perpetrators of workers' suffering. Furthermore, history will condemn them as well. Tonna continues:

> . . . and what a spectacle does he behold! not among the savage and barbarous nations, who never heard of the great Creator and his laws, of the blessed Redeemer and his love; not among people kept in comparative ignorance of both, by the substitution of the commandments of men for the doctrines of revelation,—but in a country where the knowledge of his will in all things is attainable by every human being who enquires concerning it, does this system exist. Here, in England, the Queen of Nations,
>
>   The dread and envy of them all,
> here, where the Bible is every man's book, and freedom is every man's birthright, do we find for the partial aggrandisement of a very few, for their indulgence in luxurious living, and the rivalry of display, multitudes chained by the strong fetter of extreme poverty, to a thraldom that leaves them absolutely unable to acquaint themselves with what is no less essential to the pauper than to the peer; what the latter may indeed neglect, and at his own peril

> choke with the riches and pleasures of this life, but
> which no man may withhold from another with-
> out braving the extremest wrath of God. (*Perils*,
> p. 20–21)

In the fervent rhetoric of a jeremiad, Tonna calls England to repentance. National pride and Christian duty demand that the powerful of the age preserve God's special grace bestowed on England—the genius of Protestantism and of evangelical-ism especially—the privilege of every individual to learn from scripture his or her status as child of God. There is neither master nor hand in Christ. Dives, Tonna's language implicitly warns, cannot deny Lazarus his "birthright" without ultimately suffering the consequences.

Tonna's argument would be taken up in a secular form by the Chartists, who saw literacy as the key to working-class liber-ation. But it is important to notice the power Tonna's argument derives from its evangelical context, as well as the special im-plications her argument has for women. Again and again Tonna claims that the universal accessibility of scripture is the special genius of Protestantism, a contention which appears in-controvertible. Hence, while arguments might be made against more general demands that attention be given to working-class literacy, over a century of evangelical teaching supported her allegation that "the Bible is every man's book." Tonna well knew the liberating potential of scripture that had enabled her to achieve her own powerful voice and authority. To make broader claims for working-class education would unneces-sarily lay her open to attack as a political radical. Scripture itself could teach the marginalized that "freedom is every man's birthright." Of course, it would teach every woman the same thing, which is more than could be said for secular Chartist propaganda.

As in *Helen Fleetwood*, Tonna never makes a feminist argu-ment directly, but she clearly treats her subject matter with par-ticular sensitivity to women's issues. Regardless of the abuse she is exposing, Tonna tends to illustrate it with incidents in which women rather than men are the victims. Not sur-prisingly, she emphasizes the vulnerability of women's morals to the crushing dehumanization of factory work, but when advocating safety measures in factories, she quotes from a *Bolton Free Press* story about one Isabella Gibly, fourteen, who was torn apart by a machine in the factory owned by Messrs. Cartwright, Whalley, Banks, and Blackburn.[30] Or, when discussing prostitution, Tonna enjoins magistrates to punish employers who compromise the modesty of their female workers.

Tonna is not so simplistic as to cast her argument simply in terms of sex, however. Wealthy women are as likely as wealthy men to exploit the poor of either sex. In the hope of converting her peers, Tonna acts as intermediary between the working-class women she reports on and their sisters and potential benefactresses among her audience. She holds up the "undeniable facts" of the *Second Report of the Children's Employment Commission* on the incidence of blindness among dressmakers. Tonna quotes the report's conclusion that "'the immediate cause of the disease in the eyes [of a seventeen-year-old girl] was excessive and continued application to making mourning.'"[31] In her chapter on "Female Influence," Tonna exhorts her wealthy female readers to inform themselves as to the realities of their society and their Christian duty towards society's victims.

> These things ARE: to be willfully ignorant of them, or to know that they exist, and take no decided step toward putting them away from before the eyes of the Lord God of Sabaoth, is a matter between the English Lady and Him to whom she must give account, when all these glittering vanities have passed away, and nothing remain of them, but what is recorded in those books out of which the dead shall be judged. (*Perils*, p. 363)

Tonna casts her female readership in the role of Dives and reminds them that they will be accountable to God for their neglect of the poor. But she goes beyond that to argue, albeit indirectly, for female participation in social discourse.

Addressing her male readers in her male persona, Tonna declares that "in all our great national crises has the feminine mind appeared clad with masculine energy, and evinced a fortitude, an endurance most admirable" (*Perils*, p. 346). Not only does the present crisis imply an extraordinary call to women to employ their "masculine" talents, but men should consider it a matter of national pride that Englishwomen are so well-prepared to do so.

> . . . they comprehend our political or commercial objects, share our anxieties, and assist us by their intelligent counsel, to an extent which renders their power, for good or evil, almost irresistible; and, contrasted with the insignificance of women in foreign lands, truly marvelous. No human beings, perhaps, are so quick at detecting injustice, resenting oppression, relieving the necessitous, and soothing the unhappy. (*Perils*, p. 345)

There is an implicit threat in this celebration of English womanhood. Beyond the standard argument that women will misuse their influence if men do not teach them how to use it properly is the suggestion that the wrongs of women, like the wrongs of the workers, must be alleviated to avert revolution. Women have been, and are being, enlightened concerning their own condition, and should not be counted on to "suffer and be still."

The influence of *Perils* was impressive. According to Tonna's husband, it

> had a marked and decided influence, not only on the tone of public feeling, but directly on the Legislature. . . . It was quoted on platforms and discussed in private circles; three important societies may be attributed to its influence, viz., the Society for Improving the Condition of the Labouring Classes, the Church Extension Fund, and the Clerical Education Aid fund; and what were its effects in aiding the passing of the Mines and Collieries' Bill, and the Ten Hours Bill, and in bringing forward the Health of Towns Bill, will only be known when the secrets of all hearts are revealed.[32]

Even if one acknowledges the possible exaggeration of the work's influence on legislation, *Perils* undoubtedly entered the social debate and genuinely transformed it. Nevertheless, as the passage on female influence quoted above indicates, Tonna bought her own evangelistic influence at a price. By adopting a masculine persona in *Perils*, she risked complicity in the efforts of monological patriarchy to suppress women's voices. If we reconsider the passage above from the point of view of a reader hostile to women's influence, we might conclude that the writer was subtly encouraging us to pursue more effective means of controlling women's power. Her authoritarian genre and male persona undercut her attempt to open the public discourse to marginal voices. The trap Tonna falls into in assuming a male persona for her nonfiction she avoids when writing novels and stories. In *Wrongs of Women* (1843–44) she again turns to fiction to prophesy on behalf of women.

The Wrongs of Women

"'In Christ Jesus, there is neither male nor female,'" Tonna writes in the introduction to *The Wrongs of Women*. She returns her reader to scripture and the radical equality of persons imposed on Christian culture by the original evangelistic mission of the apostles. Tonna conceives of her present work as a contribution to that mission, and asks for the gift of the Holy Spirit to enable this "weaker vessel" to be a fit instrument of God's will. That vessel vows to deliver her message as unadulterated by fiction as is possible to an audience consisting of the "educated females of England."[33]

Tonna justifies her use of fiction in terms of its combination of realistic and dialogic, evangelistic qualities. In the introduction to the final story of *The Wrongs of Women*, Tonna explains that it has been her intention "to engage the reader's sympathies, while concentrating her attention more effectually than the pages of a formal report, necessarily prolix and full of repetitions" (*WW*, p. 441). The formal report not only bores its reader, it thwarts his or her response with its pretense to completeness. Fiction is a superior tool for social evangelism because, as an "internally persuasive discourse," it demands the reader's response.[34]

In the four stories that make up *The Wrongs of Women*—"Milliners and Dressmakers," "The Forsaken Home," "The Little Pin-headers," and "The Lace-Runners"—Tonna uses various literary devices to elicit a response to the sad realities of working women's lives. In the first story, Tonna encourages her reader to identify with the dressmakers' lives by introducing familiar details from middle-class domestic life as one might find it in a domestic novel. However, when the young dressmakers gather in a circle to sew, it is not for recreation. They do not draw their chairs around a hearth, but perch on rough stools in a stifling room and strain for hours to see their stitches in the dim light. A book is brought into the room, and the reader expects the Bible to be read: "one of the elder assistants, with a strong voice, prepares to read it aloud" (*WW*, p. 404). But this "strong voice" gives itself over to a story of "heroes and heroines," whose tale consists of "murder, and violence, and situations of fearful peril, and bursts of unbridled passion." Rather than liberating its audience, this discourse enslaves their imaginations to the very world of luxury that exploits their labor. For these girls, trapped in a life of painful drudgery, this reading is not a harmless diversion. The naïve heroine, Ann, is taken up with the story, and longs for any means of escape, ignorant of its cost. Only her pious upbringing combined with the physically debilitating effects of her labor check Ann's desires.

Having established this sisterhood of sympathy, Tonna allows working women to testify against middle-class women in a dialogue between Ann and a doctor. Afflicted with a multitude of ailments after two years as a dressmaker, Ann seeks a doctor's help. He is shocked by her state, and interrogates her about her work. The description Ann gives of her working conditions and their effects on her health could be found in parliamentary reports on the millinery industry:

> "Sometimes we had to work all the Sunday, but not often, though we very often worked till almost day; and one or another of us had usually some finishing to do, and things to send home to ladies in the morning." (*WW*, p. 406)

"Shame on such ladies!" the doctor responds, condemning the readers of Tonna's tale. The doctor elicits further information from Ann, asking "Do you receive no extra pay for your extra work?" "Does your employer never call in additional help when there is such a press of work?" Of course, the answer is "no."

Though this voice of authority (the doctor) is useful for gathering information and locating blame, like the parliamentary report, it is rather ineffective in motivating people to reform. After Ann finishes her testimony, the "doctor is silent, and silence, as Ann knows, implies consent" (*WW*, p. 407). The authority figure in this dialogue, like the magistrates in *Helen Fleetwood*, can hear the cry of the poor, but seems powerless to escape the expectations of his own discourse in order to respond. The magistrates follow the dictates of an inadequate law, and Ann's doctor writes a useless prescription.

Tonna turns to her readers as the only hope for society's "Anns." In the last chapter of "Milliners and Dressmakers," entitled "Consequences," Tonna initiates a dialogue directly with her readers. "Do you ask what wrought this painful change?" she asks.

> It was wrought by THE LOVE OF MONEY. Not on her part, poor girl! she only desired to be taught a respectable business, that she might become the helper of her parents, and secure a moderate competence to herself. But the root of all evil was planted where her lot was cast; and for filthy lucre's sake the claims of justice were overlooked, the pleadings of womanhood for a youthful female charge overborne. . . . (*WW*, p. 413)

Tonna appropriates the language of scripture to indict her audience. In their hearts the love of money has taken root, and they need look no farther than their wardrobes for a means of alleviating their sisters' suffering.

In her peroration, Tonna rises to the language of a "Mother of Israel," yet maintains her questioning, dialogic rhetoric.

> And there are surely wrongs, that cannot be palliated, that ought not to be tolerated in a Christian land. Oh, when the great Apostle of the Gentiles warned his female converts from paganism, "women professing godliness," against too great a love for "putting on of apparel," or adorning themselves in "costly array," did the spirit that was in him foreshow what should come of that worldly lust in fair

and free and happy Britain, when at the height of
national glory and spiritual privilege? (*WW*, p. 417)

This question demands an answer from her readers, as if
Tonna were requiring them to justify themselves before the
judgment seat. Again it is Paul to whom Tonna directs her
readers' attention, the source of evangelical women's rhetorical
power. If the doctor is silent, women must not only put aside
their "costly array," but speak on their sisters' behalf. That is
Englishwomen's "spiritual privilege."

"It is the peculiar work of Christianity, wherever it is established, to elevate woman from the debased position in which
she is elsewhere placed" (*WW*, p. 417). So Tonna concludes in
The Wrongs of Women. This could also be said of the legacy of
evangelical fiction she left to Elizabeth Gaskell. Throughout
her career, Tonna was critical of writers like Harriet Martineau
because they took for granted the evangelical hermeneutic that
empowered women's writing. In the *Christian Lady's Magazine*
she demanded:

> Is it necessary to mention the name of Martineau, in
> order to show into how dangerous a track the female
> mind may be led, and made instrumental in leading
> others? Many branches of science may safely be
> superadded to a solid foundation of scriptural re-
> ligion, when that foundation has been evidently
> owned by God: but this I will maintain, though a
> host of reproves should start up against me, that it is
> most perilous, yea most ruinous, to put such weapons
> into a female hand, before their right use has been
> both explained AND UNDERSTOOD. And were
> the blessed woman [Hannah More], the casual in-
> troduction of whose honoured name has given rise
> to this paper,—were she now alive, I am confident
> that she would most fully concur with me.[35]

Outside the tradition defined by Tonna, More, and their precursors, this sounds like the standard anti-Jacobin, antifeminist
attack one would expect to hear coming from a reactionary
Evangelical. But within the context of that tradition, one can
understand why Tonna might consider Martineau's attitude to

be potentially "ruinous" of an entire female discourse, built as it was on a "foundation of scriptural religion."

Tonna would consider Martineau dangerous not simply because of her politics, but because she put her faith in the discourse of man rather than God. That faith would certainly be betrayed, as she made clear in a "Female Biography of Scripture" sketch of Rebecca.

> Man by nature the constituted head of the woman, her protector and guide, has in all climes and ages more or less betrayed his trust. He has proved but a broken reed, wounding the hand that leant on him for succour; and hence the natural divergence of the affections of trust and confidence from the unstable to the stable.[36]

Stability could come only from an authority transcending man's. Martineau, writing for the Political Economists, was being "led" and "made instrumental." Unlike More, when she found herself in the same situation in writing "Village Politics" and the *Cheap Repository Tracts*, Martineau would find no higher authority than her mentors to value the intrinsic worth of her talents. Tonna perceives her as secondary to a discourse that no woman could ever be allowed to dominate. The weapons she wields can as easily be turned against other women, as the laws of political economy grind the life out of Tonna's female characters and undercut the true source of women writers' power. Tonna, like Deborah, would press on into battle.

Politically, Tonna's position may be untenable. But it cannot be denied that a host of female writers, secular as well as religious, recognized the power of the woman preacher's role. Elizabeth Gaskell, Julia Kavanaugh, Geraldine Jewsbury, and Frances Trollope were among the women who accepted the role. Elizabeth Stone, and Harriet Martineau herself, adopted many of the tradition's techniques. And Charlotte Brontë, one of the strongest female voices of the nineteenth century, resisted classification as a woman writer in part because by 1840 to be a woman writer meant to write social evangelism.[37] Of all these writers, Gaskell most thoroughly internalized the role, and transformed its discourse. Yet, like More and Tonna, she too would come to appreciate its cost.

Eight

The Evangelist of Reconciliation:
Elizabeth Gaskell

The *Gentleman's Magazine* reviewer who deemed Britain's "lady novelists" to be "our great evangelists of reconciliation" doubtless believed that he was paying Elizabeth Gaskell, among others, a high compliment.[1] He was, after all, not merely sanctioning women's writing as a harmless domestic entertainment, but elevating it to the status of a spiritual mission with high public import. His review might have encouraged Gaskell, who was upset by other vehement attacks on *Ruth* as an immoral novel, "unfit for family reading,"[2] which made her identify with the fallen woman of her novel. "I think I must be a very improper woman without knowing it," she wrote to Eliza Fox, "I do so manage to shock people."[3] Whether or not Gaskell made this remark facetiously, she was not immune to *ad feminam* attacks, reporting to Fox a *Gazette* reviewer's "deep regret that we and all admirers of Mary Barton must feel at the author's *loss of reputation*" [my emphasis].[4] Reaction to *Ruth* did not come as a complete surprise to Gaskell—she had already weathered the storm precipitated by *Mary Barton* (1848)—but underscored her sense of the tenuousness of a female mission dependent on patriarchal sanction for its legitimacy. It would ultimately be a male authority who decided if her speech was inspired prophecy or dangerous lies, whether she was a "Mother of Israel" or a fallen woman.

Gaskell did not accept such dependence on men's good will as a fact of life. Sent to the matriarchal household of her aunt Lumb after the death of her mother, Elizabeth Stevenson was never without the companionship of women remarkable for their independence from masculine control. First with her aunt Lumb, and later with the friends of her adulthood, like Eliza Fox and the Winkworths, as well as her own daughters, Gaskell was part of a female interpretive community, where women's authority to make moral and political judgments was assumed.[5] Although her husband, William, seems to have presented no serious obstacles to her will, throughout her married life she resented his reading her letters before they were posted, relishing her freedom to correspond without censure when William was away.[6] Thus, Gaskell's claims that she never considered her audience when writing for publication appear to be less unfettered creative genius than a female writer's self-defense against potential male censorship.

From her earliest published writings, Gaskell investigates the sources of female authority, displaying a fascination with marginalized women that became a constant feature of her fiction. At the same time, her letters to female friends are filled with anxious arguments reconciling women's "natural duties" with writing. Margaret Homans has drawn attention to a related feature of Gaskell's diary: she describes the first speech of her own daughter—referring only to "Papa"—as "leaving poor Mama in the background."[7] The imperative Gaskell felt to accommodate the fictive marginalized woman within patriarchal society, bestowing God's blessings on her charitable labors or solitary suffering, parallels her profound need to justify herself as an author. Female characters standing outside the boundaries of the patriarchally legitimated roles of daughter, wife, and mother could be divinely sanctioned by doing God's will. So too might the woman writer transgressing the boundaries of male-controlled public discourses.

Like that of the early Methodist preachers, who were also part of a marginal sect, Gaskell's religious experience encouraged her to appropriate divine authority in opposition to social norms. Unitarians had long suffered ostracism and persecution, and derived their sense of legitimacy not from dominant ideology, but from confidence in the individual's ability to discern the will of God. And, as with the evangelical Methodists and Anglicans, the power to discern God's will carried with it the obligation to testify to that truth, calling on others to repent of their sins.[8] If anything, Gaskell's religious beliefs enabled her to recognize the essential disjunction between critical approval of her own writing and its truth or validity; even when she was encouraged by other Unitarians to be an "evangelist of reconciliation," Gaskell understood that her duty as a preacher might call her to assume the subversive voice of the fallen woman. In so doing, she would move beyond the women who had preceded her in the preaching tradition, eventually rejecting the role of evangelist of reconciliation and speaking on behalf of women as a class which had been wronged.

At the beginning of her career, Gaskell's anxiety about authorship was complicated by the fact that the woman preacher's role itself had begun to fall into the category of "natural duties." That is, as the review discussed above indicates, women's preaching was being incorporated into the symbolic construction of woman as domestic moral guardian.[9] Gaskell's own literary talent was treated by William Gaskell and William Howitt as a spiritual gift to be pressed into serving the community—or more immediately, the interests of her male mentors. Such a calling helped Gaskell, as it had earlier women preachers, to overcome the fear that writing was contrary to God's will. But it also threatened to alienate her linguistic authority from her, locating it in the mentors who claimed control over religious and literary discourse. Her earliest writings consist of discursive struggles to secure validation for herself both as author and as woman, disentangling divine from patriarchal linguistic sanction.

"Sketches Among the Poor" (1837), co-authored by Gaskell and her husband, is a prime example of a woman writer seeking legitimacy through her male mentors in a masculine tradition. Although the Gaskells conceived of the poem as a philanthropic project, which would place them in the tradition of Tonna or Caroline Norton, Elizabeth deliberately named as her predecessors Crabbe and Wordsworth.[10] In preparation for her poetic endeavor, William set her to doing imitations of "greats," including Coleridge, Wordsworth, Byron, Crabbe, Dryden and Pope.[11] Appropriately, her husband placed their poem in *Blackwood's Magazine*, that arbiter of official taste which twenty years later would accept George Eliot's first piece of fiction from the hands of George Henry Lewes. In this

ing tale, advocating hard work, patience, and charity for the working class, thus turns on its pious, affluent readers. Libbie serves as a moral model for the working class, but the middle-class readers must recognize themselves in Libbie's exacting employers.

By treating working-class life, where poverty, unemployment, disease, and sheer independence of will often prevented domestic relationships from conforming to the bourgeois ideal, Gaskell calls that ideal into question. She insists that the domestic ideal may not, in fact, serve women's interests, nor those of society at large. Though Gaskell does not focus our attention on a feminist issue until Libbie's dialogue with Anne Dixon near the story's close, various women's concerns pervade "Libbie Marsh." Most of the principal characters are working women; in the course of the story Libbie construes her spinster-hood as independence; the plot grows out of the charitable services by which single women establish bonds with one another, while the patriarchal family binds wives and mothers. Family life is represented as violent and abusive, and female independence as desirable over a chimerical domestic ideal. Moreover, whereas Mary in "Sketches" remains veiled in the language of conventional piety, Libbie's own voice, with its working-class, provincial dialect, emerges as a principal spiritual and moral authority in this story.

Though Gaskell does not name her models for "Libbie Marsh," as she did with "Sketches Among the Poor," her narrative strategies clearly mark the author's precursors as those women writers, such as Charlotte Elizabeth Tonna, who were feminizing social discourse through adaptations of preaching techniques. With Libbie's "preachments," Gaskell begins to experiment with the woman preacher's voices in fiction as a means of legitimating women's critiques of masculine authority. It is hardly a radical statement that Libbie utters, but it is important for its message about women's stake in social reform and the spinster's vocation; its implied dual audience—men and women, employers and employees; and its mode—an exhortation delivered under duress, in the context of a dialogue.

Anne, a factory worker with whom Libbie boards, provokes Libbie's "preachment" by speaking imprudently of marriage.

". . . what is marrying? Just a spree, Bob says. He
often says he does not think I shall make him a good
wife, for I know nought about house matters, wi'
working in a factory; but he says he'd rather be un-
easy wi' me than easy wi' anybody else. There's love
for you! And I tell him I'd rather have him tipsy
than any one else sober." (*LM*, pp. 483–84)

Though Libbie has been a virtually silent presence in her story
to this point, she now exclaims,

"Oh, Anne Dixon, hush! you don't know yet what it
is to have a drunken husband. I have seen something of it: father used to get fuddled, and, in the
long run, it killed mother—let alone—oh! Anne,
God above only knows what the wife of a drunken
man has to bear. Don't tell," she said, lowering her
voice, "but father killed our little baby in one of his
bouts; mother never looked up again, nor father either, for that matter, only his was in a different
way . . . Oh!" she said, recovering herself from her
train of thought, "never say aught lightly of the
wife's lot whose husband is given to drink!" (*LM*,
p. 484)

It is not a mystical calling that inspires Libbie's exhortation, but
a superior knowledge of reality, unmediated by male authorities. Like an Old Testament prophet, she gives lie to the
comfortable fictions that obscure suffering, bringing the truth
of domestic violence out into the light of day. Anne, in her sar-
castic dismissal of Libbie's "preachment" indirectly reveals the
connection between Libbie's superiority as a social prophet and
her exclusion from patriarchal relationships.

"Dear, what a preachment! I tell you what, Libbie,
you're as born an old maid as ever I saw. You'll never
be married to either drunken or sober." (*LM*,
p. 484)

Libbie's calling is to speak life's "strong truths," that are rather
unlike those Hannah More had meant. Instead, Libbie's task is

to present the reality that exposes oppressive myths and challenges renderings of the prophet as a marginal figure. When we read the character's own pious-sounding statement of her mission, it is with an ear for the subtext that is consistent with her earlier declaration on marriage.

> Libbie's face went rather red, but without losing its meek expression.
>
> ". . . I must not lose time in fretting and fidgeting after marriage, but just look about me for somewhat else to do. I can see many a one misses it in this. They will hanker after what is ne'er likely to be theirs, instead of facing it out, and settling down to be old maids, just looking round for the odd jobs God leaves in the world for such as old maids to do. There's plenty of such work, and there's the blessing of God on them as does it." Libbie was almost out of breath at this outpouring of what had long been her inner thoughts. (*LM*, pp. 484–85)

Gaskell would echo Libbie's speech in a 1850 letter to Eliza Fox: "I do believe that we all have some appointed work to do . . . what *we* have to do in advancing the Kingdom of God (and that first we must find what we are sent into the world to do,) and define it and make it clear to ourselves. . . ."[13] Gaskell's language to Fox, reminiscent of Sarah Crosby's, contrasts sharply with Libbie's, not simply for its diction, but in its directness and authority. Writing for the audience of *Howitt's Journal* at the beginning of her career, Gaskell has Libbie describe her mission as doing "odd jobs" as against the patriarchal norm for women. Nevertheless, we have just been told that wives and mothers are not the moral centers of their families (Libbie's father clearly did not look to her mother "to make all things straight") but are victims instead, while Libbie claims divine sanction for women's role outside the family.

The narrative strategies in this passage, marking her consciousness of earlier women writers, contribute significantly to Gaskell's purpose. By investing the working-class voice with power, as More and Tonna had, Gaskell legitimates a marginal perspective. Gaskell grounds Libbie's convictions in personal experience—the death of her only sibling at her drunken father's hands. That brief narrative, embedded in her speech, calls to mind the testimony, a favorite technique of preachers and tract writers. For a woman it was especially effective; by revealing the congruence of so-called public and private spheres, it helped her to avoid charges of speaking of things beyond her ken. Above all, it insists on the authority of female subjectivity.

Setting Libbie's "preachment" in the context of a dialogue proves strategic as well. Tract readers would recognize in this exchange a standard technique in which two workers, one impudent and ignorant, the other wise and virtuous, engage in a discussion of some pressing issue that ends when the wise worker has defeated the other's rash argument and convinced him of the error of his ways.[14] With her virtue firmly established by this point, Libbie can easily be identified as the voice of reason, while Anne's frivolousness verges on caricature. However, Libbie urges Anne—and beyond her, female readers regardless of class—to a specifically feminist conversion, to repent of a naïve and unholy subjection to men in marriage.

This bit of rebellion exacts from Gaskell the same price paid by women preachers. Gaskell feels she must qualify Libbie's speech by emphasizing her distracted state following the death of Franky, a crippled child she had cared for. Though, as we are told, Libbie has pondered these issues long and hard, she has never before voiced her convictions, much less held forth on them, and is exhausted by the effort required by this exceptional event. Hers is an "extraordinary call." In discussing "oracular novels," George Eliot would deplore the "notion abroad among women, rather akin to superstition, that the speech and actions of idiots are inspired, and that the human being most entirely exhausted of common sense is the fittest vehicle of revelation."[15] Though Gaskell appears to be guilty of trading on this superstition, she is also determined to counter the belief that only a madwoman would articulate any opinion not already held by sensible men—or articulate in public any opinion whatever. Libbie is clearly exhausted, but not of common sense. At the same time, authoritative female speech, however sensible, remains an extraordinary rather than a necessary part of social discourse.

The issue of female legitimation raised by the "extraordinary call" emerges more clearly in the story "Lizzy Leigh," begun before Gaskell embarked on a social novel.[16] This is Gaskell's first treatment of the "fallen woman." She does little to reveal the fallen women as subject: the stock plot of the seduction of the poor seamstress Lizzy Leigh by an aristocratic rake, who abandons her to bear their child alone, takes place before the story begins, and we see relatively little of the title character. Gaskell is more interested in examining the way the fallen woman was "read" in her society, focusing on the characters who judge Lizzy: Susan Palmer, to whom Lizzy anonymously entrusts her baby; Lizzy's mother, Mrs. Leigh, who seeks her out to rescue her; her brother, Will, who like his father, condemns her. Fallen women were among society's most despised outcasts, yet there was a clear scriptural precedent for their forgiveness and return to society. In this story Gaskell examines the power and limitations of scriptural authority to recuperate the "fallen woman."

The story begins with what is essentially a deathbed conversion: the dying patriarch, Lizzy's father, repents of condemning his fallen daughter, and begs for God's forgiveness. His wife, Anne, acts as God's voice, conferring her blessing on James Leigh's repentance, whereupon he dies. Thus ends Anne's years of "hidden, sullen rebellion" (*LL*, p. 1) against the man who has alienated her from her only daughter, and she begins her search for Lizzy. She asks her younger son, Tom (who "was gentle and delicate as a girl" and "had always clung to his mother" [*LL*, p. 4]), to read the parable of the Prodigal Son to inspire her on her quest. This story, by contrast to that of the Magadalen, figures the sinner as deserving not only forgiveness but a privileged status in the family. What is more, it anticipates the resistance of the elder brother, Will (who "was like his father, stern, reserved, and scrupulously upright" [*LL*, p. 4]), construing it as jealousy and selfishness rather than righteous indignation. In Gaskell's moral scheme, the Prodigal must be restored, but her accuser, represented by Will, must also repent. Susan Palmer is the medium for achieving both goals.

Susan Palmer might have stepped out of a Methodist's memoirs, or a saint's life. She leads the life of self-sacrifice we anticipate for Libbie Marsh at the end of her tale. In her modesty, piety, and quiet charity, she closely resembles Dinah

Morris. But unlike George Eliot, who will insist on maintaining some ironic distance from her character, Gaskell establishes Susan as a woman beyond reproach in order to attack her society's pharisaical condemnation of the most abandoned of female sinners. When Will follows his mother to Manchester, where she hopes to find Lizzy, he meets Susan and falls in love with her. Awed by her purity—and appearance—he never entertains the possibility that the child she cares for is not an orphan but a bastard, much less the daughter of his own sister.

Like Anne in "Libbie Marsh," Will's role is to preempt the reader's objections to Lizzy. Terrified that a woman of Susan's purity might reject the brother of a fallen woman, he abandons his sister's cause in order to win his angel. Instead, thanks to the sexual power Susan exerts over Will, she is able to shame him into repentance.[17] While Lizzy's father could bring himself to forgive his daughter only on his deathbed, and her brother considers her an abomination and a source of deep shame, Susan, "the holy and pure one [does] not veil her eyes" before Lizzy's fall (*LL,* p. 28). When Lizzy leaves her baby on Susan's doorstep, Susan acts the part of the good Samaritan, knowing full well the child's likely parentage. Later, when the child dies and its origin is revealed, she becomes the agent of the Leigh family's reconciliation, an angel of mercy to the weak and suffering, and a prophet of New Testament morality to the pharisaical. Susan displays many of the qualities of, and seems to have much the same effect on others as, the ideal domestic woman. But importantly, she employs that power towards a decidedly antidomestic, antipatriarchal end: the defense of a sexually active unmarried woman and her illegitimate child.

It is Mrs. Leigh however, who acts as prophetic authority rather than medium of reconciliation. She is clearly a more realistic character than Susan; neither angel nor demon, she is, rather, a loving mother and obedient wife who defies propriety and convention, speaking bravely and heroically because she believes God is on her side. When Will expresses shock at the idea of Susan caring for a bastard child, Mrs. Leigh responds,

> "Think of that, Will. Here's Susan, good and pure
> as the angels in heaven, yet, like them, full of hope

and mercy, and one who, like them, will rejoice over
her as repents." (*LL,* pp. 21–22)

Then, inspired, she assumes authority and calls her son to repentance:

> "Will, my lad, I'm not afeard of you now, and I
> must speak, and you must listen. I am your mother,
> and I dare to command you, because I know I am in
> the right and that God is on my side. If He should
> lead the poor wandering lassie to Susan's door, and
> she comes back crying and sorrowful, led by that
> good angel to us once more, thou shalt never say a
> casting-up word to her about her sin, but be tender
> and helpful towards one 'who was lost and is found,'
> so may God's blessing rest on thee, and so mayst
> thou lead Susan home as thy wife."
>
> She stood, no longer as the meek, imploring, gen-
> tle mother, but firm and dignified, as if the inter-
> preter of God's will. Her manner was so unusual
> and solemn, that it overcame all Will's pride and
> stubbornness. He rose softly while she was speak-
> ing, and bent his head as if in reverence at her
> words, and the solemn injunction which they con-
> veyed. When she had spoken, he said in so subdued
> a voice that she was almost surprised at the sound,
> "Mother, I will." (*LL,* p. 22)

Like a prophet released from a trance, Mrs. Leigh now collapses in exhaustion. Here at last, the silently brooding mother
has spoken God's message, transfixing and transforming her
child, Will, and in turn, the society he represents. Her authority derives not from her domestic role, but from her cause,
which is just; she is no longer a mother subservient to her adult
son, but a "Mother in Israel." Mrs. Leigh's words are those of
the Ten Commandments spoken in the dialect of a humble
woman: "thou shalt never say a casting-up word to her about
her sin . . . so may God's blessing rest on thee." What she commands is Christian charity. But more than that, she vitiates the
claim that fallen women are sinners by demanding that Will
never mention Lizzy's sin.[18] We see clearly the efficacy of Mrs.

Leigh's "preachment," suggesting the female prophet's tremendous social potential.[19]

The prophetic role guaranteed to women by the evangelical mission enables Mrs. Leigh to appropriate privileged language on behalf of a fallen woman. But the fallen woman herself is silent. In *Mary Barton,* Gaskell achieves an unprecedented audience for her own prophetic voice, but the haunting silence of the fallen woman remains.

Mary Barton: *Preachers, Prophets, and a Fallen Woman*

Elizabeth Gaskell's first novel, *Mary Barton,* illustrates more fully than her early stories the significance of the tradition of the woman preacher in her career. The woman preacher required a clear sense of calling to justify her extraordinary vocation; she presented herself as a medium for a divine message; she created an authoritative voice by invoking the texts of divinely inspired scripture and male-authored theology. Having been invited into the male domains of politics, history, economics, and theology, Gaskell would not only fulfill her "feminine" duty, but attempt to feminize these discourses as well. She would oppose reigning constructions of social hierarchies on behalf of a God for whom there are no distinctions of rich or poor, male or female. It is true that she relied on male-authored pretexts, that she figured her subject, the masses, as the male monster of Dr. Frankenstein, and incorporated the distinctively feminine rhetoric which would enable Carlyle to identify the author as a woman.[20] Yet, Gaskell's apparent concessions to the patriarchal censors who oversaw her work in fact enabled her to challenge their hegemony by implicating them in the deaths of the exploited worker, John Barton, and the exploited woman, Esther.

For many years, readers of *Mary Barton* accepted William Gaskell's claim that his wife undertook the novel to distract herself after the death of their only son, William. Construing one of the most influential social-problem novels of the nineteenth century as a therapeutic, private narrative saved readers— including the Reverend Gaskell—the trouble of picturing the author, not as the pious minister's wife and grieving mother, but as a woman whose political convictions forced her to cir-

cumvent masculine social and literary authority. In her autobiography, Mary Howitt credited her husband, William, with
inspiring Gaskell to write *Mary Barton*. Mary records that
William wrote to Gaskell and "urged his correspondent to
use her pen for the public benefit."[21] "The public benefit," as
Gaskell already knew from her association with *Howitt's Journal*,
meant orderly reconciliation, denying the incompatibility of
class interests. Moreover, "the public" ignored the fact that
women did not necessarily benefit from improvements in the
lot of men.

The relationship Mary describes between William Howitt
and Elizabeth Gaskell follows the pattern of male reformer and
female writer we have seen in the careers of Anne Dutton,
Hannah More, and Charlotte Elizabeth Tonna, among others.
Upon discovering that Gaskell could write, Howitt enlists her
in his philanthropic activities, her literary ability virtually obli-
gating her to join the woman's crusade as a prophet. Convinc-
ing Gaskell that her vocation derived from a higher authority,
Howitt's encouragement, coupled with the sense of urgency
pressed upon her by the contemporary economic crisis,
enabled Gaskell to risk the *ad feminam* attacks that were the inevitable lot of women who published. This was no insignificant
contribution. Matching Mary Bosanquet Fletcher's anguish
over her vocation, Gaskell took great care to ensure her
anonymity, suggesting that her novel be published under the
masculine pseudonym "Stephen Berwick,"[22] and delaying
acknowledgment of authorship until it had been guessed by
most of her friends and several critics.[23] However, as her publisher, Edward Chapman, was well aware, Gaskell's reticence
about her own vocation did not prevent her from vigorously
promoting her novel.

Elizabeth Gaskell had few doubts about the public, evangelistic mission of *Mary Barton*. When Chapman and Hall appeared to be postponing the novel's publication, she fired off a
series of impatient letters. Mimicking the tone of the female
philanthropist, she began:

> I cannot help fancying that the tenor of my tale is
> such as to excite attention at the present time of
> struggle on the part of work people to obtain what

they esteem their rights; on the other side it is very possible that people are now so much absorbed by public work as to have very little time or interest to bestow on works of fiction.[24]

After several weeks, and another impatient letter, Gaskell dropped all but the most mechanical gesture of feminine subservience:

> Allow me to remind you of your promise. I am (above every other consideration) desirous that [my novel] should be read; and if you think there would be a better chance of a large circulation by deferring its appearance, of course I defer to your superior knowledge, only repeating my own belief that the tale would bear directly upon the present circumstances.[25]

Gaskell derived confidence from her calling to preach a unique and salvific message. In the language of correspondence between author and publishers, Gaskell tells Chapman what Mrs. Leigh told her son: "my lad, I'm not afeard of you now, and I must speak, and you will listen."

What Gaskell doesn't make explicit is her desire that "Will" repent of his abuse of workers and women. *Mary Barton* is characterized by such rhetorical subterfuge. Gaskell writes *Mary Barton* with a patriarch peering over her shoulder, who confronts her as a censor, preventing her from "writ[ing] so naturally & heartily" as she did to female correspondents.[26] That presence stands as a constant reminder to Gaskell that her legitimacy as an author depends on patriarchal approval. At the same time, publishing a novel "for the public benefit" affords Gaskell the opportunity to convert the very authorities who would censor her by recasting the social discourse in feminist terms. Again and again, Gaskell transforms gestures of submission to patriarchal authority into acts of subversion.

Beginning with her preface, the novel offers evidence of Gaskell's considerable strategic powers. "I know nothing of Political Economy," she writes, "or of the Theories of trade. I have tried to write truthfully; and if my accounts agree or clash with any system, the agreement or disagreement is unintentional."

is to be done. "Wilson's eyes [fill] with tears" when Barton returns with food and fuel, knowing that these purchases cost his friend his own coat and silk handkerchief. These "observers" bring to their task "the useful skill of a working man" (*MB*, p. 56).

However, Barton, like Buckland, is filled with disgust, not at the Davenports, but at the masters responsible for making their lives wretched. In effect, Barton translates the delirious raving of Davenport, dying of a fever, into a persuasive and rhetorically powerful denunciation of the millowners. Wilson sadly compares the patience and resignation Davenport displayed in health with the dying man, "looking like the prophet of woe in the fearful plague-picture" (*MB*, p. 57), and the curses uttered by his tongue "unbridled" by fever. He recalls reading a letter from Davenport for his illiterate wife which was "as good as Bible-words; ne'er a word o' repining; a' about God being our father, and that we mun bear patiently whate'er he sends" (*MB*, p. 60). But Barton would appropriate that same Bible language to justify Davenport's current rage against the masters. "Han [the masters] done as they'd be done for by us?" (*MB*, p. 60) Barton asks. Masked by illness, Davenport's curses are the rational response of a just man, like Job, driven by the plague of industrial capitalism into poverty and death.

If the masters recognize God as their father, Barton asks Wilson, then "how comes it they're rich and we're poor?" (*MB*, p. 60). "You'll say," Barton continues,

> they'n getten capital and we'n getten none. I say, our labour's our capital and we ought to draw some interest on that. . . . Besides, there's many on 'em has nought to begin wi' . . . and now they're worth their tens of thousands, a' getten out of our labour . . . but look at yo, and see me, and poor Davenport yonder; whatten better are we? They screwed us down to th' lowest peg, in order to make their great big fortunes, and build their great big houses, and we, why we're just clemming, many and many of us. Can you say there's nought wrong in this? (*MB*, p. 60)

Gaskell's form is the catechetical dialogue so popular in conservative propaganda. But where Hannah More would have

Wilson overcome Barton simply by counseling Christian resignation, Gaskell lets Barton's argument stand, for who could gainsay its most compelling evidence: the Davenport family.

Finally, Gaskell reverses the alienating effect of Buckland's narrative by observing the master through the worker's eyes. In a scene modeled on Mrs. Green's interview with the mill-owner in Tonna's *Helen Fleetwood*, Wilson goes to Davenport's employer of three years, Mr. Carson, to obtain an infirmary order for the dying man. Admitted to the Carsons' kitchen, Wilson overhears the "keen remarks" of the domestic servants upon "the parlor" (*MB*, p. 62). This insider's view confirms Barton's accusations that the masters are a self-absorbed, capricious lot, constructing their reality according to the fantasies of sentimental fiction. Behind the parlor doors, Gaskell shows Carson a slave to his pampered children's wishes, but when Wilson enters his manner is brusque and impatient. Davenport is an unfamiliar name to him, and the best he will do for this anonymous sufferer is an outpatient order, only a bit better than Dives stepping over Lazarus at his door. Davenport dies thanking God "'that the hard struggle of living is over'" (*MB*, p. 66), thereby authorizing Barton's interpretation of social and economic realities.

Gaskell narrates these scenes without a specifically female point of view. There is no female prophet to correspond to John Barton. Mrs. Davenport's only words protest her own insignificance: "'Oh, Ben, Ben!'" she cries to her dying husband, "'have you no thought for me? Oh, Ben! Ben! do say one word to help me through life'" (*MB*, p. 66). Instead, Gaskell herself performs the prophetic role; unlike Buckland, she reports a woman's speech and exhorts the women of her class to do likewise. Whereas Amelia, the millowner's daughter in *Helen Fleetwood*, overhears Mrs. Green's appeal on Helen's behalf, thus circumventing her father's effort to censor this "discourse so unfit for a delicate mind," Carson's daughter Amy, whose interests are limited to "flowers and scents," "dance[s] off into the conservatory . . . before the gaunt, pale, unwashed, unshaven weaver [is] ushered in" (*MB*, p. 65). This scene presents an exchange between men about a man, ending when Carson's son Harry gives Wilson five shillings for the "'poor fellow'"— before riding off to pursue his flirtation with John Barton's daughter, Mary. Gaskell's revision of this exchange uncovers the disturbing consequences of Mr. Z.'s censorship. Amy, "little Miss Extravagance" (*MB*, p. 64) as her brother calls her, remains oblivious to the business practices which insure her a supply of eau de Portugal and roses at half a guinea, while no one speaks on behalf of Mary Barton, whose future is threatened by the millowner's son. Gaskell, like Mrs. Green, plays the role of Ancient Mariner, passing from one woman to another the obligation to tell the tale of injustice, to prophesy against their age and the powers that would render them deaf and dumb.

While critiques of classism and sexism necessarily intersect in Tonna's single plot, Gaskell structures her narrative so as to underscore the way in which women's true complaints are rendered unspeakable. While she combines class and sexual exploitation in the novel's dominant plot (Mary Barton's renunciation of Harry Carson in favor of the working-class Jem Wilson), Gaskell relegates her attack on the wrongs of woman to a subplot, and chooses a fallen woman—Mary's aunt Esther—as her prophet. In this way, she establishes a distinctly feminist point of view, which cannot be subsumed into, or easily reconciled with, narratives attacking other social ills.

In a brief paragraph ending the novel's penultimate scene, Gaskell graphically joins John Barton and Esther as fellow victims by laying "these two wanderers" in the same grave.

> And there they lie without name, or initial, or date.
> Only this verse is inscribed upon the stone. . .
>   Psalm ciii.v.9.—"For He will not always chide, neither will He keep his anger for ever." (*MB*, p. 371)

The scripture verse, Gaskell's last word on these characters, is the most qualified description of God's mercy in a positively exuberant psalm, which continues "He hath not dealt with us after our sins; nor rewarded us according to our iniquities." Like Mrs. Leigh, Gaskell enjoins her readers not to speak a "casting-up word" to those that man, not God, condemns as sinners. Yet Esther has been condemned to death in the novel—by the lover who abandons her, by the men who use her as a prostitute, by the conspiracy of silence that hides her life from women like Mary, who might save her, and by John Barton himself. She has not been considered by critics to be of much importance in the novel beyond serving as a cautionary example for Mary; but Mary is never disabused of her belief that Esther married a man of means. Rather, Esther constitutes a devastating presence in the novel, undercutting any reforming agenda that does not address women's victimization and any social discourse that can exclude women's voices.

With Esther, Gaskell encompasses prophet, mother, and whore: the combination of roles distinctly associated with women preachers. This often frivolous-minded, vain, and headstrong character shares her name with the Hebrew Queen of Persia who successfully pleads with the King to spare the Israelites from attack and thereby becomes the savior of her people, the figure who had served as role model for Tonna, More, and the Methodist women preachers. Gaskell's Esther, too, will plead for her people—first warning Jem about Harry Carson's dangerous flirtation with Mary, and then providing Mary with the crucial evidence to prove Jem innocent of Carson's murder. Though literally the mother of a bastard who died in infancy, Esther appears to a distraught and abandoned Mary as her mother and, in comforting her, unites the "madonna/magdalen" opposition.[31] But it is her status as prostitute which defines her in society, effacing all her other features. She will not speak from a privileged position, nor will she be recognized as a savior; the very marginality which enables her to see the truth that others have overlooked leaves her irrevocably alienated and ends only in death. Instead, it will be the pure, virginal Mary who must serve as the medium for Esther's text.

The parallels between Mary Barton and her aunt Esther suggest an ironic twist to the novel's original title, *A Manchester Love Story.* Undoubtedly the title refers to the love between Mary Barton and Jem Wilson. But Esther experiences her own love story, which begins like a sentimental romance and ends as a tragedy. The naïve expectation that her soldier-lover will marry her is soon shattered by the reality of facing pregnancy and poverty alone, barred by the patriarch John Barton from returning to the only family left to her. He is determined that Mary's life will not follow the same script, yet it is not John Barton, nor Jem Wilson, but, finally, Esther who can save her, precisely because of her story.

Esther the outcast lurks on the periphery of her family, peering into the "court where John lived," "peep[ing] through the chink in the window-shutter to see the old room, and sometimes Mary or her father sitting up late," and "watch[ing] over Mary" (*MB*, p. 153). From her concealed position she discovers Mary's secret rendezvous with Harry Carson, and comprehends the likely outcome. Consumed with a desire to rescue Mary, yet barred from approaching her, Esther is removed still further from the family circle, first by illness, then by prostitution, prison, and alcoholism—the last warm refuge remaining to her. Nevertheless, her only desire upon leaving prison is to tell someone the truth that will save Mary. Knowing that John Barton would never give her a hearing, she turns to her childhood friend, Jem Wilson, stepping out of the shadows to accost him with words that echo Mrs. Leigh's: " 'You must listen to me, Jem Wilson. . . . You must listen,' she said again authoritatively, 'for Mary Barton's sake' " (*MB*, p. 150).

Jem rejects this disreputable character's authority to speak of his beloved Mary until he recognizes Esther. The memory of "his boyhood's friend" obliterates the image of the fallen woman, and he shakes Esther's hand "with a cordiality that forgot the present in the past" (*MB*, p. 150). But Esther refuses to play the role of demon or angel, and Jem's thoughtless question " 'Why, Esther! Where han ye been this many a year?' " provokes her to tell her tragic love story, one that Jem and all Esther's "readers" have too long denied.

> "Nay! don't change your fickle mind now, and say you don't want to hear it. You must hear it, and I must tell it; and then see after Mary, and take care she does not become like me. As she is loving now, so did I love once; one above me far." (*MB*, p. 151)

Mary, not Jem, is the appropriate audience for this story, but the same rules of propriety that Mrs. Green innocently transgressed in telling the factory-owner's daughter of the workers' suffering,[32] require Esther to employ Jem as the unsatisfactory medium of her message. Indeed, there is none so deaf as he who will not hear; all Jem hears in Esther's speech is that he has a rival for Mary's affections.

To Esther's story of the happy years of her romance and the birth of her baby, Jem responds "'Don't tell me any more about yoursel,'" eager as he is to hear more of his rival. But Esther retains control of the dialogue:

> "What! you're tired already, are you? but I will tell you; as you've asked for it, you shall hear it. I won't recall the agony of the past for nothing. I will have the relief of telling it." (*MB*, p. 151)

As Hetty Sorrel would do in *Adam Bede*, Esther tells the tale of her fall, assuming more guilt than a sympathetic reading of circumstances would require. When her husband is posted to Ireland, Esther uses the £50 he has left her to "set up a small-ware shop," providing an adequate living for her and her daughter until the baby becomes ill and the cost of her medicine exhausts Esther's resources. No one shows her mercy. The shop owner seizes her inventory for rent, and her landlord threatens to throw her out into the street. Esther continues in words which her namesake Hetty Sorrel would echo:

> "it was winter, cold bleak winter; and my child was so ill, so ill, and I was starving. And I could not bear to see her suffer, and forgot how much better it would be for us to die together;—oh her moans, her moans, which money could give me the means of relieving! So I went out into the street one January night—Do you think God will punish me for that?" she asked with wild vehemence, almost amounting to insanity, and shaking Jem's arm in order to force an answer from him. (*MB*, p. 152)

Esther does no more than John Barton would have done to save his starving son, had it been in his power. Yet when Barton asks if it would have been a crime to steal food to feed his boy, it is a self-consciously rhetorical question, filled with a clear sense of the injustice of poor workers starving within sight of their sleek masters. Gaskell cannot confer such moral authority on Esther, nor can she assume it for herself but must reach out and clutch the male reader's arm to beg his approval. "'But it's no matter?'" Esther concludes. "'I've done that since which separates us as far asunder as heaven and hell can be'" (*MB*, p. 152). It is unclear who is in heaven, who in hell, only that Esther concedes that she is inscrutable to Jem.

Gaskell makes one final appeal, and like the women preachers before her, it is to the authority of scripture. Esther, in agony over the memory of her dead child, cries out

> "My darling! my darling! even after death I may not see thee, my own sweet one! she was so good—like a little angel. What is the text, I don't remember,— the text mother used to teach me when I sat on her knee long ago; it begins 'Blessed are the pure—'" (*MB*, p. 152)

Jem finishes the text for her: "'Blessed are the pure in heart for they shall see God.'" The matriarchal lineage of this text, passed from one good mother to another, has been broken by a misogynistic patriarchal interpretation. Esther believes that it would break her own mother's heart to see her now, but unlike John Barton, Esther's mother might recognize her daughter's heart to be as pure as her infant grandchild's and that all three would be joined before God. Esther can be at once preacher, mother, and fallen woman—indeed the three are inseparable.

Jem interprets Esther merely as an object of pity, but he finds her entire story a frustrating digression from the tale which involves him, "the subject of Mary, and the lover above her in rank, and the service to be done for her sake" (*MB*, pp. 152– 53). And even after Esther satisfies his curiosity, Jem attempts to rewrite her text in such a way as to place himself in the center. In a passage of free indirect discourse that allows Gaskell to distance herself from Jem's romantic melodrama, we read:

> And now the mists and the storms seemed clearing away from his path, though it still was full of stinging thorns. Having done the duty nearest him (of reducing his heart to something like order), the second became more plain before him. (*MB*, p. 157)

Jem's imagination transforms Esther's text into a ludicrous travesty of the Romantic sublime. Jem figures himself as Teufelsdröckh—"doing the duty nearest him"[33]—but the narrator's parenthetical remark reduces *him* to a quite ordinary jealous lover. Furthermore, Esther's faith in Jem as Mary's protector is unfounded, for he dismisses "poor Esther's" interpretation of Mary's relationship as the too hasty conclusion of a woman warped by her experience. Precisely the experience which gives her speech authority enables him to dismiss it. Thus, he considers his "second duty" to be to force Carson to make good on his imagined marriage proposal to Mary.

When Jem confronts Harry Carson, Esther's original story is subjected to another misreading, since all Carson cares to hear in the rude worker's speech is evidence that "Mary loved him in spite of her frequent and obstinate rejections; and that she had employed this person (whoever he was) to bully him into marrying her" (*MB*, p. 168). Jem's "service" ends up in a skirmish with Harry Carson, thereby putting him in a position to be saved by Mary when he is wrongly accused of Carson's murder. If anyone saved Mary from Carson, it was Mary herself.[34] Of course, although Carson's death finally moots the question of her seduction, Esther's agency nevertheless plays a crucial part in Mary's love story.

Gaskell reunites her paired female characters, Esther and Mary—one possessing the stories of experience, the other the ethos of innocence—in order to create, if only briefly, a vision of female heroism. Esther's return to the Barton house to give Mary the bit of text that will be Jem's reprieve contrasts sharply with Arthur Donnithorne's dramatic arrival just in time to deliver the pardon saving Hetty Sorrel from the gallows. Indeed, Esther fears stepping in from the shadows[35] where she has found the vital evidence, the fragment of Jem's valentine to Mary that was last in John Barton's possession. "She had felt as if some holy spell would prevent her (even as the unholy Lady Geraldine was prevented, in the abode of Christabel) from crossing the threshold of that home of her early innocence" (*MB*, p. 223). Only in men's imaginations is Esther barred, however, and the reunion "complicates, by foregrounding female relationships, what has seemed to be a purely masculine drama only mediated by women."[36] Indeed, it calls for a feminist rereading of the entire novel.

Both women are hampered in this meeting from "opening their hearts" by the patriarchal prejudices they have internalized. Fearful of shocking Mary, Esther disguises her actual circumstances so effectively that "Mary felt a kind of repugnance to the changed and altered aunt . . . who had, by her own confession, kept aloof from and neglected them for so many years" (*MB*, p. 225). Even after their traumatic exchange, in which Mary believes she has been given proof of Jem's guilt, the women remain alienated from each other. Esther comprehends Mary's love for Jem, but for her part, "[n]o faint imagination of the love and the woe of that poor creature [Esther] crossed [Mary's] mind, or she would have taken her, all guilty and erring, to her bosom, and tried to bind up the broken heart" (*MB*, p. 227). Esther cannot even allow Mary to kiss her—the act symbolic of class reconciliation in an episode near the novel's close.[37] It is left to Gaskell's novel to subvert the masculine misreadings that disrupt women's salvific dialogue, rendering them illegible to one another.

The social mechanisms rendering women inscrutable except as instruments of patriarchy, and the state's power to enforce women's patriarchal roles are dramatized in the novel's trial scene. Here, Gaskell elaborates on the contrast drawn by Hannah More in *Daniel* and Charlotte Elizabeth Tonna in *Helen Fleetwood*: namely, that between the pharisaical legalism of ruling men and the spiritual understanding of women. Jem's trial for the murder of Harry Carson highlights the testimony of Mary Barton and Will Wilson. In the public space of the courtroom, Mary, theatrically lit by a ray of sunlight, is imagined as "the fatal Helen" by Mr. Carson, and likened to a portrait of Beatrice Cenci by the spectators. Her status as a speaker is overdetermined by literary and artistic constructions of femininity. The prosecutor's relentless probing after details of Mary's affair with Carson is rendered in terms which suggest rape. For her part, Mary keeps "the tremendous secret [of her father's guilt] imprisoned within her" (*MB*, p. 306). The narrator makes clear that, far from "bearing witness to the truth," as Mary imagines is her duty, the court hears only what it wants to hear—the melodramatic tale of seduction that drives a jealous lover to murder—and imprisons the narrative naming the father.

At most, Mary can effect her intention of exonerating Jem, not through her own words, but by securing a male speaker,

Will Wilson, to testify on Jem's behalf. Jem's attorney is well aware that Mary has authored and executed the scheme that brings Will vaulting into the courtroom over benches and railings to deliver the testimony that saves Jem from the gallows. He knows but suppresses the story of Mary's valiant trek to Liverpool to reach Will before his ship sails. This story of Mary's heroism becomes a male-owned commodity, which Jem's attorney imagines publishing to great acclaim. Will not only hurdles physical boundaries but, unlike Mary, discursive ones as well, turning back attempts to discredit his testimony by demanding sarcastically that "someone with a wig on" ask his ship's captain to give a character for him. Will's testimony is perceived as self-authorizing in a fashion clearly related to his position in a patriarchy. He can, therefore, "bear witness to the truth" he came to tell, and effect Jem's acquittal. Upon hearing the verdict, Mary acts out the final gesture of the silenced woman, collapsing in a faint.

Of course, the law's search for truth has suppressed an even more vital story than that of Mary's quest for Will: the testimony of the fallen woman, Esther. She, in fact, could produce evidence not simply of Jem's innocence but of John Barton's guilt. Esther possesses this knowledge by virtue of her marginal status. She finds John Barton's gun-wadding in a hedge where she is hiding. And it is also because of her marginal status that she is outside the purview of the law. Indeed, the situation invites us to see that patriarchally constituted discourses exclude her story precisely because the outlawed woman knows the father's guilty secret.

Gaskell readmits Esther into her own narrative obliquely with a return to religious rhetoric. A sermon spoken by a minor female character, a Liverpool boatman's wife, Mrs. Sturgis, applies the good Samaritan parable to fallen women. Exhausted from her attempt to reach Will's boat before it sails, Mary collapses on the quay, and Sturgis takes her to his home to be cared for by his wife, much as the good Samaritan brings the robbery victim to an inn. The good Samaritan, however, has no reason to think this victim is anything but innocent. Neither the boatman nor his wife know anything of Mary's character, and given her circumstances—a poor woman traveling alone, apparently to prevent a sailor from abandoning her—they can only assume her character is bad—as bad as Esther's. Gaskell's doubles are reunited.

Sturgis, a person of rather grudging action and few words, leaves his wife, "sorely puzzled as to the character and history of the stranger within her doors" (*MB*, p. 295), to articulate their obligation in a homely, but moving speech. At Mary's feeble attempt to rise, Mrs. Sturgis exclaims

> "Nay! nay! whoe'er thou be'st, thou'rt not fit to go out into the street. Perhaps" (sinking her voice a little) "thou'art a bad one; I almost misdoubt thee, thou'rt so pretty. Well-a-well! it's the bad ones as have the broken hearts, sure enough; good folk never get utterly cast down, they've always getten hope in the Lord; it's the sinful as bear the bitter, bitter grief in their crushed hearts, poor souls; it's them we ought, most of all, to pity and help. She shanna leave the house to-night, choose who she is,—worst woman in Liverpool, she shanna. I wish I knew where th' old man picked her up, that I do."
> (*MB*, p. 295)

To be sure, Gaskell's challenge is somewhat blunted by the religious rhetoric that calls Esther and similar women sinners, a designation earlier undercut by Esther's own "confession."[38] Nevertheless, despite its limitations, Gaskell's revision of the good Samaritan parable attacks the patriarchal authority to marginalize women. Mrs. Sturgis, whose practical charity Gaskell shrewdly balances with touches of conventional prejudice, is tempted to reject Mary as many have scorned her Aunt Hetty, but relents, not only pitying this stranger, as Jem pities Esther, but helping her as well.

This incident points out the possibility of the reconfiguration of social relationships along feminist lines utterly absent from the courtroom, and likewise denied in Esther's visit to Mary. Mrs. Sturgis admits the suspected fallen woman into her home, reasoning that the recentering of society around those who have been marginalized is an ethical imperative. By contrast, the meeting between Esther and Mary reinscribes the patriarchal rules of feminine legitimacy, preventing these women from telling one another their own stories, much as legal discourse ventriloquizes Mary and excludes Esther. Esther is the mother restored to Mary, though Mary cannot see it; Mary is the daughter Esther cannot legitimately claim. Instead, they both continue to live the patriarchal lies that deny their social and narrative kinship.

Esther and Mary, then, are alienated from one another in a fashion analogous to the way the female writers of one generation have historically been denied access to their precursors. The recovery of literary mothers demands a recognition of their "impropriety" that marks the female reader as fallen herself, and renders her own writing inscrutable to her proper female readers.[39] Likewise, Mrs. Sturgis's gesture towards Mary Barton marks a stage in the development of feminist reading, eventually leading to the point at which "the feminist reader takes the part of the woman writer against patriarchal misreadings."[40] The importance Gaskell attaches to this female interpretive community is made obvious in the contrast between those two occupants of the unmarked pauper's grave: John Barton and Esther.

Although mediated by considerable pathos, John Barton's prophecy succeeds in securing his reader's repentance. Barton's confession, like Esther's, is in fact a scripturally sanctioned vindication, but while the penitent response of Carson to John Barton's suffering can be represented within the novel as patriarchal fellow-feeling, Esther's "forgiveness" seems unthinkable. Identifying with his son's murderer as a father who has likewise grieved over the death of his own Absalom, Carson rereads scripture with a heightened sympathy for Barton's claim "'I did not know what I was doing'" (*MB*, p. 346), and finds there his spiritual brotherhood with Barton. Barton dies in Carson's arms as the repentant millowner prays the "Our Father," at once forgiving Barton and accepting his own guilt. To forgive Esther would entail the same assumption of guilt, an action that only Gaskell as author can take upon herself. She has authorized Esther's story by telling it, and both marginalized women wait for their readers to repent or condemn.

With *Mary Barton* Gaskell made her first major contribution to social-problem writing, and in so doing became the target of those patriarchs who sought to dominate it. Her attempts to maintain anonymity having failed, Gaskell became subject matter for incenses millowners, social reformers, and other political writers, notably Carlyle and Dickens. Even praise was not an unmitigated blessing, as Carlyle's letter to the author of *Mary Barton* makes clear. Gaskell cherished this letter, quoting to one correspondent a conviction she claimed to share with Carlyle: "May you live to write good books," Carlyle had written, "or *do silently good actions which in my sight is far more indispensable*" [Gaskell's emphasis].[41] Carlyle, needless to say, failed to take his own advice. The disapproving gazes of her Manchester friends and the attacks of reviewers stung Gaskell, who, like her predecessors, looked to God to vindicate her. Shortly after the novel's publication, Gaskell wrote: "God will cause the errors [of *Mary Barton*] to be temporary[,] the truth to be eternal, that I try not to mind too much what people say either in praise or blame."[42] But the focus of her next novel, the fallen woman, suggests that in fact she did.

Ruth: *The Sisterhood of Preachers*

Ruth is about a woman who has "fallen" outside patriarchal law, but remains within God's law. Unlike Esther in *Mary Barton*, who as a prostitute is literally a criminal, *Ruth*'s heroine suffers from a more subtle, but nonetheless devastating marginality, by which Gaskell aligns her experience with the improper woman writer's. Yet *Ruth* cannot be reduced to an allegory of writing. On the contrary, the very peculiarities of characterization and plot that are often perceived as flaws—violations of aesthetic norms—emphasize the interrelation of textuality and sexuality. The connection Gaskell makes between patriarchal strategies to suppress and control women's speech and repressive norms of female sexuality illuminates her contributions to the tradition of female preaching, which are both literary and political.

Ruth's sexual transgression, rendering her story unspeakable within the novel, mirrors Gaskell's own discursive transgression in giving voice to a story which violates the laws of feminine decorum. Gaskell counters both manifestations of patriarchal law, specifically their claims to divine sanction, with feminist interpretations of scriptural texts that privilege marginalized women. Indeed, very much like the early women preachers, Gaskell appreciates the ideological conflicts in scripture which, by contrast with more homogeneous patriarchal narratives, can actually raise feminist consciousness and lead to an evangelical witness on behalf of women. Far from being unspeakable, women's stories may be prophetic. Gaskell has no illusions about the power of this narrative to bring the patriarchy to repentance—Ruth does die while her seducer lives on in narcissistic oblivion of his guilt. Yet the novel gives us two examples, albeit imperfect, of "conversions" to Gaskell's nonpatriarchal Christianity: Thurston Benson and Jemima Bradshaw. These two readers of Ruth's character dramatize Gaskell's hope that the readers of *Ruth* will likewise repent of patriarchal ideology and become woman preachers.

Traditionally, *Ruth*'s proponents have defended this critically unpopular novel as a courageous plea for Christian charity on behalf of England's most despised class. But they are largely responsible for defining *Ruth* according to its weakest elements and deflecting its strongest—and most troubling—statements. Indeed, the reviewer who numbered the author of *Ruth* among the nation's greatest "evangelists of reconciliation" hoped the novel would result in social reforms beneficial to fallen women, but ignored the incompatibility of feminist reform with established patriarchal interests presented in the novel. Exactly what Gaskell might have hoped *Ruth* would accomplish in the way of social reforms is unclear; to the extent that the novel is taken as a piece of social advocacy, it appears confused and inadequate. Modern critics have sneered at Ruth's absurd innocence and the plot's sentimental culmination in her deathbed scene, and accused Gaskell of being a timid, bourgeois prude, either ignorant of the realities of sexual exploitation or determined to conceal them.[43] Certainly, she is allowed to have regretted the double standard of sexual conduct, enforced by law, that might allow men to ruin women's lives without consequence to themselves. But even this conviction is used to deride her, as symptomatic of a pervasive ideology of female propriety.

Ruth's most indignant enemies, the Victorian fathers who denounced the novel as unfit for family reading, perhaps better understood its power. Certainly *Ruth* is not for the reader demanding polite subject matter, or conventional plot development and verisimilitude—discursive patterns confirming patriarchal values. Presenting an almost surrealistic vision of women's fallen status in the patriarchal order, Gaskell endows her characters with divine authority to reject conventional definitions of feminine virtue. She explores the subversive, resistant possibilities of female silence, and questions the assumption that silence always implies consent. What is more, Gaskell once again asserts the need for women to witness on behalf of one another, crossing lines of class and propriety to defy patriarchal censorship of women's stories.

For most of the novel Ruth functions as an icon, the subject of patriarchal misreadings. To her seducer, the narcissistic aristocrat Bellington, Ruth is a commodity he acquires to gratify his ego. To the pharisaical manufacturer, Mr. Bradshaw, who unwittingly hires her as the governess to his children, Ruth must be either saint or demon. Even the Dissenting minister, Mr. Benson, Ruth's most sympathetic male "reader," gives her a proper alibi, introducing her to his Eccleston parish as a widow. Women, too, construe Ruth in terms of patriarchal narratives: as a poor seamstress, a magdalen, a foolish chit, or a captivating beauty. Only Jemima Bradshaw, who begins by idolizing her beautiful "widowed" governess as the tragic heroine of a sentimental romance, eventually undergoes a traumatic conversion to a feminist reading of Ruth.

Until well into the novel, Gaskell's narrator provides Ruth with virtually no interiority that would definitively contradict the other characters' misreadings of her. This narrative strategy, which some critics have disparaged as nothing more than prudish reticence, might also be seen as focusing attention on the social structures that prevent women from constructing a public identity. Revelations of Ruth's character are inseparable from rebellions against patriarchal authority. When Ruth finally speaks out against her oppression, asserting her independence from the foolishness of men, she will touch off a series of feminist rebellions that topple the novel's arch patriarch, Mr. Bradshaw. Ruth's speech finally locates the marginalized, misread woman as the novel's moral center.

Gaskell's theology informs this entire process. Ruth's first advocate, Thurston Benson, who saves her from suicide when

Bellingham absconds, demonstrates the importance of Christian teaching as a means of enabling men to imagine women with subjectivity, independent of conventional types. Though associated with middle-class Christian piety, and enjoying access to both sacred and secular scripture, Benson himself occupies a marginal position in a patriarchal society. As a Dissenting minister he is outside the dominant religious and political communities; in his poverty he is vulnerable to the will of his wealthy parishioners; his fragile health and physical handicap make him dependent on his sister, Faith, and his housekeeper, Sally, and at a crucial point, Ruth herself, thus separating him from the more robust and dominant members of his sex. His situation then, resembles that of women: politically, economically, and physically vulnerable.

In comparing Benson with his sister, Gaskell describes Faith as having a more masculine character because she is clear-sighted and inclined to act without prolonged deliberation, trusting to God that all will go well, while Thurstan "was so often perplexed by the problems of life, that he let the time for action go by" (*R*, p. 203). This seems an idiosyncratic assignment of gender categories. Women were typically thought to act as Faith does, intuitively, without attention to the intricacies of the problem they addressed.[44] Gaskell herself, in letters to her daughter Marianne, blamed women for oversimplifying complex social issues and for lacking judgment. Something more subtle is implied here. Women, as well as men, may be guilty of misogyny, and ideology, more than sex, determines one's ability to tolerate difference. The marginal status Thurstan Benson shares with women as a class—largely as the result of his evangelical calling—makes him more reflective and sympathetic than other members of his sex to the fallen woman's plight. Viewing the world from the perspective of victim rather than victor, as fellow sinner rather than pharisee, Benson understands the inadequacy of conventional moral and social categories and does not assume that he possesses a complete or authoritative vision. Rather, he feels compelled to forgive as he would be forgiven, to assume that Ruth is within God's community.

Benson comes upon Ruth when despair over Bellington's removal with his mother drives her to attempt suicide. He runs after her as she rushes towards a cliff, calling on God to have pity and save her. Benson's words are lost on Ruth, but his infirmity causes her to recognize a fellow sufferer. Ruth's response to Benson's "few homely words" is inarticulate, denying her the confession as vindication that allows Esther to dominate her dialogue with Jem in *Mary Barton*. But this narrator is as cagey as *Mary Barton*'s when she claims that Ruth is saved by a sense of duty to others, for Ruth forgets Benson's presence and indulges her own sorrow. That she is wanted in the world does not mitigate the fact that some—like Bellington and his mother—would gladly see her rush out of it. "Covering her face with her hands" may suggest Ruth's recognition of her unwanted, undeserved exclusion from society.

Instead, Gaskell gives us access to Benson's motivations as he undertakes Ruth's defense as his Christian duty. In dialogues between Thurstan and Faith Benson, Gaskell discloses the misogyny pervading conventional Christian morality, and opposes to it the more egalitarian theology characteristic of the women's preaching tradition. Gaskell creates Faith with a well-developed sense of delicacy as well as duty, underscoring the difficulty of converting even relatively charitable women to a sense of solidarity with their fallen sisters, when the very mention of their existence is construed as a threat to feminine virtue. Faith Benson, shaped by social norms, does not readily accede to her brother's more radical application of Christian forgiveness. But Gaskell's strategy implies that there is no real argument against assisting Ruth, only an irrational—and irreligious—aversion to it.

Faith repents of her condemnation of Ruth only because the girl appears to be near death, and therefore is nullified as a vital threat to Miss Benson's moral order. But the discovery that the friendless waif she has agreed to nurse is pregnant shocks Faith and threatens to destroy her nascent sympathy for Ruth. Faith declares that "the worst part of all" is that Ruth seems pleased to be pregnant. "Oh, my God, I thank Thee!" cries Ruth when Faith tells her she is pregnant; "Oh, I will be so good!" "I had no patience with her then," Faith declares, "so I left the room" (*R*, p. 117). Women's greatest threat to the patriarchal order lies in their ability to produce this illegitimate fruit, a power shared metaphorically by female writers of feminist texts. Rather than seeing it as a confirmation of her depravity, however, Benson, like Wesley, interprets Ruth's fruit as evidence of God's blessing, legitimating Ruth herself. "In the eye of God," Benson argues, "she is exactly the same as if the life she has led had left no trace behind," and the child "may be God's messenger to lead her back to Him" (*R*, p. 118). "These are quite new ideas to me," replies a resistant Faith (*R*, p. 118). In terms of patriarchal morality, bent on preserving itself against the claims of bastards and their illicit mothers, Benson's argument is patently unorthodox, yet he claims to be "act[ing] as my blessed Lord would have done" (*R*, p. 119).

Benson's opposition of God's law to man's is good as far as it goes, but the preacher himself confesses to uncertainty, falling back on a mother's natural duties as Ruth's salvation rather than sanctifying her sexuality. Patsy Stoneman has pointed out that Gaskell becomes trapped by a rhetoric of repentance into casting Ruth as a sinner in order to redeem her. But Benson's interpretation of Ruth does not go unchallenged in the novel. His compliance with Faith's plan to pass Ruth off as the widow "Mrs. Denbigh" in their community of Eccleston reveals his squeamish desire to avoid the peculiar stigma of the fallen woman. The narrator implies that this lie has significance primarily with respect to the unborn child and the Bensons, and secondarily with respect to Ruth's reformation. What Gaskell leaves implicit is the significance this lie will have with respect to the novel's world, and by implication, to the reader's. Informed of her pregnancy, Ruth speaks her first words since being rescued from her suicide attempt. She awakes to a new role, and a new authority. No society can acknowledge the fallen woman's authority when it substitutes a fiction for her actual voice. The tragic consequences of employing polite fictions to obscure the fallen woman point up the moral responsibility central to evangelicalism—to testify to the truth.

It is not long before someone guesses Ruth's story. Sally, the Bensons' elderly housekeeper, greets Mrs. Denbigh's arrival in her characteristically direct manner: "'If I'd been her mother, I'd ha' given her a lollypop instead on a husband. Hoo looks fitter for it'" (*R*, p. 134). Good-hearted and loyal as well as shrewd, Sally perceives that Ruth is an unlikely widow, but says nothing to the Bensons and treats her new guest civilly. Rather than denouncing Ruth, Sally, "with judge-like severity of demeanour," subjects her to a ritual of penance through which Ruth's character is redeemed in Sally's eyes.

On the day after Ruth's arrival, Sally marches into her room declaring that a young widow should be in mourning, and that Ruth's long tresses must be shorn and her head covered with a widow's cap. Sally anticipates some resistance from Ruth, but she submits quietly to her "merciless" cutting. In meekly accepting this penance, Ruth is her own best witness to her innocence, for Sally is "touched . . . with compunction" (*R*, p. 144). Further, Ruth's shearing and her donning of the widow's cap can be compared to a woman's entry into a religious order. Indeed, as an unmarried woman, Ruth joins the sisterhood of Gaskell's spinsters and widows whose lives are devoted to charity. Her concern for Leonard, her son, her piety and kindness, will make Ruth a model woman admired by all of Eccleston. However, this model of respectability is founded on a patriarchal fiction of the sort Tonna's Mr. Z. would feed his daughter Amelia. Rather than face the strong truth, society's privileged would prefer to see its Ruths through the medium of sentimental piety, where she can play the grieving widow.

Like the decorous fiction that separates Mary Barton from her aunt Esther, Ruth's assumed identity interferes with any conversion that might be effected by a "confession" of her actual circumstances. Among Ruth's admirers is Jemima Bradshaw, daughter of Mr. Benson's most prominent parishioner and the embodiment of the society's most unforgiving attitudes towards fallen women. From their first meeting, Ruth's beauty and the melancholy fiction concerning her past enchant Jemima: "the pretended circumstances of her life were such as to catch the imagination of a young romantic girl" (*R*, p. 182). What for Mr. Bradshaw signifies proper resignation to her sphere—Ruth's "reserve and retirement"—for Jemima enhances Ruth's aesthetic appeal. Yet neither Bradshaw correctly interprets Ruth: while the father's approval is founded on his prejudices, Jemima's is based partly on a lie. Nevertheless, she imaginatively enters into Ruth's life enough to understand that hers is the beauty of an innocent soul. For Jemima, Ruth is a lovely story unfolding before her eyes and for her benefit.

Bradshaw's authoritarian rule has made a fearful servant of

his wife, and a devious cheat of his son, but it has not managed to crush Jemima's rebellious spirit. When Bradshaw invites Ruth to become the governess of his two younger daughters, he is pleased by Jemima's attachment to her, hoping this re-calcitrant child will imitate Ruth's retiring manner. When the novel resumes five years after Ruth's entry into the Bradshaw household, Jemima is still devoted to her but is given to arguing matters of politics and economics with her much-chagrined fa-ther and his business partner, Mr. Farquhar. This combination of behaviors hints at a strength of character that will enable the defiant Jemima to defend Ruth passionately when the truth about her seduction comes to light.

At the same time, Bellingham's appearance in Eccleston as "Mr. Donne," a candidate for Parliament, threatens to expose Ruth's fictitious identity, not only to Jemima, but to a pharisai-cal Mr. Bradshaw. But rather than exposing her, the confronta-tion between them enables Ruth to reject this epitome of immoral power on behalf of her son, Leonard, and, by impli-cation, on behalf of all his victims. Just as he had once used his power of speech to seduce female innocence, the glib Bellingham now hopes to seduce the voters of Eccleston to send him to Parliament, where his ego would enjoy ever greater range. He succeeds in winning Bradshaw's assistance in carrying out his unethical election schemes, and the part-nership between "Donne" and Bradshaw brings about his en-counter with Ruth. But this new attempt at seduction will finally be dominated by Ruth, who, like a prophet, confronts Bellingham with his sin and calls on him to repent. By virtue of her spiritual authority, Ruth effectively opposes the com-bined sexual, political, and verbal power of the reprobate Bellingham.

Bellingham's voice still has some power to control Ruth, drawing her into a dialogue in which her own identity is mean-ingless. Bellingham remains unwilling to imagine Ruth apart from his own shallow desires. The beauty of the Bradshaw fam-ily's governess first attracts his attention, particularly the detail of her dimples, which seem to rank among his most profound recollections of Ruth. Recognizing Bellingham, Ruth is thrown into an agony of mixed emotions—fear, guilt, longing—most threatening, the narrator tells us, for their potential to block her access to God in prayer, the source of her authority. When he approaches Ruth as she walks to church with the Bradshaw girls his "well remembered voice" makes her tremble as she recalls its "power to thrill" (*R*, p. 281). But though made "weak . . . in body, she [felt] strong in power over herself" (*R*, p. 277), walking on in silence with her eyes fixed on the church. His questioning, a more seductive version of the rape-like examination Mary Barton undergoes on the witness stand, repells Ruth, who resists him with a tone of such "quiet authority" that it surprises the Bradshaw children (*R*, p. 278).

Gaskell here introduces the scriptural text which reveals the archetypal pattern of Ruth's persecution, identifying the fallen woman with Jesus. In church, Ruth gazes at a gargoyle, its unusually beautiful face, like hers, a silent icon of suffering relieved only by the promise of God's help (*R*, p. 280).[45] Calmed by the artist's faith in the face of "infinite sorrow," she hears the words of the scripture lesson, Matthew 26, where Jesus prays in Gethsemane that the cup of suffering be taken from him. Ruth, too, has been met by her betrayer—Bellingham is her Judas, who betrays with a kiss. Like Jesus, she may be empowered by God to endure this trial, and indeed, she may be delivered. "And when they prayed again Ruth's tongue was unloosed, and she could pray, in His name who underwent the agony in the garden" (*R*, p. 280).

Ruth's "trial" resembles just that, associating Bellingham with the pharisees and Pilate, who questioned Jesus before condemning him to death, as well as the institutions of patriarchal society that oppress women. Fearful lest Bellingham assert his legal right to Leonard, Ruth agrees to meet him on an isolated beach. He plays with her like a barrister confident of his ability to control the witness. Bellingham's attempts to endear himself to Ruth with reminiscences of their love are met with silence. When he finally provokes her to admit she had loved him, it is more a confession of guilt than of present affection. Bellingham cannot imagine Ruth as anything but a beautiful object for his pleasure, and therefore takes this confession as encouragement to urge his plan on her. He will educate Leonard if she will become his mistress.

However, Ruth at last answers his melodramatic proposal

with a firm rebuke, and her confession becomes her vindication.

> "Listen to me!" said Ruth, now that the idea of what he proposed had entered her mind. "When I said that I was happy with you long ago, I was choked with shame as I said it. And yet it may be a vain, false excuse that I make for myself. I was very young; I did not know how such a life was against God's pure and holy will—at least, not as I know it now; and I tell you the truth—all the days of my years since I have gone about with a stain on my hidden soul—a stain which made me loathe myself, and envy those who stood spotless and undefiled; which made me shrink from my child—from Mr. Benson, from his sister, from the innocent girls whom I teach—nay, even from God Himself; and what I did wrong then, I did blindly to what I should do now if I listened to you." (*R*, p. 296)

Ruth turns the tables on Bellingham, convicting him of alienating her from her own voice, and forcing on her a fictional identity; what is worse, he now threatens to exclude her from converse with God, her only protector and source of the only authoritative language available to her.

Although she commands him to listen, Bellingham cannot hear: "He was so struck anew by her beauty, and understood her so little, that he believed that she only required a little more urging to consent to what he wished" (*R*, p. 296). When his threat to expose Ruth fails to persuade her, musing on her "stately step" and "majestic and graceful" air as she turns away, Bellingham decides to offer her marriage, concluding that "'[Leonard] and [Ruth] would grace any situation" (*R*, p. 299). He understands Ruth no better than a stranger. He cannot comprehend her refusal—he cannot read her—because he will not repent of his own selfish desires. "'We are very far apart,'" Ruth tells him.

> "'The time that has pressed down my life like brands of hot iron, and scarred me for ever, has been noth-

> ing to you. You have talked of it with no sound of
> moaning in your voice—nor shadow over the
> brightness of your face, it has left no sense of sin on
> your conscience, while me it haunts and haunts; and
> yet I might plead that I was an ignorant child—only
> I will not plead anything, for God knows all—" (*R*,
> pp. 299–300)

"'You have heard my mind now,'" Ruth concludes, and indeed she has testified eloquently on her own behalf. But Bellingham remains impenitent, as if she had mumbled gibberish.

The depth and authority of Ruth's character is established here through her rhetorical power; conversely, Bellingham's consistent misinterpretation, or sheer bafflement at her speeches, confirms his egotistical one-dimensionality, and the resistance of a masculine discourse to a woman's voice. Bellingham can persist in attempts to oppress Ruth because his egotism renders him insensitive to her language. As a reader he cannot repent; as a speaker he merely repeats clichés of romance and revenge. To Ruth, however, it no longer matters, for she has achieved her independence of his voice and his narrative.

Her voice will effect a repentance, producing the closest thing to a feminist reading of Ruth's story. While Gaskell left Esther isolated in sexist social codes, she uses Jemima to dramatize her own relation to the novel's reader, a relationship which has already transgressed rules of propriety. Just as the middle-class proper lady, Miss Jemima Bradshaw, undergoes a traumatic conversion from patriarchal constructions of feminine virtue in order to become Ruth's advocate, the reader of *Ruth* must forgo *ad feminam* attacks on its author, interpreting the novel according to its feminist "spirit" rather than patriarchal law. Although that spirit involves the rhetoric of sin and redemption, it allows Gaskell to present feminist solidarity as a Christian ideal.

Earlier in the novel, when Mr. Farquhar seemed to transfer his attention from fiery, opinionated Jemima to the placid, reserved Ruth, the jealous Miss Bradshaw began to attend even more minutely to Ruth's behavior in the hope of finding some deviousness or pride which would justify her resentment. Jemima, who once romanticized Ruth, assumed the stance of judge. But she is frustrated until a shopkeeper remarks to her on Mrs. Denbigh's resemblance to a young woman formerly in her sister's employ, who came to a bad end. In this woman's telling, the tragedy we have followed for three hundred pages becomes a sordid tale told for the titillation of hypocritical gossips. This is one "official" version of Ruth's past, replete with the prejudices of her society. The truth proves a bit more than Jemima bargained for, and it poses a threat to the foundations of her own character. In a striking psychosexual image, Gaskell describes Jemima's shock.

> The diver leaving the green sward, smooth and known, where his friends stand with their familiar smiling faces, admiring his glad bravery—the diver, down in an instant in the horrid depths of the sea, close to some strange, ghastly, lidless-eyed monster, can hardly more feel his blood curdle at the near terror than did Jemima now. Two hours ago—but a point of time on her mind's dial—she has never imagined that she should ever come in contact with any one who had committed open sin. . . Without being pharisaical in her estimation of herself, she had all a pharisee's dread of publicans and sinners, and all a child's cowardliness—that cowardliness which prompts it to shut its eyes against the object of terror, rather than acknowledge its existence with brave faith. (*R*, p. 320)

Jemima's experience of strong truths force her to penetrate— to "dive down"—beneath the surface of romantic portrayals of woman's nature. Her own terror speaks to the experience of the readers of *Ruth*. They too might trust that no such tale would intrude on their well-defended ignorance of women's oppression. Gaskell here shapes that response, showing it to be pharisaical on Bradshaw's part, but on Jemima's a stage of childhood naïveté, which the adult—particularly the Christian adult—must abandon.

Jemima's ability to reinterpret Ruth's character in light of the truth and to appreciate its real beauty become synonymous with her own maturity and achievement of independence. "The very foundations of Jemima's belief in her mind were shaken" by the knowledge of Ruth's seduction. If Ruth in whom she had tried mightily but failed to detect a hint of guile could not be trusted, who could? Her fictional understanding of woman's virtue, the one imposed on her imagination by male authority, is shattered by these strong truths. From this state of despair and confusion, Gaskell rebuilds Jemima's attitude towards Ruth.

Jemima has the power over Ruth she once desired. She might enlighten Mr. Farquhar and destroy her rival. Immediately, however, Jemima's generous instincts assert themselves.

> It might be—she used to think such things possible, before sorrow had embittered her—that Ruth had worked her way through the deep purgatory of repentance up to something like purity again; God only knew! If her present goodness was real—if, after having striven back thus far on the heights, a fellow-woman was to throw her down into some terrible depth with her unkind, incontinent tongue, that would be too cruel! (*R*, p. 323)

While women's special duty as defenders of domestic sanctity was to abhor the fallen of their sex, Gaskell stays Jemima's vengeance by this recognition of sisterhood. It is not woman's special duty to abhor the fallen of her sex, but to protect and respect them for enduring "the deep purgatory of repentance." Jemima wavers in accepting this duty, uncertain of Ruth's repentance and jealous of her as the object of Mr. Farquhar's affection. However, all Jemima's doubts are overcome when she alone can defend Ruth against her father's wrath.

Mr. Bradshaw, enraged by his discovery of Ruth's sin, confronts the governess in Jemima's presence. Ruth stands numb and helpless as Bradshaw viciously accuses her of wantonness and hypocrisy, but at the height of her father's rage Jemima steps forward.

> "Father! I will speak. I will not keep silence. I will bear witness to Ruth. I have hated her—so keenly, may God forgive me! but you many know, from that, that my witness is true . . . dear Ruth"—(this was

spoken with infinite softness and tenderness, and in spite of her father's fierce eyes and passionate gesture)—"I heard what you have learnt now, father, weeks and weeks ago . . . and I shuddered up from her and from her sin; and I might have spoken of it, and told it there and then, if I had not been afraid that it was from no good motive I should act in so doing, but to gain a way to the desire of my own jealous heart. Yes, father, to show you what a witness I am for Ruth, I will own that I was stabbed to the heart with jealousy . . . I watched her, and I watched her with my wild-beast eyes. If I had seen one paltering with duty—if I had witnessed one flickering shadow of untruth in word or action—if, more than all things, my woman's instinct had ever been conscious of the faintest speck of impurity in thought, or word, or look, my old hate would have flamed out with the flame of hell! my contempt would have been turned to loathing disgust, instead of my being full of pity, and the stirrings of new-awakened love, and most true respect. Father, I have borne my witness!" (*R*, p. 335).

Bradshaw's command, "'Look at that woman,'" echoing Pilate's words to the crowd that would condemn Christ, have precisely the opposite effect on Jemima. Rather than forcing Jemima to betray Ruth, it inspires her to bear witness to her. Like many of Gaskell's earlier female characters, Jemima speaks passionately and eloquently in defense of the weak at a moment of crisis. Jemima's conversion is possible precisely because she has looked clearly at the real Ruth, her vision no longer obscured by the polite, cowardly lies that have surrounded this fallen woman. She stands side by side with her sister against her father, bearing witness as though her defense were a divine message.

Bradshaw's rejection of this message is complete. But this does not diminish the power of Jemima's testimony; rather, it underscores Bradshaw's hardness of heart. From this point, Gaskell destroys any sympathy for Bradshaw, while portraying Jemima as a redeeming and revitalizing force in the novel.

Bradshaw proceeds from denouncing Ruth to denouncing her son. As his final curse on Leonard, Bradshaw shouts at Ruth that "'the best thing that could happen to him would be for him to be lost to all sense of shame, dead to all knowledge of guilt, for his mother's sake.'" (*R*, p. 337) At that

> Ruth spoke out. She stood like a wild creature at bay, past fear now. "I appeal to God against such a doom for my child, I appeal to God to help me. I am a mother, and as such I cry to God for help—for help to keep my boy in His pitying sight, and to bring him up in His holy fear. Let the shame fall on me! I have deserved it, but he—he is so innocent and good." (*R*, p. 337)

Ruth, like Jemima, must defend one weaker than herself. But Ruth knows better than to appeal to man; instead, she calls on God to defend her son. This prayer too fails to move Bradshaw, who casts Ruth out with a warning "'if ever you, or your bastard, darken this door again, I will have you both turned out by the police!'" (*R*, p. 337)

For a third and final time, Gaskell presents Bradshaw with an opportunity to repent. Mr. Benson, summoned by Bradshaw to answer for his protégée, defends Ruth's innocence. But for Bradshaw, Ruth's depravity is absolute and unmitigated by any evidence of alleged virtue. At this point, Benson becomes a prophet to this unrepentant sinner:

> "Now I wish God would give me power to speak out convincingly what I believe to be His truth, that not every woman who has fallen is depraved; that many—how many the Great Judgment Day will reveal to those who have shaken off the poor, sore, penitent hearts on earth—many, many crave and hunger after a chance of virtue—the help which no man gives them—help—that gentle, tender help which Jesus gave once to Mary Magdalen." Mr. Benson was almost choked by his own feelings. . . . "I take my stand with Christ against the world. I declare before God, that if I believe in any one human truth, it is this—that every woman who, like Ruth,

has sinned should be given a chance of self-redemption—and that such a chance should be given in no supercilious or contemptuous manner, but in the spirit of the holy Christ." (*R*, pp. 347–48)

Benson resists a classification of women that diminishes real and important differences, attributing the ability to distinguish individuals from stereotypes to divine judgment. His words— "'the women who have fallen should be numbered among those who have broken hearts to be bound up'" (*R*, p. 348)— recall Mrs. Sturgis's words to Mary Barton that identify society's marginalized members as the center of Christ's world. Even though in Benson's mind Ruth's status still depends on repentance, his theology does not ask more of her than it does of all believers, each of whom must repent. Indeed, Bradshaw's rejection of this call to repentance underscores his moral inferiority to Ruth. Like Mr. Carson in *Mary Barton*, Bradshaw will be brought to his knees only by tragedy.

From the point of her defense of Ruth, Jemima replaces her father as the dominant force in her family. Her act of defiance, itself resulting from a challenge to her identity, fatally cracks the foundation of Bradshaw's authority. She remains steadfast in her duty towards Ruth, and watches for an opportunity to do her good which will outweigh her duty to obey her father's command that all contact with Ruth be terminated. Jemima's loyalty and courage cause Farquhar, who pities Ruth though he can no longer love her, to rekindle his interest in Jemima. Not only does Gaskell show that a virtuous woman need not be stigmatized for defending a fallen sister, but furthermore she maintains Jemima's moral superiority over Farquhar.

> The unacknowledged bond between them now was their grief, and sympathy, and pity for Ruth; only in Jemima these feelings were ardent, and would fain have become active; while in Mr. Farquhar they were strongly mingled with thankfulness that he had escaped a disagreeable position, and a painful notoriety. (*R*, p. 367)

Granted, we would prefer to see Jemima acting independently rather than as a salutary influence on her fiancé, whose sympathy as a fellow bastard seems rather contrived. However, Gaskell shows Jemima to have gained much, despite the fact that those gains are cloaked within the acceptable language of renunciation. Jemima's increasing independence from woman's "natural duties" stems from an understanding of her duties to her own sex.

> ". . . if you knew all I have been thinking and feel-
> ing this last year" [she tells Benson], "you would see
> how I have yielded to every temptation that was able
> to come to me; and, seeing how I have no goodness
> or strength in me, and how I might have been like
> Ruth, or rather worse than she ever was, because I
> am more headstrong and passionate by nature, I do
> so thank you and love you for what you did for her!
> And will you tell me really and truly now if I can
> ever do anything for Ruth?" (*R*, pp. 361–62)

As Mrs. Farquhar, Jemima represents Gaskell's ideal for the married middle-class woman, who recognizes her sisterhood with more obvious victims of exploitation.

Nevertheless, while the Jemima Bradshaws might plead the fallen woman's case, it would be the Mr. Bradshaws who would decide her fate. The events of the novel's close emphasize the fatal consequences of the domination of patriarchal law over the conciliatory spirit of scripture. While campaigning for Parliament near Eccleston, Bellingham falls ill, and Ruth volunteers to nurse him. Bellingham is restored to health; Ruth contracts the fever and dies. Unlike Esther's death in *Mary Barton*, which seems a blessed release for a lost and tormented soul, Gaskell presents Ruth's death as her apotheosis, describing it in terms worthy of a saint's life:

> They stood around her bedside, not speaking, or
> sighing, or moaning; they were too much awed by
> the exquisite peacefulness of her look for that. Sud-
> denly she opened wide her eyes, and gazed intently
> forwards, as if she saw some happy vision, which
> called out a lovely, rapturous, breathless smile. They
> held their very breaths.
> "I see the Light coming," said she. "The Light is

coming," she said. And, raising herself slowly, she stretched out her arms, and fell back, very still for evermore. (*R*, p. 444)

If Ruth's readers conceive of her as a saint, she must be assumed into heaven. In a society ruled by pharisees, Ruth drinks from the bitter cup of her own martyrdom. Some readers many feel that in Ruth's death Gaskell indulges in clichéd rhetoric, which she elsewhere rejects, but other readers (like Charlotte Brontë) may be prompted to ask why Ruth must die and to resent the "plot" that calls for her demise.

Indeed, Gaskell refutes the notion that a woman's death produces a salutary effect; rather, it serves no other purpose than to remove one troublesome woman from a man's world. Over Ruth's corpse, Bellingham unashamedly reveals to Mr. Benson his "youthful follies" with her, and offers to compensate Leonard with a large sum of money. Benson, barely suppressing his anger toward this heartless perpetrator of Ruth's misery, responds icily, "Men may call such actions as yours youthful follies! There is another name for them with God" (*R*, p. 450). Bellingham, unfazed, continues to urge his money on Benson. After Benson shuts the door in his face, Bellingham, still oblivious to this tragedy of his making, complains of Ruth's benefactor

> "An ill-bred, puritanical old fellow! He may have the boy, I am sure, for aught I care. I have done my duty, and will get out of this abominable place as soon as I can. I wish my last remembrance of my beautiful Ruth was not mixed up with all these people." (*R*, p. 450)

The worst fate, suffered by this incarnation of exploitive ideologies is to be denied an aesthetically pleasing end to a troublesome affair. Ruth's suffering cannot be wholly erased, even if Bellingham will not accept responsibility for it.

Among men, who dominate the novel's close, Ruth's death functions merely as the means of patriarchal reconciliation. The effect on Bradshaw is rather like Lancelot's crude admiration of the corpse of the Lady of Shalott. He orders a monument for Ruth's grave to testify to "his respect for the woman, who," as the narrator tells us, "if all had entertained his opinions, would have been driven into hopeless sin" (*R*, p. 453). In the novel's final scene, Bradshaw and the stoneman go to the chapel yard where they find Leonard weeping over Ruth's grave. This picture of a boy's innocent suffering and Leonard's simple words, "'My mother is dead, sir'" (*R*, p. 454), evoke a more human tribute to Ruth than the stone monument Bradshaw had planned. He places his hand on Leonard's shoulder and offers to take him home, where the novel ends in a scene of reconciliation.

> The first time, for years, that he had entered Mr. Benson's house, he came leading and comforting her son—and, for a moment, he could not speak to his old friend, for the sympathy which choked up his voice, and filled his eyes with tears. (*R*, p. 454)

For all the emotion Gaskell generates in this scene, it describes a reconciliation between two old friends, Benson and Bradshaw. Though we might wish for some token of the fallen woman's presence in this final scene, the best Gaskell will offer is the rigid, domineering man of business humbled before the "feminine" Mr. Benson. Even Benson's response to Bradshaw's penitence is withheld. Gaskell's conclusion emphasizes all the more the need for a sisterhood of preachers who will not allow the fallen woman's story to be effaced by patriarchal plots. Ruth and Jemima deconstruct the dominant ideology of femininity and relations between the sexes in a patriarchy only to be displaced by Bradshaw's inarticulate emotion. Gaskell harbors no illusions about the patriarchy which resists woman's voices even when speaking the word of God; as the novel itself predicts, their message could be co-opted by the patriarchy, or silenced. Yet, Bradshaw embraces Ruth's bastard son and *Ruth*'s readers might heed the woman writer's illegitimate fruits.

The critique of Bradshaw's phariseeism in *Ruth* did not discourage some reviewers from responding to the novel in words worthy of the old Pharisee himself. A *Christian Observer* reviewer wrote that "in *Ruth*, [Gaskell] instructs us, that a woman who has violated the *laws* [my emphasis] of purity is entitled to occupy precisely the same position in society as one who has never thus offended."[46] Some saw the novel as a threat to innocence, as had the critics of *Coelebs*. Like Mr. Z. in Tonna's *Helen Fleetwood*, they equated innocence with ignorance. That is, all the responses to Ruth within the novel itself were played out in its aftermath. Gaskell had correctly anticipated her audience. She enjoyed substantial encouragement from other women writers, however, who could appreciate the support the novel leant to woman directly involved in bettering the lot of their "fallen" sisters—and defending women's voices. Charlotte Brontë, Elizabeth Barrett Browning, and Mrs. Jameson were among the novel's admirers. The controversy stirred up by *Ruth* followed Gaskell for many years and, in some readers' eyes, she herself was stigmatized by her knowledge of, and identification with, fallen women.

Dickens would encourage Gaskell after her traumatic experience with the press. He enthusiastically praised *Ruth* and the plan for her next novel, *North and South*. Despite Dickens' support, however, Gaskell began work on the novel in a rather fitful manner, showing signs of disillusionment with her evangelical mission.

Subversion of the Preacher: North and South

Despite the dichotomy implied in the title, the world of *North and South* appears less polarized than that of *Mary Barton* or *Ruth*. Dickens and the eventual publishers of *North and South*, Chapman and Hall, saw the novel as an argument for class understanding and social responsibility. Yet Gaskell's critique of sexual relations threatens to displace her more sanguine analysis of other social conflicts. *North and South* is Gaskell's revision of that classic novel of sexual misunderstanding and conflict, Austen's *Pride and Prejudice,* done in such a way as to foreground the politics of the romance narrative and the ideological barriers to women's recognition of themselves as an exploited class. Like Austen, she analyzes social power in terms of speech and silence, creating a heroine with an authoritative voice and strong convictions. Gaskell ups the ante considerably, however, by giving her heroine, Margaret Hale, an explicitly public vision, extending the rationale for her personal battles against feminine socializations to general ethical and political principles. In *North and South* sexual politics exposes the artificiality of boundaries between private and public spheres that had so long excluded woman from public discourse.⁴⁷ But it is precisely because Gaskell is aware of the power of sexist ideology to enforce this division that she resists Austen's utopian closure, leaving Margaret Hale in self-imposed silence. Gaskell's aim in *North and South* is to explore the ways in which the most powerful female speakers—particularly evangelists— can be convinced to become their own censors, how women succumb to patriarchal ideology, adopting its values as she herself did in defending "natural duties."

To the extent that the central relationship of Gaskell's novel between Margaret Hale and the millowner Thornton is genuinely adversarial, the conflict derives from gender difference rather than regional or class antagonism. By the time Margaret and Thornton meet, Margaret's father has given up his living as a Church of England clergyman over a matter of conscience, and the Hales live in genteel poverty, while Thornton, as a wealthy millowner, has put his working-class origins behind him. Margaret represents the south of England, but the south in turn represents not the gentry, but Gaskell's conception of the feminine, in its inculcation of the "seeing-beauty spirit," in the necessary social interdependence of a rural economy, as well as in the severe demands of its natural duties. Thornton's north is the world of men's power, individualism, technological triumphs over nature, and material wealth. In the old myth of symmetry,⁴⁸ Margaret and Thornton represent two interdependent halves of human experience. However, the only social relation uniting men and women—marriage, the event which begins and ends the novel—is not one of interdependence but is founded on the principle of male domination and female silence. Gaskell darkens the vision of marriage offered by Austen at the end of *Pride and Prejudice,* where Lizzy continues her subversive assault on Darcy; instead Gaskell leaves her heroine gratefully clinging to the man who saves her from her own power by making her his wife.

Gaskell originally planned to name the novel after her heroine, the focus of her creative energies; instead, she was persuaded to emphasize the novel's regional theme. In the conflict between men and masters, Margaret acts much as Gaskell her-

self had done in *Mary Barton,* as a proper evangelist of reconciliation, defending the poor, but reminding both sides of their
moral obligations. Margaret's fate in *North and South* suggests
that Gaskell now saw the futility of subordinating issues of gender to class conflict, for even if the pious middle-class woman
marshaled arguments from scripture in defense of exploited
workers, if she preached only on behalf of those supposedly
weaker than herself, she would nevertheless be pilloried as
a fallen woman. Conversely, to be readmitted to patriarchal
propriety by assuming her duties as a wife costs Margaret her
voice. Having violated an unwritten rule of feminine propriety
by asserting her will against men's, Margaret finds the fright-
ening result to be that, in the ideological economy, she is both
criminal and executioner, dutifully punishing herself. The
crushing guilt caused Margaret by her superior intellect, ethics
and oratory—by her independence—foreshadow Gaskell's
future explorations of female psychology in *Sylvia's Lovers*
and her *Life of Charlotte Brontë.* Margaret Hale, a full-blown
preacher of social reform, helps to subvert her own authority.

Winifred Gérin has remarked that *North and South* finally
gets underway when Gaskell, having set out the contrast between her "two Englands," turns her attention to developing
the character of Margaret Hale.[49] Yet even in the early exposition of rural versus urban life one finds clear evidence that
Gaskell draws her contrast not only along social lines but according to gender lines as well, describing the growth of the
female writer's mind. The novel's first chapter, entitled "Haste
to the Wedding," opens with a scene of quintessential bourgeois femininity: a parlor, in which Margaret's cousin Edith has
drifted off to sleep as the two girls were talking about Edith's
imminent marriage, her wedding dresses, the ceremony, and
her exotic future with Captain Lennox on Corfu. As her
spoiled and childish cousin sleeps, Margaret "broods" happily,
but silently, over her own future, "filling the important post of
only daughter in Helstone parsonage" (p. 36). In this world of
white muslin, blue ribbons, and lap dogs, where women's sole,
and apparently rather boring, goal is marriage, Margaret's alternative course of action renders her a cipher, sinking into the
background of the wedding festivities. Gaskell raises the dis-

turbing possibility that the women preachers who rejected domesticity in favor of their vocation simply became irrelevant to the majority of other women.

As George Eliot's Romola would fill the void in Signor Bardo's life, left when his son betrays him by joining the Dominicans, Margaret appears to be returning to Helstone to become her father's son, replacing her brother Frederick. She is temperamentally and intellectually better suited to carry on her father's work as a preacher than was Frederick, whose personal quest for adventure led him into the navy, and whose high-minded morality got him involved in a mutiny. "If Frederick had but been a clergyman, instead of going into the navy, and being lost to us all" (*NS*, p. 47), Margaret mourns. But of course, if he had become a clergyman, his sister would remain at her aunt Shaw's house until a suitor could be found, rather than return to her father's home to take Frederick's place. Even Margaret's instinctive preference for "cottagers and labourers, and people without pretence" over "shoppy people" (*NS*, p. 50) indirectly reveals her resistance to conventional feminine behavior, since Mrs. Hale's unstated motive for meeting her bourgeois neighbors is to find a wealthy suitor for Margaret—and her own ticket to a luxurious existence.

Margaret's early experiences in the village of Helstone develop in her the "seeing-beauty spirit" Gaskell attributed to William Wordsworth in 1837, when she and her husband were at work on their first publication. But Helstone is also a sacred, hidden place, an Eden where the integrity of Margaret's identity and her authority to name are guaranteed by her father. Margaret resists the requests of her suitor, the lawyer Henry Lennox, to describe her home, guarding it against intrusion by one who might incorporate her tale into some unsympathetic category of his own experience, like the picturesque, or the country estate. "'I cannot tell you about my home,'" Margaret objects. "'I don't think it is a thing to be talked about unless you knew it'" (p. 42), she demurs, echoing Mary Barton's discomfort at the improper questions asked her at Jem's trial.

Margaret rejects Lennox's proposal of marriage, rebelling against being yoked with a man she could not love, who, by his own admission, is "'not given to romance in general—prudent, worldly'" (*NS*, p. 62) but views life as a business operation. In such a marriage, Margaret must necessarily take up her place in the patriarchy as a mere wife. Later, Margaret feels "disturbed and unhappy," "while [Lennox], not many minutes after he had met with a rejection of what ought to have been the deepest, holiest proposal of his life, could speak as if briefs, success and all its superficial consequences of a good house, clever and agreeable society, were the sole avowed objects of his desires" (p. 64). Gaskell draws Lennox far more sympathetically than Austen's Mr. Collins, attributing his callousness to the affairs of business, which cause men to ignore beauty and tranquility, and, consequently, their own deeper emotions. Yet Margaret imagines that Lennox's response manifests an essential difference between men and woman, not to be mitigated by circumstances (*NS*, p. 64). This essentialist argument and its radical consequences become the focus of the novel's romantic/political conflict.

To a far lesser degree than Margaret, Thornton seems to have resisted gender socialization. His early life in the industrial town of Milton is an extreme example of a young man channeled into the practical, material world and away from the contemplative existence encouraged by a pastoral environment like Helstone. He is a self-made man, who has struggled up from the position of sole provider at age sixteen for his impoverished mother and sister, to that of prominent captain of industry, able to support his family in luxury. Thornton's life has left him incomplete, but he does not share Lennox's superficiality. He is not insensitive to beauty or suffering, but his responses have been shaped by experiences of struggle and material want. Indeed, when Margaret and Thornton are introduced, he immediately appreciates her worth, if only in a crude fashion. He is awed by Margaret's demeanor, and although "Mr. Thornton was in habits of authority himself," she seemed to assume some kind of rule over him.

Margaret, for her part, tolerates this man of business, against whom all her prejudices rebel. She accepts Thornton's basic decency, but refuses to see anything else in his character which does not "revolt [her] from its hardness" (*NS*, p. 128). This conflict of values inspires the preacher's daughter to speak out her mind quite passionately against Mr. Thornton, attacking as she does so the northern industrialists' opportu-

nism, exploitation of workers, and pollution of the environment (*NS,* pp. 122–23). On each occasion, Thornton accepts
some of Margaret's criticisms but manages to defend himself,
provoking Margaret to intensify her charges. Margaret's attacks on the factory system will eventually extend to workers,
although her "seeing-beauty spirit" enables her to sympathize
with Thornton's workers, whom he barely knows.

The humanity of the workers overcomes Margaret's original
aversion to their coarse manners, establishing a bond of communication between them. When Margaret decides to smile at
a careworn old worker, who has complimented her appearance,

> he seemed to understand her acknowledging
> glance, and a silent recognition was established
> between them whenever the chance of the day
> brought them across each other's paths. (*NS,* p. 111)

Margaret has entered into a conversation with members of the
working class. This man, Nicholas Higgins, and his daughters,
Bessy and Mary, provide Margaret with insight into the hardships as well as the virtues of the workers' lives. The interest
she takes in this family involves her emotionally in the life of
Milton, making it "a brighter place to her" (*NS,* p. 113). As well as
Thornton might think he knows his workers—their imagined
tendencies to profligacy, or ignorance of sound economics—
Margaret enjoys an experience of their lives from which the
millowner's adversarial stance excludes him. This novelistic experience of the workers' inner lives Gaskell associates with the
female imagination; it triggers Margaret's "womanly instincts,"
compelling her to exhort Thornton to fulfill his biblical, and
universal, duties towards his workers.

Margaret achieves only slightly better success with Thornton
than Ruth had with the utterly uncomprehending Bellingham.
Margaret reacts with indignation to Thornton's assertion that
it is his right to withhold information from his workers about
the bad trade which prevents him from meeting their wage
demands, making a strike inevitable. "'A human right,'"
Margaret mutters. To Thornton's request that she repeat
her response Margaret replies, "'it related to a *feeling* [my em-
phasis] which I do not think you would share'" (*NS,* p. 164).

Margaret is right. When she proposes that a religious obligation binds him to his workers, Thornton tries to deflect Margaret from the subject of his duties onto the sectarian disagreements between them. But this is a moral imperative, Margaret reminds him, not a sectarian doctrine.

> "I do not think that I have any occasion to consider your special religious opinions in the affair. All I meant to say is, that there is no human law to prevent the employers from utterly wasting or throwing away all their money, if they choose; but that there are passages in the Bible which would rather imply—to me at least—that they neglected their duty as stewards if they did so. However, I know so little about strikes, and rate of wages, and capital, and labour, that I had better not talk to a political economist like you." (*NS*, pp. 164–65)

This could be Gaskell in her introduction to *Mary Barton,* disclaiming technical expertise while asserting the ethical validity of her position. Deaf to Margaret's sarcasm, Thornton takes this disclaimer at face value, and, rather than confronting the accusation of unfaithful stewardship, offers to instruct Margaret in the mysteries of economics. However, Thornton's tone changes when he discovers that Margaret has had firsthand experience of the manner in which these two interdependent classes behave toward one another through her conversations with factory workers. He accuses Margaret of misunderstanding his own attitude towards the workers, yet demands that she reveal the identity of the men she heard speak against their masters. Margaret will not be cowed. "I am not fond of being catechised," she responds, "I refuse to answer your question. Besides, it has nothing to do with the fact."

Margaret anticipates Thornton's inability to entertain criticism of his business practices, not only because they are in ideological disagreement, but because she is a woman. Though Thornton seems to deny it to himself, the sexual dynamic of this exchange is clear. He wants simultaneously to draw out in conversation the woman to whom he is attracted, hoping she will in turn be attracted to him, while at the same time trying to limit the power of her language (which enjoys the authority of the Bible) by trivialization, condescension, and finally threat. As Jem hears only his own fate in Esther's narrative, Thornton will turn Margaret's argument into a love story. Citing her experience of another authoritarian male, Margaret tells Thornton

> . . . that it was considered to the advantage of the masters to have ignorant workmen—not hedge-lawyers, as Captain Lennox used to call those men in his company who questioned and would know the reason for every order." (*NS*, pp. 165–66)

At the name of Captain Lennox, a potential rival, Thornton experiences "a strange kind of displeasure," as the subtext of the conversation becomes obvious. He is reduced to insulting Margaret's judgment: "'in short, Miss Hale, it is very evident that your informant found a pretty ready listener to all the slander he chose to utter against the masters'" (*NS*, p. 166). That is, Margaret must be something of a loose woman listening indiscriminately to discourses "unfit for a delicate ear." However, Margaret will not be manipulated.

Nothing happens in this exchange that would have been unfamiliar to intellectual women of the period. One way or another, their convictions could be discredited, misrepresented, or suppressed, when they weren't simply ignored, because men would not see their discourse in any but sexual terms. What Gaskell proceeds to do in this novel is to chronicle Margaret's ideological and verbal self-destruction as the character comes to discipline and censor her own transgressive behavior.

Margaret's most dramatic display of what she herself labels as "womanly instinct" comes when she risks her life protecting Thornton in defense of a principle. Trapped at the Thorntons' by a mob marching on the millowner's house to demand the expulsion of Irish laborers imported to undercut their wages, Margaret rises to the occasion. Like her preaching foremothers, Margaret has doubted her ability to face a crisis courageously, "but now, in this real great time of reasonable fear and nearness of terror she forgot herself, and felt only an intense sympathy—intense to painfulness—in the interests of the moment" (*NS*, p. 230). Overcome by the desire to protect the workers from the brutality which the approaching soldiers will undoubtedly inflict on them, she demands that Thornton go down to the crowd and urge them to disperse peacefully.

> "Mr. Thornton!" said Margaret, shaking all over with her passion, "go down this instant, if you are not a coward. Go down and face them like a man. Save those poor strangers, whom you have decoyed here. Speak to your workmen as if they were human beings. Speak to them kindly. Don't let the soldiers come in and cut down poor creatures who are driven mad. I see one there who is. If you have any courage or noble quality in you, go out and speak to them, man to man!" (*NS*, p. 232)

Here an avatar of the prophetess Deborah orders a cowardly Barak to keep the peace. Although Margaret, somewhat shocked by her own authority, attempts to retreat ("'Oh! Mr. Thornton! I do not know—I may be wrong—only—'" [*NS*, p. 232]) and, although Thornton goes out to the crowd for the wrong reason (to prove his bravery to Margaret), nevertheless, the action is right. A massacre is averted.

With the balance of power tipped in favor of the workers, Margaret's womanly instinct compels her to intervene on Thornton's behalf, literally throwing herself, her feminine sympathy and strength, between Thornton and "that angry sea of men" (*NS*, p. 233). At first her "eyes smit[e] them with flaming arrows of reproach," but when they advance threateningly, she "[holds] out her arms towards them," desiring to act as a medium of peace between men and master. Margaret warns the men of the soldiers' approach and promises them that their grievances will be addressed, but neither men nor master intend to cooperate. At the threat of violence, now against Thornton, Margaret shields him with her own body. Unlike Thornton, this mob is quite capable of overlooking Margaret's sex and has no compunction about risking her injury to attack the master. Rather than diminish Margaret's act as the foolish heroics of a woman trading on privileges afforded her sex, however, this incident validates her as a redemptress. A worker bent on violence hurls a clog at Thornton, and Margaret

pleads, "'For God's sake! do not damage your cause by this violence. You do not know what you are doing'" (*NS*, p. 235). As
she speaks Christ's words from the cross, Margaret is struck
with a rock intended for Thornton, and the sight of her "pale,
upturned face, with closed eyes, still and sad as marble," the
blood from her wound and the water of her tears, awes the mob
and causes its retreat.

Gaskell's "Pietá" places a woman in the role of victim and redeemer. Like Christ, who accepted the death befitting a common criminal, Margaret allows herself to be stoned—the
traditional punishment for an adulteress—in order to save
her people. Further, her symbolic death sparks a limited conversion for Thornton, initiating the process of his redemption. The sight of her death-like expression causes Thornton
to admit to himself his love for Margaret. From the barbarian
fascinated by a beautiful and unfamiliar object, Thornton
changes into the philistine lover who desires Margaret as his
wife. Thornton confesses his love for Margaret to his mother
who, though she is torn between perceiving her as a competitor
for her son's love and as the key to his happiness, cannot resist
declaring that Margaret's defense of Thornton before the mob
is a clear sign of her affection. Encouraged by this reductive
assessment of Margaret's motives, he decides to propose marriage to her.

In the following chapter, entitled "Mistakes," Gaskell shifts
to Margaret's point of view and makes the folly of Thornton's
judgment clear. Margaret is mortified to discover that the
crowd likewise has construed her behavior as that of a woman
in love, but that is only part of her anxiety over her actions. Her
primary concern is one she shares with women preachers: she
has exposed herself in a public (male) forum, and been "the
object of universal regard" (*NS*, p. 249); she has dared to transgress the limits of feminine decorum on behalf of principles of
duty. In an agony of self-doubt Margaret cries

> "I, who hate scenes—I, who have despised people
> for showing emotion—who have thought them
> wanting in self-control—I went down and must
> needs throw myself into the melee, like a romantic
> fool! Did I do any good? They would have gone

away without me, I dare say." But this was overleap-
ing the rational conclusion, —as in an instant her
well-poised judgment felt, No, perhaps they would
not. I did some good. But what possessed me to defend that man as if he were a helpless child! Ah!"
said she, clenching her hands together, "it is no
wonder those people thought I was in love with him,
after disgracing myself in that way. I in love—and
with him too!" Her pale cheeks suddenly became
one flame of fire; and she covered her face with her
hands. When she took them away, her palms were
wet with scalding tears. (*NS*, p. 247)

Margaret's association of "woman's work," "maidenly pride,"
and "pur[ity] before God" marks the most explicit statement in
Gaskell's fiction to this point that a woman should not only be
uncompromised by her entry into the public forum but be
sanctified by it. At the same time, that sense of vindication is
wholly undercut when, precisely imitating Ruth,[50] Margaret
covers her face and cries tears of shame. Of course, it is also
obvious and unfortunate that Margaret protests too much, implying her nascent attraction to Thornton, and establishing the
novel's romantic plot, which will reduce her liberating declaration of woman's power in the public sphere to displaced sexual
desire. Margaret subverts her own moral and political agency.

By contrast to Margaret's agony, Thornton's misinterpretation of her actions and his desire to co-opt her as his wife seem
ridiculously petty and inadequate. Margaret responds to him
with shocked indignation, and disabuses him of his mistaken
impressions, attacking the two contradictory images of woman
he presents her. First, his passionate declaration that he owes
his life to her and loves her more than "'man has [ever] loved
woman before,'" Margaret labels "'blasphemous'" (*NS*, p. 253).
And, that she returns his affections and would consent to be his
wife, Margaret finds offensive. Her defense of justice entitles
him to claim her neither as his angel nor his happy slave.

"I do feel offended; and, I think, justly. You seem to
fancy that my conduct of yesterday"—again the
deep carnation blush, but this time of eyes kindling
with indignation rather than shame—"was a per-

> sonal act between you and me; and that you may
> come and thank me for it, instead of perceiving,
> as a gentleman would—yes! a gentleman," she
> repeated . . . "that any woman, worthy of the name
> of woman, would come forward to shield, with her
> reverenced helplessness, a man in danger from the
> violence of numbers." (*NS*, p. 253)

The confusion of this scene's emotional undercurrent results from Margaret's indecision regarding the nature of her
power. Is it enough to be an evangelist of reconciliation between men and masters, or is Margaret's relationship to both
groups essentially adversarial? That to speak on behalf of the
weaker *is* to speak on behalf of women, the weakest, least-
represented, least-organized victims in her society because
they are ignorant of their status as victims? Margaret declares
woman the impartial defender of the weak. She might be the
perfect example of the ideal Victorian male citizen—free of
any party interest or selfish motivation—but, a woman not of
man's party is a threat. She will become an adversary because
cooperation with her would destroy the foundation of that
party: established gender roles.[51] In order to avoid this conclusion, Margaret convinces herself that she is incomplete without
Thornton.

The narrator justifies Margaret's harsh speech to Thornton
in the scene described above as resulting from his "cruel[ty]." If
there is any need to justify Margaret, this will hardly do.
Thornton is not acting cruelly, but blindly. Margaret's tearful
response suggests that her indignation might be mixed with an
unacknowledged desire for him. Furthermore, that "seeing-
beauty spirit" turns out to have a blind spot. "'I know you
despise me.'" says Thornton, "'allow me to say, it is because
you do not understand me.'" "'I do not care to understand,'"
replies Margaret. "'No, I see you do not. You are unfair and
unjust'" (*NS*, p. 254). This is Gaskell's reworking of Elizabeth
Bennet's rejection of Darcy, where this heroine's prejudice
follows from her pride in her sense of social justice. Only by
accepting Thornton's point of view will Margaret correct her
own vision.

The excessive quality of this lack in Margaret's "seeing-beauty spirit" manifests itself in the elaborate contortions of plot required to bring about its remedy. Margaret's brother, Frederick, who has been in exile because he has been implicated in a ship's mutiny, sneaks into England to visit their dying mother. When he is leaving Milton, accompanied by Margaret, he is involved in a scuffle at the railway station, which results in a man's death. In order to give Frederick time to escape, Margaret denies her presence at the station when the authorities question her about the incident. Thornton discovers Margaret's lie and covers for her. When Margaret realizes his role in quashing the investigation, she is mortified.

> Oh! had anyone such just cause to feel contempt for her? Mr Thornton, above all people, on whom she had looked down from her imaginary heights till now! She suddenly found herself at his feet, and was strangely distressed at her fall. She shrank from following out the premises to their conclusion, and so acknowledging to herself how much she valued his respect and good opinion. (*NS*, p. 356)

Margaret had been called on to be a witness, that all-important event wherein a woman's voice is solicited in the public sphere, and she had given false testimony.

Yet Margaret's response appears extreme and melodramatic. In a fit of guilt, she bewails her fall, both in the eyes of God and Thornton.

> If she had but dared to bravely tell the truth as regarded herself, defying them to find out what she refused to tell concerning another, how light of heart she would not have felt! Not humbled before God, as having failed in trust towards Him; not degraded and abased in Mr Thornton's sight. She caught herself up at this with a miserable tremor; here was she classing his low opinion of her alongside with the displeasure of God. How was it that he haunted her imagination so persistently? . . . She believed that she could have borne the sense of Almighty displeasure, because He knew all, and could read her penitence, and hear her cries for help in

> time to come. But Mr Thornton—why did she
> tremble, and hide her face in the pillow? What
> strong feeling had overtaken her at last? (*NS*, p. 358)

With as exaggerated a response to a lie as we find in *Ruth,* this
woman preacher falls from the "imaginary heights" and ele-
vates man to the position of God above her. Margaret's mor-
tification suggests that a woman's power cannot be manifested
as dominance rather than influence, and that Margaret herself
must be sacrificed to this belief.

From the point of her "fall," Gaskell deals with Margaret in a
most anxious fashion. Though it is clear that Margaret initi-
ated Thornton's conversion, Gaskell robs her of that honor. We
are told that the men and master want no intermediary, and
Thornton and Higgins are brought into contact, and commu-
nion, by the great reconciler: grief, in this instance, economic
in nature. Meanwhile, despite the fact that Margaret has
gained economic power over Thornton as his landlady, Gaskell
does not use this occasion to demonstrate a woman's ability to
exercise power over a man. Instead, the two characters retreat
in shame over their wounded gender images; like the master
and men early in the novel, they are joined only by the cash
nexus. During this time, Thornton seems to be undergoing a
conversion, brought about by necessity, into Gaskell's ideal
Christian man of business, while Margaret undergoes a disturbing metamorphosis into a silent angel of mercy. She visits
the poor and sick, like Libbie Marsh, or Alice Wilson, or Ruth,
but seems to have lost the power of speech—especially in the
public sphere. She is chastened and shows her willing submission to the social order at just the time when her economic
power could enhance the authority of her speech.

This problem is certainly more than the product of Gaskell's
romantic plot overshadowing her social argument, as Gérin
suggests. For the novel to end "happily"—for the marriage to
take place—Margaret must resign herself to a woman's traditional role as the incomplete half of a whole—Thornton—who
himself has become strikingly independent of women. She
must be converted from women's duties as she had redefined
them early in the novel to those acceptable to a male-
dominated society: the angel of mercy, the wife and mother.

What has so corrupted Margaret's femininity as to necessitate this conversion? It can only be the exercise of public speech, the voice she inherits from her father. Mr. Hale has encouraged her education, engages her in debate, demands of her logical rigor, and treats her as an intellectual equal. Just as he acts and speaks on matters of conscience, resigning his living, taking his family's fate in his own hands rather than subscribing hypocritically to a doctrine he does not believe, Margaret "speaks out her mind" on Thornton's religious duties as manufacturer, and takes her own life her hands to defend the weak against violence. Clearly, the next logical step would be Margaret's recognition of her own sex's need for such a champion as she, but instead, Margaret retreats, allowing her own word, her lie about Frederick, to condemn her. All her speech must be equally invalid, Margaret believes.

The lovers' union in the novel's final scene completes Margaret's submission. Margaret's offer to bail out Thornton's bankrupt mill should make her his redemptress. Instead, she appears to be buying Thornton's esteem, lost when she told the fatal lie. She makes her offer with none of the queenly self-possession which first attracted Thornton's admiration.

> She went on rapidly turning over some law papers and statements of accounts in a trembling hurried manner. "Oh! here it is! and—he drew me out a proposal—I wish he was here to explain it— showing that if you would take some money of mine, eighteen thousand and fifty-seven pounds, lying just at this moment unused in the bank . . . you could bring me much better interest, and might go on working Marlborough Mills." . . . she was most anxious to have it all looked upon in the light of a mere business arrangement, in which the principal advantage would be on her side. While she sought for this paper, her very heart-pulse was arrested by the tone in which Mr Thornton spoke. (*NS* pp. 528–29)

Margaret then collapses in silent shame, once again covering her face with her hands. So humbled, she appears to Thornton to be accepting his offer of marriage with this offer of money.

He lifts her up, removes her hands from her face, and accepts her as his wife. He now possesses Margaret's devotion, her money to maintain his social power, and, thanks to a visit he has made to Helstone, his very own seeing-beauty spirit. For her part, Margaret receives roses cut at Helstone (a symbol of her restored childhood state of dependence?), and a husband.

Having created this powerful female voice, Gaskell subverts her. This revision of *Pride and Prejudice* closes with a more disciplinary message than the original. Austen, after all, allows Elizabeth Bennet's subversive voice to survive domestication; that character retains the role of social critic while taking up the duties of a wife. *North and South* offers a grimmer view of the romance plot and its goal of domestic union. Margaret is so diminished by the novel's close that, despite her large inheritance and Thornton's bankruptcy, her social role and her power of self-representation are covered over with her fiancé's magnanimity, as she will be legally "covered" in marriage. So bleak and so frank a presentation of romance closure looks back to women preachers who tried desperately to elude domestic bonds and hints at the growing disjunction in Gaskell's writing between the preacher understood as reconciler and the preacher as trouble-making prophet. Margaret's fate points to a new direction her creator would take. The death of Charlotte Brontë, and Gaskell's experience as her biographer, radicalized her understanding of her vocation as a woman writer.

The Life of Charlotte Brontë: *The "Two Currents"*

As a writer, Gaskell had been willing to risk ridicule in order to defend her religious convictions. In return, she had once believed, the patriarchy that had claimed to share those values would protect her. But as Margaret Hale's fate demonstrates, service to that patriarchy ultimately meant submission and silence. In *North and South*, Margaret Hale, motivated by the principles her father taught her, spoke out, and was stoned by the crowd like a magdalen—or like Mary Bosanquet and other woman preachers. Her "salvation" came only through submission to a husband. As early as 1851 when she started work on *Cranford*, Gaskell had begun devising narrative strategies that would elude patriarchal censorship in order to represent a utopia where men's voices, not women's, might be silenced, and female-centered discourses reigned. There, a community of Libbie Marshes, Alice Wilsons, and Faith Bensons were the authors, critics, economists, and legislators. The death of Charlotte Brontë, Gaskell's friend, a member of her community of correspondents, would fill Gaskell with a new sense that real-life Cranfords existed in a hostile world, and that their members must come to one another's defense.

Initially naive as to conclusions she would be forced to draw with respect to Charlotte's Brontë's fate, but fearing only the wrath of Patrick Brontë, Gaskell almost immediately responded to her friend's death by proposing to write her biography. For Gaskell, Charlotte Brontë would become a symbol of the martyred woman of letters. By 1855, the year of Charlotte Brontë's death, Gaskell had learned on her own the subtle ways gender roles could systematically confine, manipulate, and often even terrorize women. One need not be a social outcast like Ruth or Ester, or a downtrodden spinster like Libbie Marsh, to be persecuted *qua* woman. As a dutiful middle-class woman— even one famous for her literary talents—one was equally vulnerable to the institutionalized oppression of women. Marriage crowned Margaret Hale's ambiguous fate in *North and South,* and marriage, too, led to Brontë's tragic death. The connection surely did not escape Gaskell. She had visited Brontë after her engagement to Nichols, and her joy was dampened by Brontë's clear and persistent recognition of Nichols as her inferior. In a matter of months, Brontë, whose health had been sacrificed to her duties as daughter to a demanding father and sister to a drunkard, would die as Nichols's wife, of complications resulting from her pregnancy.[52]

In addition to inspiring a critique of woman's "natural duties," Brontë articulated for Gaskell the fear she had addressed in *North and South*: that the evangelistic goals of the social-problem novel might no longer serve to liberate women writers but to discipline them. Her research into the Brontës' correspondence and Charlotte's journals revealed a bitter analysis of the critical standards that pilloried female authors who did not preach reconciliation, whose texts were not male-centered. This experience radicalized Gaskell on women's issues as Buckner and Layhe had convinced her of the plight of the working class. Now, however, Gaskell was not to veil her convictions in a fiction; instead, in the tradition of the biographers of female preachers defending their sisters from patriarchal revisions of their contributions and trials, she would be speaking in her own voice as the interpreter of a real life.

Discussing Charlotte Brontë's new life as woman of letters following the success of *Jane Eyre,* Gaskell wrote:

> Henceforward Charlotte Brontë's existence becomes divided into two parallel currents—her life as Currer Bell, the author; her life as Charlotte Brontë, the woman. There were separate duties belonging to each character—not opposing each other; not impossible, but difficult to be reconciled. . . [By contrast with a man's duties,] no other can take up the quiet, regular duties of the daughter, the wife, or the mother, as well as she whom God has appointed to till that particular place: a woman's principal work in life is hardly left to her own choice; nor can she drop the domestic charges devolving on her as an individual, for the exercise of the most splendid talents that were ever bestowed. And yet she must not shrink from the extra responsibility implied by the very fact of her possessing such talents. She must not hide her gift in a napkin; it was meant for use and service of others. In an humble and faithful spirit must she labour to do what is not impossible or God would not have set her to do it. (*CB,* p. 242)

Following her preaching predecessors, Gaskell argues that literary talent is a divine gift which the recipient is obliged to exercise. Exercising that gift does not, however, exonerate a woman from her "natural duties," her "principal work in life." Gaskell describes not only Brontë's, but also her own, balancing act between domestic obligations and literary production, made less onerous for Gaskell than Brontë by her domestic help and four daughters. This might constitute the last, half-hearted assertion of Gaskell's long-held beliefs about the nature of woman's life and the source of her obligations. Almost a century earlier, Bosanquet and the other women preachers had rejected this view of women's duties.[53] Women could not maintain both "currents" for the same reason that man could not serve God and mammom: their demands were often in conflict. Through her journal and letters, Brontë joins her voice to those of the preachers and rises up to condemn woman's enslavement to "natural duties."

Gaskell uses Brontë's voice as she once had used scripture to sanction women's indignation and despair. Gaskell quotes a letter Brontë wrote to her on August 27, 1850, in which she discusses one of the myriad of "Woman's Mission" articles, this one appearing in the *Westminster Review.* Finding "a great deal" in the article which was "just and sensible," Brontë delivers these reflections on the condition of women:

> Men begin to regard the position of women in another light than they used to do; and a few men, whose sympathies are fine and whose sense of justice is strong, think and speak of it with a candour that commands my admiration. They say, however—and, to an extent, truly—that amelioration of our condition depends on ourselves. Certainly there are evils which our own efforts will best reach; but as certainly there are evils—deep rooted in the foundation of the social system—which no efforts of ours can touch; of which we cannot complain; of which it is advisable not too often to think. (*CB,* p. 315)

These untouchables were, of course, largely women's "natural duties," the yoke fastened on women by a patriarchal society. Gaskell will not allow herself to draw this conclusion explicitly, but allows it to emerge from her treatment of the events of Brontë's life.

For example, Brontë's literary talents are shown to have been consistently sacrificed to the unreasonable and futile demands on her as a relative creature: a daughter, a sister, a wife. The economic hardships and isolation she endured for most of her young life resulted directly from Branwell's profligacy. Brontë wrote to a friend on July 6, 1835, that "Emily is going to school, Branwell is going to London, and I am going to be a governess."

> I am sad—very sad—at the thoughts of leaving
> home; but duty—necessity—these are stern mis-
> tresses, who will not be disobeyed. Did I not once say
> you ought to be thankful for your independence?
> (*CB*, p. 99)

Of course "being a governess" meant that Brontë was giving up
the opportunity of going anywhere in pursuit of her own
desires. Gaskell comments bitterly that "these are not the first
sisters who have laid their lives as a sacrifice before their
brother's wish. Would to God they might be the last who met
with such a miserable return!" (*CB*, p. 99). By 1841 the sacrifice
was becoming unbearable. Describing a gift and letter received
from friends traveling in Brussels, Brontë wrote to Ellen
Nussey,

> I hardly know what swelled to my throat as I read
> her letter: such a vehement impatience of restraint
> and steady work; such as strong wish for wings—
> wings such as wealth can furnish; such an urgent
> thirst to see, to know, to learn; something internal
> seemed to expand bodily for a minute. I was tan-
> talized by the consciousness of faculties unexer-
> cised,—then all collapsed, and I despaired. My
> dear, I would hardly make that confession to any
> one but yourself; and to you, rather in a letter than
> *viva voce*. These rebellious and absurd emotions
> were only momentary; I quelled them in five min-
> utes. I hope they will not revive, for they were
> acutely painful. (*CB*, p. 147)

Brontë's obsessive fear of expressing her anguish publicly was
not unjustified. Later, when she came to incorporate some of
the emotional trauma of her life—including the debacle with
M. Heger—into her fiction, reviewers attacked Currer Bell,
supposing that name masked a woman, as de-sexed and "unwomanly." As a *Gentleman's Magazine* writer asked in an 1853
essay on "The Lady Novelists of Great Britain," "Can the au-
thoress [of *Jane Eyre, Shirley,* and *Villette*"] live among wives and
mothers?"[54] Conversely, in this same essay, the writer praises
Ruth's author for promoting understanding.

Mutual comprehensions—mutual understanding of each other, how inestimable a privilege it is! This is what women can especially forward; and those *other ministers* [my emphasis] of the people—our physicians, watching over their bodily health—our clergymen, labouring after their spirituals—how much may they do to promote this great object of mutual good understanding! Scarcely less important is the novelist's part. Of all men, the novelist should not divide, but unite.[55]

Brontë saw that the woman preacher's role and voice could win the approval of such a reader as this. It gained women access to a public forum, but it also limited them as artists—particularly as female artists. As preachers, women's first obligation was to an ideology created by men, even if they employed that discourse in the defense of certain female victims of men's power. However, it blinded them to the ways in which that ideology defined their subject matter and shaped their perception of it. The preaching vocabulary could deal with the fallen woman, the prostitute, the virgin, the widow. But what could it say about woman's sexual desire, her artistic creativity (apart from its service to others), her sense of wholeness and self-reliance (was the will of God too close to the will of man?), or her anger?

Brontë did not disparage women writers of social-problem fiction, but she wishes to remain free to explore other topics. Discussing *Villette* (significantly), Brontë made this self-effacing remark to a correspondent:

You will see that *Villette* touches on no matter of public interest. I cannot write books handling the topics of the day; it is of no use trying. Nor can I write a book for its moral. Nor can I take up a philanthropic scheme, though I honour philanthropy; and voluntarily and sincerely veil my face before such a mighty subject as that handled in Mrs. Beecher Stowe's work, *Uncle Tom's Cabin*. To manage these great matters rightly, they must be long and practically studied—their bearings known intimately, and their evil felt genuinely; they must not

be taken up as a business matter, and a trading speculation. (*CB,* p. 364)

One senses the extreme self-control that must have gone into
this analysis of social-problem fiction by women as a profitable
commodity. Women preachers, as Brontë sees it, have been
swallowed up by the marketplace and lost much of their power
to challenge the social relations it dictated. Becoming expert in
the matters of which social problem novels are made required
more than hard work for novelists like Elizabeth Gaskell and
Harriet Martineau. It demanded that they subordinate their
literary goals to a discourse whose values and hierarchies had
already been determined by men. When Gaskell moved to include fallen women in their discussion of reform, she could do
it only by means of appealing to preexisting formulations.
That is, in order for men to behave consistently with the
Christian social gospel—as articulated by men—to avoid phar-
isaism, they must treat fallen woman charitably. By placing the
fallen woman squarely within the matrix of Christian duties,
Gaskell, Brontë would grant, accomplished a significant goal.
"But," as Brontë asked, "why must [Ruth] die?" Why must she
be denied survival *qua* woman, independent of her role as an
object of Christian charity? Because the conceptual framework
of the social-problem novel (Christian duty) and its voice (the
woman preacher's) provides neither structure nor vocabulary
for doing anything else.

Hagiography, conversion narratives, utopian closures, exhortation, prophecy—the strategies from which Gaskell's fictions derive their strength—can explain women's roles in a
male culture, but they cannot articulate a thorough rejection of
that exploitive world or imagine Ruth's, Mary Barton's and
Margaret Hale's existence apart from it. Gaskell herself seems
to have recognized these limitations in *North and South,* in the
conflict between Margaret's public role and her personal
desires. The confused presentation of both manifests the author's struggle with the desire to develop her female characters
apart from their potential contribution to man's world. In vigorously defending Charlotte Brontë against the range of *ad
feminam* attacks made on her as a woman writer,[56] Gaskell may
have come to a new understanding of her own literary goals
and position as a writer.

The Life of Charlotte Brontë (1857) inflamed more hostility than had *Ruth*. As Brontë herself had seemed to prophesy, it was easier to ignore a social-problem novel about issues that did not directly touch most readers' lives than to feel untouched by a biography that strongly reflected on the middle-class culture of which Brontë was a part. Gaskell disappointed a variety of readers, namely, those who awaited an uncritical Brontë hagiography, those whose sense of decorum was offended by Gaskell's prying into "private" matters, those who found Gaskell's treatment of the men in Brontë's life unjustifiably harsh. A common complaint connected such responses: Gaskell had lifted the veil from a life in which women were to "suffer and be still." Here was documented evidence of the polite, socially acceptable oppression of a woman and its lethal consequences. What is not said in these attacks is as significant as what is. These reviewers refuse to deal with Gaskell's most important revelation—the life of a woman author—because the life of Currer Bell, in its independence and self-containment, threatened their social and psychological fictions with "strong truths." Like Bellingham standing before Ruth's corpse, these reviewers could not interpret the icon that was the life of Charlotte Brontë.

Several writers attempting to describe the shape of Gaskell's career cite the *Life of Charlotte Brontë* as a turning point after which her newly awakened feminist consciousness released her from the obligation to write social-problem novels—to be a woman preacher—and write art for art's sake.[57] While accepting the importance of these categories, I wish to blur the distinction a bit. Gaskell's social-problem narratives prior to the *Life* insist that the wrongs of women be placed squarely on the agenda of reforms as a necessary part of any efforts to address injustices. Long the target of women preachers, the cult of domesticity by which women's exploitation might be sanctified is exposed as a subterfuge. Furthermore, it could appropriate women's work, both material and intellectual, to further reform on behalf of other oppressed groups while denying to women the right to prophesy against their own subservience. As Hannah More and Charlotte Elizabeth Tonna feared, Gaskell recognized that men set themselves up as a higher power than God in order to discipline women. While these earlier writers had generally sought reconciliation with their male critics through the medium of scripture, Gaskell saw that her preaching might simply be co-opted in the name of God. Gaskell responded by rejecting the complicitous narratives that earned her praise as an "evangelist of reconciliation." Like her predecessors, she innovated discursive strategies that would maintain the integrity of women's prophecies. In Gaskell's case, they would take her beyond the limits of women's preaching.

Apocalyptic Prophecy: "Speaking Like a Woman"

When, in her last three novels, *My Lady Ludlow* (1858), *Sylvia's Lovers* (1864), and *Wives and Daughters* (1865), Gaskell turned from social-problem writing, she did not turn her back on social issues. Rather, as I have argued elsewhere, these later fictions experiment with narrative techniques that fracture or deny the recuperative closures by which challenges to patriarchal authority could be domesticated.[58] For example, the eccentric structure of *My Lady Ludlow,* comprising stories with stories with no center, no privileged narrative; or the radical destabilization of romance closure in *Sylvia's Lovers,* offer modes of rewriting cultural history which emphasize discontinuity and heterogeneity, particularly of women's experiences in a society constructed according to male desires.

Significantly, these two novels treat an apocalyptic period in British history: the French Revolution through the Napoleonic Wars. The mission of evangelical prophets to call on their society to repent and be saved had been inspired by biblical interpretations of human history. As empowering as we have seen those evangelical narratives to have been, they were finally circumscribed by the resolution of apocalypse, symbolized by the marriage of Christ and the church at the end of history. Gaskell reads traditional biblical history as romance that demands women's reconciliation to their subordination as a prerequisite for human salvation. This narrative pattern rationalized the suppression of religious dissent (including Unitarians), political protests, feminist aggitation, and women's preaching during the period treated in *My Lady Ludlow* and *Sylvia's Lovers.* To be a prophet in this tradition, as women preachers had been, meant consenting to this patriarchal representation of human events. What Gaskell aims for instead is a narrative to inspire feminist prophecy, a history without reconciliation, an apocalypse without marriage.

With a literary ingenuity that has disturbed generations of critics, Gaskell insists on the incompatibility of prophesying against the wrongs of women with the conciliatory politics of social sermonizing, including male-centered conventions of historical writing, biography, and of social-problem fiction. The heroine of *Sylvia's Lovers* is a women whose life, like Libbie Marsh's at the beginning of Gaskell's career, is marked by hardship. Her father is executed for his role in a press-gang riot, her lover is pressed into the navy to fight against Napoleon, his rival, so that Sylvia will marry him, leads her to believe that the lover is dead. Miserable in her marriage, Sylvia discovers her husband's deceit, and he absconds in shame. In this treatment of the wrongs of woman, blame is placed squarely on men and their institutions—government, the military, marriage. Moreover, Sylvia, unlike Gaskell's earlier heroines, refuses to be reconciled to her fate. When another character blames Sylvia for her own misfortune, Sylvia angrily rejects her culpability and denies anyone else the right to judge her. Her resistance is dismissed as childish petulance; she is scolded for "speaking like a silly child." "No," Sylvia declares, "I'm speaking like a woman; like a woman as finds out she's been cheated by men as she trusted, and as has no help for it. I'm noane going to say any more about it. It's me as has been wronged, and as has to bear it" (*SL*, pp. 443–44).

To speak like a woman no longer means to preach reconciliation but, like Job, to protest one's innocence and decry the injustice of one's suffering. This model of oppositional discourse better suits the representation of women's history than the amelioristic romance narrative of Christian providential history. Sylvia's "contemporaries" of the 1790s–1810s, including both women preachers and feminists, contributed to social reforms which could be narrated progressively: the increase in working-class literacy, the proliferation of philanthropic organizations, the growth of antislavery sentiment, the slow movement towards democratic government marked by the first Reform Bill. But from Gaskell's point of view in 1864, women had "been cheated by men as [they] trusted." Women's preaching had not brought about patriarchal repentance, but only new forms of repression which must be opposed in their turn. Indeed, any history that represented women's experience as part of some providential progress had to maintain that women's silencing, repression, exploitation in the workplace, or domestic confinement served some higher goal.

The alternative was to prophesy apocalypse without resolution or reconciliation. Gaskell's allusions to apocalyptic biblical texts in the final chapters of *Sylvia's Lovers* rupture the coherent, continuous progress of patriarchal history through repentance to salvation. In these chapters, Sylvia's broken and repentant husband returns, but the couple is reconciled only after he is too weakened by injuries and starvation to survive. "With God all things are possible," Sylvia recalls, whereupon the narrator solemnly entones, "But oft times He does his work with awful instruments. There is a peacemaker whose name is Death" (*SL,* p. 489). In contrast to the providential romance that ends with marriage, Gaskell's narrative posits an author of history—a God—who imagines an alternative ending for *Sylvia.* This God, like Sylvia a few chapters earlier, seems to think she would get along much better without her husband and uses his "awful instrument" to remove him from her life.

Looking down at the corpse of Sylvia's husband, his pious cousin offers a benediction from the book of Revelation: "The former things are passed away—and he is gone where there is no more sorrow, and no more pain" (*SL,* p. 501), and, she might have added, as Mary Wollstonecraft paraphrased an apocalyptic verse of Matthew, where there is no more marrying or giving in marriage. Sylvia's denunciation of patriarchal structures, her refusal to accept betrayal patiently and meekly, her rejection of the sanctity of her wifely duty, signal Gaskell's break with the politics of reconciliation, the evangelical mission, and the providential narrative on which that mission depends. Instead, women's prophecy could only be an outbreak of female desire and anger, an apocalypse without marriage.

In this feminist revision of Christian doctrine, Gaskell implies the history of her own experience as a woman preacher. Her novel affords no evidence that Sylvia's "preachment" brings about anyone's repentance. The narrative resumes, apparently unimpeded after Sylvia's speech, suggesting Gaskell's awareness that at this historical moment there is yet no real base from which to attack patriarchy. As Sylvia concludes, "and now I've said my last word," Gaskell, too, renounces continued complicity in the patriarchal discourses of repentance and confession by which women are disciplined.

Commenting on Frederic Rowton's *Female Poets of Great Britain,* published in 1848, the year of Gaskell's first novel, *Mary Barton,* Nancy Armstrong concludes that "if nature decrees women to write 'not as rivals' but as 'partners' of men, it follows that women's writing will complement that of men and never be able to engage male writing in a critical manner."[59] For a woman writer of the nineteenth century who genuinely swerved from the preaching tradition, we would have to turn to Gaskell's subject, Charlotte Brontë. In the *Life,* Gaskell quotes Brontë's letter to George Henry Lewes, responding to his review of her social-problem novel *Shirley.* Brontë complains, not about Lewes's criticisms of the novel, but about his consideration of her as a woman writer rather than as a writer.

> I will tell you why I was so hurt by that review in the "Edinburgh"; not because its criticism was keen or its blame sometimes severe; not because its praise was stinted (for, indeed, I think you give me quite as much praise as I deserve), but because after I had said earnestly that I wished critics would judge me as an *author,* not as a woman, you so roughly—I even thought so cruelly—handled the question of my sex. I dare say you meant no harm, and perhaps you will not now be able to understand why I was so grieved at what you will probably deem such a trifle; but grieved I was, and indignant too.[60]

Why did Brontë's first, and only, social-problem novel inspire Lewes to treat the subject of the author's sex? By 1850 the tradition of the woman preacher as the writer of the social narrative had been thoroughly integrated into Victorian culture. Women were expected to place their literary talents in the service of social reform, and deliver a predictable, ameliorist message. Brontë already saw what Gaskell later learned: that so

Nine

The Extraordinary Prophet: George Eliot

It is tempting to imagine the public career of a Mary Ann Evans born, not in 1819, but in the 1760s, the contemporary of her aunt, the Methodist preacher Elizabeth Evans. Like the historical Mary Ann, she would have grown up among strong female mentors who combined religious commitment with intellectual rigor. As Mary Ann actually did, she would devour evangelical biographies and tracts, share with William Law a nostalgia for a bygone age of female sainthood, and begin to fulfill her own sense of calling by leading prayer groups. So too would she resist "worldly pleasures"—and early marriage—on the grounds that they interfered with more lofty pursuits. Her letters, like the historical Mary Ann's, would be filled with biblical allusions and commentary on pious literature. But when her father died, would she have defied her beloved brother Isaac's objections to what he regarded as fanaticism in order to answer her extraordinary call to a preaching career? And when the Wesleyan Methodists forbade women's preaching, would she join her aunt in founding the Arminian congregation at Wirksworth, extending the radical possibilities of women's preaching, or would she retire from public view?

The point of such an exercise, in addition to noting the striking parallels between George Eliot's beginnings and those of the preachers treated in the first section of this study, is to suggest the ways in which this imaginary Mary Ann both inspired and haunted the author George Eliot. George Eliot's youthful evangelicalism, critics have noted, persisted in exerting an influence on the author long after she had rejected its dogmas.

U. C Knoepflmacher, and more recently Mary Carpenter, have demonstrated that evangelical doctrines of providence and teleological time schemes inform the structure of George Eliot's narratives, while Valentine Cunningham has identified the significant dissenting themes of the novels.[1] Likewise, her feminist biographer, Jennifer Uglow, has connected George Eliot's evangelicalism with her opinions on the "Woman Question," noting that evangelicalism "provided a model for expressing the spiritual power of women."[2] George Eliot's understanding of authorship inextricably links the "Woman Question" and religious beliefs. Long after she rejects evangelical theology, Eliot continues to assert that the evangelical call was of peculiar value to women. Likewise, she retains the evangelical configuration of genius through the various stages of her intellectual history. The mature novelist and the woman, it would appear, continued to draw on the evangelicalism that earlier commanded her devotion.

George Eliot stands out on the Victorian literary landscape, like a woman field preacher, as an extraordinary figure. Yet despite her learning, literary talent, and professional ambition, which undeniably distinguish her from the common man and woman, our perception is in part the result of both Eliot's cultivation of an "extraordinary call," familiar to women preachers, and the persistence of the patriarchal values served by such a formulation of female genius. From her early essays, most notably "Silly Novels by Lady Novelists," to her lament in *Middlemarch* over the decline in female heroism (which so provoked Florence Nightingale), "she constantly separates the extraordinary woman from the mass," as Jennifer Uglow puts it.[3] As we have seen, Wesley conceived of the extraordinary call as a means of sanctioning a few highly successful women preachers without appearing to encourage the practice among women generally. In turn, women invoking the call in their own defense might understand it as merely a strategic move, a sop to their enemies rather than a reflection on women as a whole. Nevertheless, hierarchy and patriarchal collusion are inherent in the extraordinary call, and George Eliot's stance towards her female contemporaries shows evidence of both.

The extraordinary call enabled Eliot to eschew the socialization that would have paved the way to an early marriage and motherhood, justifying instead her development of the intellectual powers that led to a literary career. At the same time, as with women preachers, acceptance of this extraordinary status won her patriarchal approval and recognition because "her case did not make it necessary [for men] to rethink the situation of all women."[4] Gillian Beer argues that George Eliot's "sequestration made her assimilable back into society as it stood, not bringing about general change but voicing vatic insights which enforce no action."[5] Indeed, whereas Gaskell eventually comes to see the extraordinary call as being at odds both with feminism and with her revisionist Christian theology, and identifies with the figure of the fallen woman, George Eliot, known by her society as a literal fallen woman by the time she comes to write fiction, enhances that sense of visionary superiority in her Feuerbachian narrators, often at the expense of her female characters.

In discussing George Eliot's status as the preeminent intellectual woman of the Victorian period, Deirdre David argues that the whole of her work is marked by the conflict between female intelligence and male authority.[6] This formulation likewise describes the conflict at the heart of the female evangelical mission. That George Eliot's fiction would so often achieve coherence "outside history, outside time," as David puts it, further identifies her with the traditions of women's preaching. She shares with Hannah More, Charlotte Elizabeth Tonna, and Elizabeth Gaskell the millennial or apocalyptic desire for a new heaven and earth where, in Eliot's case, "woman possesses universal, atemporal, and inherent characteristics making her immune from the stifling, subjugating restraints of male culture and society."[7] However, the world beyond man's wisdom, a place so prominent in women's preaching, Eliot transforms along the lines of Comtean and Feuerbachian metahistorical theories.[8] Faced, as Gaskell was, with the increasingly untenable conflict between female intellect and male authority, or, to put it another way, between the spirit that called women to prophesy and the temporal authorities who sought to regulate that inspiration, George Eliot constructs a paradoxical resolution: a prophetic narrator speaking on behalf of transcendent history, who preaches silent, passive obedience to its laws. The extraordinary prophet, then, calls women in general to await the apocalypse while accepting the status quo as an ideal.

"Silly Novels by Lady Novelists" (1856),[9] the starting point for so many discussions of George Eliot's fiction, may seem an unlikely source for evidence of her concern with women's preaching, yet it is at once a denunciation of false prophets and an annunciation of her own coming as a prophetic novelist. Published less than two weeks before Eliot embarked on her own novelistic career, the essay anatomizes the forms of "fatuity" to which the female imagination is heir. Adopting the voice of a male critic, Eliot takes aim at silver-fork novels ("mind and millinery"), historical novels, and "oracular" novels by women. Novels of the first sort are contrived and snobbish; the second, "ponderous" and "leaden." The third sort—the "oracular novels"—she dismisses most contemptuously, precisely because of their execrable abuse of the very preaching rhetoric that she employs in her own fiction.

By the term "oracular" George Eliot comprehends two objectionable traits: (1) works that are ignorantly and narrowly sectarian and reductive, and (2) works that trumpet their faults by an excessive use of heightened rhetoric. Such novels "set . . . before you a complete theory of life and manual of divinity, in a love story" in which the characters run the gamut from Papists to "ultra-Protestant," settling at last into "that particular view of Christianity which either condenses itself into a sentence in small caps, or explodes into a cluster of stars on the three hundred and thirtieth page."[10] "The most pitiable of all silly novels by lady novelists are," she continues,

> what we may call the *oracular* species—novels intended to expound the writer's religious, philosophical, or moral theories. There seems to be a notion abroad among women, rather akin to the superstition that the speech and actions of idiots are inspired, and that the human being most entirely exhausted of common sense is the fittest vehicle of revelation.[11]

It cannot be denied that the oracular novelists employed clumsy means (italics, capitalization, etc.) to represent the preacher's spoken voice; it is true, too, that their novels are fraught with problems (the speakers' frequent near-hysteria among them). Nevertheless, these novelists had enlisted a voice whose authority to rebuke and exhort a mixed audience George Eliot appreciated.

The spleen she pours on her contemporaries' oracular tendencies raises suspicion; safely masked as a male essayist, perhaps the lady doth protest too much. The fate of oracular speakers in her fiction suggests that George Eliot at once craved and feared the intensified power that was released when the restraints of decorum were thrown over, and its radical political implications. That way madness lay for characters, and novelists as well. Yet, surveying fiction by her female contemporaries, she sensed that her own talents, particularly for historical prophecy, the exposition of religious belief and the psychology of faith, were far superior to theirs, hence her particular scorn for "oracular novels."

Significantly, in "Silly Novels" George Eliot does not name her serious competitors were she to enter the field of fiction writing, authors such as Elizabeth Gaskell. Although Gaskell did not preach religious dogma, Eliot's criticisms of the abuses of "oracularism" might easily have been applied to many episodes in her social-problem fiction. Several years later, when Eliot responded to Gaskell's praise of *Scenes of Clerical Life* and *Adam Bede,* she cautiously expressed her own "affinity with the feeling which had inspired 'Cranford' and the *earlier chapters* [my emphasis] of 'Mary Barton.'"[12] Neither of these can be considered "oracular," and one must wonder if Eliot specified *Mary Barton*'s "earlier chapters" because she might have felt that the rest of the novel quite often could be regarded as such. In any case, a complex strategy of denial and affiliation seems to have been in operation enabling Eliot to appropriate what she appeared to condemn.

George Eliot's argument in "Silly Novels" echoes her most notable attack on an evangelical preacher: the 1855 *Westminster Review* essay, "Evangelical Teaching: Dr. Cumming." There she objects that the popular Dr. John Cumming's ignorance and arrogance, which would be damned in any other writer, are tolerated in an evangelical preacher, just as she would claim in "Silly Novels" that women writers' fatuity and triviality are forgiven out of deference to their sex. Often, the essay on Cumming's abuses reads more like a true believer's denunciation of a false prophet than as a disinterested critique:

> But of really spiritual joys and sorrows, of the life and death of Christ as a manifestation of love that constrains the soul, of sympathy with that yearning over the lost and erring which made Jesus weep over Jerusalem, and prompted the sublime prayer, "Father, forgive them," of the gentler fruits of the Spirit, and the peace of God which passeth understanding— of all this, we find little trace in Dr. Cumming's discourses.[13]

Eliot's ire against Cummings suggests an unstated conviction that she could do better—that she is the true prophet—as indeed she demonstrates. Her first works of fiction, in an important sense the sequels to "Silly Novels," would prove that Eliot was not only the better preacher, but the better *female* preacher.

Years earlier, as an ardent evangelical, Mary Ann Evans had hinted as much to Maria Lewis. "Are you fond of the study of unfulfilled prophecy?" she asked.

> The vagaries of the Irvingites and the blasphemies of Joanna Southcote [sic] together with the fanciful interpretations of more respectable names have been regarded as beacons, and have caused many persons to hold all diving into the future plans of Providence as the boldest presumption, but I do think that a sober and prayerful consideration of the mighty revolutions ere long to take place in our world by God's blessing serve to make us less grovelling, more devoted and energetic in the service of God. *Of course I mean only such study as pigmies like my self in intellect and acquirement are able to prosecute; the perusal and comparison of Scripture and the works of pious and judicious men on the subject.* (My emphasis).[14]

The "Evangelical Teaching" and "Silly Novels" essays adhere to the rhetorical pattern established in this letter. By condemning the abuses of false prophets, Eliot, who in 1838 was planning her own history of prophecy—the "Ecclesiastical Chart"—

makes room for herself as the humble, but true, interpreter of God's will in current political events.[15] With *Scenes of Clerical Life,* Eliot could step into the triune role she had been creating for herself: prophet, preacher, and philosophical novelist.

George Eliot had already braved the "de-sexing" role of woman writer before she turned to fiction. She had achieved considerable acclaim as a translator in the male-dominated disciplines of philosophy and theology. Still, even though translation afforded women considerable opportunity to treat subject matter normally reserved for men, the dominant voice of the primary text demanded subservience and prevented them from creating their own authoritative voices.[16] Despite her consciousness of the "audacious additions" she had made to Strauss's *Das Leben Jesu,* Eliot as translator, like the female scholar she would create in *Romola,* might be reduced to no more than the means of "textual transmission from one generation [or nation] of men to another."[17] In this respect, little had changed from the days in which Anne Dutton had ghosted George Whitefield's correspondence. Even for the essays which Marian Evans wrote for the *Westminster Review* she had to resort to an anonymous yet distinctly masculine voice. On the one hand, Eliot clearly prided herself on her successful male ventriloquism, yet, on the other, she frequently betrayed a longing for the female preacher's moral authority and rhetorical power *as a woman.*[18] She urged friends not to reveal the authorship of the anonymously published "Dr. Cummings" essay, knowing that such criticism from a woman's pen would be dismissed. In plans for an essay on "Woman in Germany," Eliot wrote that she hoped to show that in "the earliest historic twilight . . . its women were prophetesses."[19] That she never wrote this essay locating female prophecy at the origin of culture,[20] suggests Eliot's abivalence towards the women she identified as her precursors.

George Eliot well knew the enabling potential of the evangelical idiom for women, and as a translator and essayist must have longed for the powerful preaching rhetoric that had appeared over her own signature when she had been a pious young scholar corresponding with her female mentors. These evangelical women were far from "silly." Maria Lewis, the principal governess of Mrs. Wallington's school where Mary Ann

was a student from 1828 to 1832; the Franklin sisters, Mary
and Rebecca, who ran the finest school in Coventry where
Mary Ann was their star pupil; and of course the well-known
Methodist preacher, Elizabeth Evans,[21] Mary Ann's aunt, each
revealed to this eager and bright young woman a worldview in
which women's discursive power was represented as divinely
sanctioned. From the often awkward and withdrawn Mary
Ann Evans, they drew intense responses: her close friendships
with Lewis and the Franklins survived her rejection of dog-
matic evangelical Protestantism, and as an adult she would recall that her aunt was among the very few people to whom she
had ever spoken intimately.

In her correspondence with these mentors, Mary Ann Evans
exercised her literary talents, perfecting in this private medium one of the few modes of public rhetoric made available to
women: preaching. She infused her own speech with Bible language, preferring it to the language of her favorite poetry. In
1840, in a letter to Maria Lewis, she quoted some of her "very
pet lines" from Felicia Hemans's "A Spirit's Return," following
the lines with this comment:

> But these lines beautiful as they are, have not the
> living power of the promise "Thine eyes shall see
> the king in his beauty, they shall behold the land that
> is very far off" [Isa. 33:17]. In proportion as the
> things present and tangible are the fruit of men's ac-
> tions they are pronounced wise in their generation
> by the children of this world [cf. Luke 16:8]; in pro-
> portion as the things impalpable to sense, but pos-
> sessing substance to the perception of faith are at
> once the basis of our life and its sustenance, we shall
> take our rank among those wise ones who shall
> shine as the sun [Matt. 17:2].[22]

Indeed this facility in the evangelical idiom caused Mary Ann
some discomfort, lest her rhetorical powers outstrip her spiritual growth. Confessing to Elizabeth Evans a troubling desire
for esteem and recognition, she revealed a hypocritical gap between her words and thoughts. "I make the most humiliating
and appalling confessions," she wrote, "with little or no corresponding feeling."[23] As a result, she did "not attach much

value to a disclosure of religious feelings," suspecting that they issued from a corrupt pride in one's rhetorical powers.

Even in acknowledging these misgivings, Mary Ann was echoing the women whose preaching style she had already mastered. Among the many evangelical biographies she was reading during this period was Henry Moore's *Life of Mrs. Fletcher* (1818),[24] in which she would have encountered that famous woman preacher's anxieties that her gift came from the devil, rather than from God. She also expressed doubts about exposing herself to public ridicule and finding the voice which would best move an audience,[25] concerns which doubtless continued to resonate in Eliot's life as she too experienced the trials of female authorship and public life. Indeed, in the tradition of a community of women of the word, she encouraged her aunt Elizabeth in her ministry. With words reminiscent of Sarah Crosby's she wrote in 1839,

> I am truly glad to hear that you are less embarrassed with respect to your congregation etc., than when we saw you; I should think that if you have evidence of a blessing on your present labours, you must be in your proper sphere, but the anointing of which you partake will teach you in this as in other things.[26]

These women, several of whom provided models for characters in George Eliot's fiction, served the crucial function of authorizing her voice as a woman's. As Jenifer Uglow points out, her female friends, though they were sometimes intimidated by her superior learning, afforded George Eliot very rare, though ultimately inadequate, opportunities for intellectual exchange before she moved to London.[27] But of even greater significance for the particular course George Eliot's literary career would take is the connection between religious belief and public action—particularly public speech—that evangelicalism insisted on for both sexes. Maria Lewis vigorously supported the charismatic and controversial preacher John Jones, whose lectures in Nuneaton provoked riots in 1828, recalled by Eliot in "Janet's Repentance." The Franklins were the daughters of a Baptist minister on whom Eliot would model her politically conscious preacher Rufus Lyon in *Felix Holt*.[28]

An episode from her gallows ministry that Elizabeth Evans had recounted to her niece Mary Ann, which would form the outline of Hetty Sorrel's story in *Adam Bede*, underscores George Eliot's appreciation of the political significance the evangelical idiom held for a woman, allowing her to disclose her oppression and exploitation in the guise of a confession.

Women preachers had struggled to a position of authority in their culture, a position to which George Eliot would aspire, and one which, with the help of their language, she would eventually achieve. Her rejection of evangelical dogmatism was at odds with her nostalgia for the faith of her childhood, but also with her desire for the power invested in its language.[29] Eliot would herself become the most accomplished creator of the woman preacher's voice in fiction, but she would do so self-consciously, keeping her preachers—and her precursors—at arm's length.

Scenes of Clerical Life: *Answering the Extraordinary Call*

George Eliot's career in fiction began on January 1, 1857, with the publication of "Amos Barton" in *Blackwood's,* the same periodical that had published Gaskell's "Sketches" twenty years earlier. Gaskell had collaborated on that anonymously published work with her clergyman husband, who arranged for its publication, and thereby erased any public trace of her authorship. Similarly, the writing and publication of "Amos Barton" cloaked Marian Evans in male influences and identities and finally the masculine nom de plume "George Eliot." Eliot described the origin of her new vocation largely in terms of George Henry Lewes's agency. She acknowledged Lewes as having provided the impetus for carrying out her plan for "Amos Barton" by urging her to try a novel after she had read an early descriptive sketch to him. She settled on "The Sad Fortunes of the Rev. Amos Barton" after he declared it to be a "capital title" for the story. Not only did she appear as a woman "bending to the suggestions of her 'husband,'" as Margaret Homans points out,[30] but also, like the female preachers who attributed their calling to respected male clergy, as the extraordinary woman receiving her inspiration from an authoritative—masculine—source. "The most sympathizing of editors,"[31]

John Blackwood, accepted "Amos Barton" from George Henry Lewes, who claimed to be acting on behalf of a "clerical friend" who wished to remain anonymous. Lewes carefully chose the vague term "clerical friend," encouraging readers to speculate as to whether the author was ordained or a layman, while deflecting suspicion that a laywoman was responsible, and the success of this ruse delighted Eliot. Soon after the last installment of "Amos Barton" had appeared, its author supplied Blackwood with a nom de plume, "as a tub to throw to the whale in case of curious inquiries,"[32] and signed the letter "George Eliot." As she had already done as an essayist, George Eliot further surrounded herself with masculine disguises, mentors, and voices.

At the same time, by assuming a clerical identity as the author of *Scenes of Clerical Life,* Eliot was covertly answering an extraordinary call to preach when ordinary—male—preachers had failed. In her choice of authorial persona and subject matter Eliot extends the condemnation of abuses of the pulpit, begun in the essay on Dr. Cumming, with the authority of a brother clergyman. The narrator's calls for female readers to repent of their decadent tastes for romance and melodrama are themselves "tubs thrown to a whale," and the first two *Scenes* provide plenty of both. Eliot's most potent rebukes are aimed at the titular characters of "Amos Barton" and "Mr. Gilfil's Love Story" as unsuited to their clerical vocation by virtue of specifically masculine defects. The Reverend Mr. Barton, and to a lesser extent the Reverend Mr. Gilfil, each fail to meet the clerical narrator's standards as pastors and preachers until they are brought to repentance by extraordinary women. Yet it is only the narrator, not Amelia Barton or Catrina Gilfil, who ideally combines female vision with the authority culturally reserved for men.

In the economy of patriarchal social institutions, women "are holy sacrifices through whom men's lives are given spiritual meaning."[33] If she were given a voice, Milly Barton would clearly make the better preacher in her husband's church, offering to the parishioners the same spiritual encouragement she gives her family, rather than the theological abstractions behind which the Reverend Mr. Barton hides his emotional superficiality. But by denying these women voices, Eliot can represent their power only through sentimental conventions in which the spectacle of the virtuous woman's death is needed to accomplish a man's repentance. They silently rebuke with their edifying deaths.

Critics have often noted the extraordinary qualities of the female characters in *Scenes*,[34] but as Gillian Beer remarks, that extraordinary status is ambiguous, for in construing them as the exception rather than the rule they are more easily dismissed. Beer counters by insisting that Eliot in fact "portrays the power and scale of ordinary experience, ordinary women." As I have argued throughout this study, extraordinary status for women certainly does hamper any claims for women's political and social equality; nevertheless, it is far from clear that George Eliot would resist this conclusion. Rather, she may create female characters with a "story-book quality," as Jennifer Uglow puts it, situating them within the conventions of "Silly Novels" while retaining for her narrator the hard-won extraordinary calling. Eliot emerges as the extraordinary preacher, establishing her power while leaving other women trapped in patriarchal plots.

"Janet's Repentance," the last of the three tales that make up *Scenes of Clerical Life,* and the only one whose principal character is female, thematizes its author's struggle to consolidate a tangle of personae—"clerical friend," clergyman/layman, "George Eliot," Marian Evans, Mrs. Lewes. "Janet's Repentance" seems directly to address George Eliot's desire to treat the wrongs of women in her fiction without compromising her patriarchal affiliation, risking classification among the silly lady novelists, or succumbing to hysteria. She does so, much the way Gaskell had done in *Ruth:* by dividing the narrative focus between the victimized woman, Janet Dempster, and the redeemer, the Reverend Edgar Tryan. George Eliot had tried on the role of clergyman in the characters of Amos Barton and Mr. Gilfil, when she wrote their sermons and depicted their anxiety over spiritual duties, but in narrating Edgar Tryan, she returned to the evangelicalism of her childhood as a source for the preaching voice which would call people forth to action and set women free. Both Tryan and Janet are prophets in this tale, partners in Janet's repentance, and through them, George Eliot works her way towards a narrative technique that might fuse the roles of woman and preacher.

Like Gaskell's Mr. Benson, Tryan is feminized. He is a social outsider, brutally persecuted for his evangelicalism by Janet's sadistic husband and his cronies, and physically frail, suffering from consumption. What is more, Tryan has earned Benson's qualities of compassion and gentleness through his own conviction and conversion. He confesses to a past which rivals that of Bellingham, Ruth's seducer, but unlike that character, Tryan has allowed the tragic story of the woman he has wronged to convict him of his guilt and to change his vision of himself and his world. In reparation for his sins, Tryan devotes his life to God and to serving others. Tryan's "feminine" qualities make him a favorite of the ladies, and the gentle irony with which George Eliot treats the circle of spinsters and widows which surrounds him shows the influence of *Cranford*.[35] But most important, his acceptance of his vulnerability draws to him a woman of immense strength and depth of character, Janet Dempster.

Janet is as unlike Ruth as a character could be. While Ruth is depicted as childlike, innocent, ignorant, submissive, and angelic, Janet Dempster is drawn on a grand scale. Anticipating the Pre-Raphaelite Romola, she could be illustrated by Dante Gabriel Rossetti's "Astarte": a tall, imposing, beautiful woman, with long, thick, dark hair, and a "delicately-curved nostril, which seemed made to quiver with the proud consciousness of power and beauty."[36] Nevertheless, she is entirely dominated by her husband. Not only is she the victim of his beatings and verbal abuse, but what is worse, she enforces her own subjection by adopting her husband's ideology. She echoes his logic, his prejudices, his construction of reality; in short, she speaks his language—literally—shocking the Milby townspeople with her vulgarity.

For Dempster and his followers "cant" sums up everything objectionable in Methodism, and they wage war on Tryan because evangelical language threatens to demystify the discourses which guarantee their power and define their identities. The discourses of law, politics, economics—as well as crude wit—with which Dempster and his cronies enforce their authority are revealed as empty words by the transcendent authority of Bible language. In Dempster's world, might makes right, dooming woman to enslavement. Only when her husband's violent treatment makes her life unbearable, does Janet stop talking his language, stop ridiculing Tryan and his religion, and recognize in it the hope for her salvation.

Tryan does not use language to bully or threaten, as does the lawyer and demagogue Dempster, nor to congratulate sinners and enhance their self-righteousness as does the the rector, Mr. Crewe. Yet his words come "to [Janet] charged with a divine power such as she had never found in human words before" (*JR*, p. 393). Consistent with her objections to the heightened rhetoric of oracular novels, George Eliot refrains from showing Tryan in the pulpit. He preaches no passionate jeremiads or exhortations. His ministry recalls that of Elizabeth Ritchie, Elizabeth Evans, and many other women preachers, who had preferred to engage the faithful in a dialogue, to draw out their doubts and fears, and allow them to confess their sins, answering them with words of admonition and encouragement. When he is beset by the Milby mob, he walks with silent composure through their "pelting shower of nicknames and bad puns, with an *ad libitum* accompaniment of groans, howls, hisses, and hee-haws" (*JR*, p. 315).

Tryan is most effective in intimate conversations with Janet in which he elicits her confession, expresses his sympathy, and gives her reason for hope.

> The great source of [Janet's] courage, the great help to perseverance, was the sense that she had a friend and teacher in Mr Tryan: she could confess her difficulties to him; she knew he prayed for her; she had always before her the prospect of soon seeing him, and hearing words of admonition and comfort, that came to her charged with a divine power such as she had never found in human words before. (*JR*, p. 393)

Evangelical dialogue liberates Janet's voice in confession. George Eliot had herself experienced the evangelicals' key to her buried life in conversations with Elizabeth Evans. In her journal entry for November 30, 1858, entitled "History of

Adam Bede," George Eliot wrote of her aunt, "She was loving and kind to me, and I could talk to her about my inward life, which was closely shut up from those usually around me."[37] Confession legitimized, and at the same time controlled, the expression of the most intimate, and possibly disturbing, details of one's life, a particularly rare luxury for women.

It is confession as liberation, then, that the Reverend Tryan offers Janet. When she is driven from her home by Dempster's beatings, Tryan tells her that at the nadir of his own life

> "I found a friend to whom I opened all my feelings—to whom I confessed everything. He was a man who had gone through very deep experience, and could understand the different wants of different minds. He made it clear to me that the only preparation for coming to Christ and partaking of his salvation, was that very sense of guilt and helplessness which was weighing me down . . . as soon as we desire to be united to [God], and made pure and holy, it is as if the walls had fallen down that shut us out from God, and we are fed with his spirit, which gives us new strength." (*JR,* pp. 360–61)

As described here, confession implies a liberation of voice and a validation of self through entry into a dialogue. Tryan's confession releases Janet from her depression and fear, and empowers her to make her own confession. It is also possible to see in this formulation a reconstruction of desire, breaking down "the walls" of isolation wherein a disenfranchised woman experiences her "helplessness" and creating a "desire to be united to [God]." Following Foucault's analysis of confessional discourses, Nancy Armstrong has argued that this was one of the means by which women's energies were directed towards the goals of domestic production.[38] Whereas confession typically signaled discursive empowerment in the early stages of women's preaching, confession followed by silent service within patriarchal structures becomes the more typical pattern, as in fact it does throughout Eliot's fiction. However, Janet's discursive self-representation, albeit limited, and the subsequent transferral of discursive authority to Tryan and to the narrator, complicates the pattern.

Like Gaskell, particularly in *North and South* and *Sylvia's Lovers*, Eliot offers a telescoped narrative of women's emergence and suppression as public speakers in the evangelical movement. Eliot clearly takes a more sanguine view of these events than did Gaskell, construing them as part of a providential evolutionary process. Indeed, her fiction often aims at justifying the ways of history to women, as we shall see most clearly with *Felix Holt*. Yet, as this episode in "Janet's Repentance" develops, Eliot also hedges her bets, retaining an authoritative voice to articulate a call to women to repent of their enslavement to specific patriarchal practices, if not to mount a systematic rebellion. Encouraged to reinterpret her own life, Janet concludes her "confession,"

> "Pray with me . . . pray now that I may have light
> and strength." (*JR*, pp. 362–63)

Tryan brings about her conversion not by a sermon, but by a story. It is a collaborative effort, with the power of authorship passing from Tryan to Janet in the dialectic of their conversation. Unlike the ventriloquistic quality of Janet's position within her husband's discursive practice, this combination of narrative strategies implies that a woman's voice may be kept alive in concert with a male's, rather than subsumed into it.

Nevertheless, after her repentance, Janet falls silent. Her confession frees her to act, but apparently not to speak further, and she becomes a silent witness—an icon, as Gaskell's Ruth had been. Though Tryan's story implies the transference of the redemptive role from one sufferer to another, that Janet could ever assume the evangelical call to be "teacher and guide to [her] fellow-men" (*JR*, p. 412) seems unlikely. Her sober appearance, her attendance at Tryan's services, and finally her widow's mourning, all testify to a "new strength" that redirects Janet's desires towards more socially acceptable and less disruptive behaviors. Only if one assents to the Eliotic faith in a providential historical process towards, among other things, harmonious relations between the sexes, can this repentance and its consequences instill hope.

The narrator, rather than her character, finally possesses the authority to construct female power. Janet's beloved confessor and friend, Tryan, dies, and she walks "in quiet submissive sorrow" (*JR*, p. 411) behind his coffin. Many years later, her witness remains one of silent service:

> Janet is living still. Her black hair is grey, and her step is no longer buoyant; but the sweetness of her smile remains, the love is not gone from her eyes; and strangers sometimes ask, Who is that noble-looking elderly woman, that walks about holding a little boy by the hand? . . . Janet in her old age has children about her knees, and loving young arms round her neck. (*JR*, p. 412)

George Eliot's description is filled with the sentimental clichés that flawed Gaskell's "Sketches:" the "sweetness of her smile," "loving young arms round her neck." The narrator presents us with a madonna-like image of Janet to serve as a living memorial to Tryan.

> There is a simple gravestone in Milby Churchyard. . . . But there is another memorial of Edgar Tryan, which bears a fuller record: it is Janet Dempster, rescued from self-despair, strengthened with divine hopes, and now looking back on years of purity and helpful labour. The man who has left such a memorial behind him, must have been one whose heart beat with true compassion, and whose lips were moved by fervent faith. (*JR*, p. 412)

Like the novelist who, in the epilogue to *Middlemarch*, bears witness to the "unhistoric acts . . . [of] the number who lived faithfully a hidden life, and rest in unvisited tombs," the narrator marks Tryan's passing. Significantly, she does so with the silent body of her title character.

In the fate of Janet Dempster we find in condensed form the fate the woman preacher's voice will undergo in George Eliot's fiction. Women's voices must be liberated from those modes of discourse which enslave them. Yet, once having spoken, Janet does not go on to become a preacher in her own right. Freed both from her husband's brutal egotism and from the egotism of her own self-pity, Janet can escape the "cold dark prison of self-despairing" (*JR*, p. 371). Still, Tryan's personal testimony and catechetical dialogue can at best liberate Janet's own confession. She cannot replace her male mentor by assuming his role. Her power is not verbal, but iconographic, or mythic. Janet's silence, like her creator's early anonymity, implies that George Eliot was as yet uncertain as to whether the male preacher and female penitent roles could be combined, as early women preachers had attempted, or even reversed. She devoted her first full-length novel, *Adam Bede*, to precisely that task, representing a woman as a preacher—agent, speaker, authority—but at the same time dissociating herself as narrator from the preacher, and finally domesticating her.

Adam Bede: *George Eliot and Dinah Morris as Women Preachers*

Dinah Morris, the character that for so long has displaced actual women preachers in literary history, enabled George Eliot to embrace her preaching precursors only to exorcise them. Dinah's sermons, extemporaneous prayers, and dialogue are among some of the best extant examples of evangelical preaching rhetoric; her language so closely resembles that found in women preachers' letters, memoirs, and biographies that one historian of Methodism treated George Eliot's character as a real person, conflating her with Elizabeth Evans.[39] The principal scene of female empowerment in the novel, Dinah's ministry to Hetty Sorrel, is based on an actual experience of Elizabeth Evans which she had related to her niece. Though able to reproduce the evangelical idiom so convincingly, George Eliot's attitude towards that language is highly guarded. Unlike Elizabeth Gaskell, whose narrators frequently underscore her characters' "preachments," George Eliot's narrator consistently maintains a critical stance towards Dinah, as if fearful of being swept away by the lyrical modulations of that charismatic character's voice; Marian Evans might still be alarmed by the insincere eloquence of her own confessions.[40]

There was another issue at stake as well, for in creating a woman preacher with the power to call men as well as women to repentance Eliot might be seen as recognizing female authority apart from masculine sanction, leading her—as it would Gaskell—to identify with women outside patriarchal social relations. In *Adam Bede*, Eliot comes as close as she ever does to

> feel her heart is hard, and she is helpless. She cries
> to me, thy weak creature . . . Saviour! it is a blind
> cry to thee. Hear it! Pierce the darkness! Look upon
> her with thy face of love and sorrow, that thou didst
> turn on him who denied thee; and melt her hard
> heart." (*AB*, p. 496)

Dinah makes her appeal to a decidedly nonpatriarchal savior, one who himself knows exclusion ("the black darkness where God is not") and whose power to save stems from his "travail and pleading." Sin is equated here with confinement and paralysis—confession, as in "Janet's Repentance," with liberation. When Hetty responds "'I will speak. . . . I will tell. . . . I won't hide it anymore'" (*AB*, p. 497), the sense is not so much of a woman reduced to repentance, but of one finding the courage to speak out her mind. Hetty's long and poignant story makes clear her guilt, but it is also an eloquent testimony to the tragic vulnerability of both women and children in a society ruled by Donnithorne's law.

Hetty describes placing her infant in a hole beneath a tree, as if Nature would take unto itself this natural child, rejected by men. In a maternal gesture, Hetty covers the child with grass and wood chips. "I couldn't kill it any other way," she tells Dinah.

> "And I'd done it in a minute; and, O, it cried so,
> Dinah—I *couldn't* cover it quite up—I thought per-
> haps somebody 'ud come and take care of it, and
> then it wouldn't die. . . . And I made myself a bed,
> ever so far behind, where nobody could find me;
> and I was so tired and weak, I went to sleep. . . . But
> oh, the baby's crying kept waking me. . . . Dinah, do
> you think God will take away that crying and the
> place in the wood, now I've told everything?"
> "Let us pray, poor sinner: let us fall on our knees
> again, and pray to the God of all mercy." (*AB*,
> pp. 499–500)

The story that never found its way into the public record of Hetty's trial enters the novel thanks to the discourse of repentance. The simplicity of Hetty's language—its plain description, repetition, its naive sincerity—would have no chance of influencing a judge and jury; it would be dismissed as "vulgar." However, precisely those qualities embue it with authority in the context of evangelical discursive practices, which are in turn validated by the novel.

Dinah Morris afforded George Eliot an opportunity to authorize women's prophecy, yet the novel subverts Dinah's power. Certainly, the author's disagreements with evangelical doctrine must figure prominently in any account of this phenomenon, but they do not offer a full explanation. In narrating Dinah's field preaching in chapter 2, Eliot credits her with splendid story-telling talents, but treats her public calls for repentance with irony. Dinah's sermon shows the seductive qualities of preaching rhetoric for women writers: Dinah calls on God as the source of her authority, feminizes scripture in her retelling of the story of the Samaritan woman, exhorts a mixed audience, employs diction ranging from that of ordinary conversation to the heightened rhetoric of visionary ecstasy—all with apparent unselfconsciousness. With apparent impunity, this voice breaks the boundaries of rhetoric, subject matter, and stance that circumscribed feminine decorum. Yet by maintaining an ironic distance from Dinah, George Eliot refuses to align herself with that power, just as she declined direct involvement in the public crusades of her day, particularly feminist ones.

Dinah's authority is impugned alternately on the basis of her religious doctrines and her sex. On the one hand, evangelical doctrine is blamed for catching women in a web of male-authored texts which efface the women's subjectivity and enforce their subjugation, while men look on unfazed. Even the progressive Seth Bede counters Dinah's rejection of his marriage proposal by arguing that her vocation is sanctioned by 1 Corinthians 7:34 and adds that a litany of texts counsel their marriage. "'It seems to me there's more texts for you marrying than ever you can find against it,'" Seth concludes (*AB*, p. 78). It appears then that Dinah is not so different from Hetty, after all, as she too can be victimized by male plots. But on the other hand, Dinah's participation in a public discourse under any terms seems a betrayal of her genuine social role as a woman, that is, her domestic ministry. Considered in the light of the novel's historical setting, the result is to cast Dinah as a fascinating but remote character from a thankfully irretrievable past. With Dinah, Eliot can at once acknowledge the power and successes of her preaching predecessors and suggest that history has progressed irreversibly beyond them. Eliot's creation of Dinah seems something of an exorcism, then, ending in the confinement of the preacher's voice in the literalizing vocations of marriage and motherhood.

The novel provides the grounds for circumscribing women preachers' vocations with a highly nuanced representation of Dinah's field preaching. Anatomizing preaching as a public discourse, attending to subtleties of rhetoric, audience, and gender, Eliot discriminates between features of the tradition that she believes have rightly met with extinction and those which have evolved into the very stratgies that authorize her own narrative techniques. To illustrate the complexity of the critique of the public-preaching tradition, I wish to consider Eliot's presentation of Dinah's field preaching in detail. First, by viewing Dinah preaching through the eyes of a skeptical male traveler, Eliot at once recognizes the masculine point of view as normative in the public sphere (rendering Dinah's status as spectacle a foregone conclusion) and ironizes the authority of the male reader. The traveler, who "knew but two types of Methodist— the ecstatic and the bilious" (*AB*, p. 66) (the same two types of characters which the skeptical George Eliot had herself professed to discover in silly oracular novels), finds Dinah to be an extraordinary example of both femininity and evangelicalism.

> Dinah walked as simply as if she were going to market, and seemed as unconscious of her outward appearance as a little boy: there was no blush, no tremulousness, which said, "I know you think me a pretty woman, too young to preach"; no casting up or down of the eyelids, no compression of the lips, no attitude of the arms, that said, "But you must think of me as a saint."
>
> "A sweet woman," the stranger said to himself, "but surely nature never meant her for a preacher."
>
> Perhaps he was one of those who think that nature has theatrical properties, and, with the con-

siderate view of facilitating art and psychology, "makes up" her characters, so that there may be no mistake about them. But Dinah began to speak. (*AB*, pp. 66–67)

Dinah has effected some sort of repentance, but as the object of speculation in this case—not as a speaker—and even the narrator's irony leaves her extraordinary nature intact. In fact, as she begins to speak the suggestion is that Dinah has mistaken her own gifts, that nature meant such exceptional women to be novelists, not preachers.

The sermon which follows redefines the power as well as the weaknesses of Dinah's preaching voice. To invoke the Lord's presence at this gathering, Dinah identifies herself and her audience with the Samaritan woman at the well, who was taken rather by surprise with Jesus' "free mercy." Told from the female perspective, the point of this story becomes one of liberation rather than rebuke. Dinah next identifies herself with the poverty, ignorance, and despair of her audience, as did Jesus, and, like Tryan, she tells them a story from her own life in which the preaching of John Wesley brought beauty into her bleak childhood. The only bit of doctrine she remembers from that sermon is a message of hope, that the "Gospel" means "good news," like a letter from a friend offering help in time of trouble (*AB*, p. 69), she explains. However, it is above all the aesthetic element of the experience that remains vivid.

"I remember [the preacher's] face well: he was a very old man, and had very long white hair; his voice was very soft and beautiful, not like any voice I had ever heard before." (*AB*, pp. 68–69)

Dinah attributes Wesley's power to his feminine qualities, especially his "soft and beautiful" voice. But it is clear from this description that George Eliot sees Wesley not as an intellectual mentor, the role he actually fulfilled for many women, but as an aesthetic object with a somewhat mystical appeal, rather in the way Gaskell's Ruth attracted Jemima Bradshaw.

Initially, Dinah holds sway over the traveler's imagination. However, when she returns to her exhortation, the stranger suddenly becomes conscious of her rhetoric.

> "The *lost!* . . . Sinners! . . . Ah, dear friends, does
> that mean you and me?"
>
> Hitherto the stranger had been chained to the
> spot against his will by the charm of Dinah's mellow
> tones, which had a variety of modulation like that of
> a fine instrument touched with the unconscious skill
> of musical instinct. The simple things she said
> seemed like novelties, as a melody strikes us with a
> new feeling when we hear it sung by the pure voice
> of a boyish chorister. . . . The stranger had ceased
> to doubt, as he had done at the first glance, that she
> could fix the attention of her rougher hearers, but
> still he wondered whether she could have that
> power of rousing their more violent emotions,
> which must surely be the necessary seal of her voca-
> tion as a Methodist preacher, until she came to the
> words "Lost!—Sinners!" when there was a great
> change in her voice and manner. . . . Her voice be-
> came deep and muffled, but there was still no ges-
> ture. Nothing could be less like the ordinary type of
> the Ranter than Dinah. She was not preaching as
> she heard others preach, but speaking directly from
> her own emotions, and under the inspiration of her
> own simple faith. (*AB*, pp. 71–72)

Eliot's description problematizes the woman preacher as author. Insofar as her voice can be disembodied and depoliticized
(that is, voided of any demands on the audience's intellect or
beliefs), it can be treated as purely aesthetic and even de-sexed
as "the pure voice of a boyish chorister." In this manner,
Dinah's sermon is easily reconciled with normative cultural
practices. Importantly, both Dinah's ability to effect social
change for the "Samaritan women" of her parable and the patriarchal authorization of her calling as a preacher depend on
her "rousing . . . more violent emotions" than does this purely
aestheticized facet of her discourse. That is, to demand repentance is also to invite invalidation and censorship. Moreover,
when "she [preaches not] as she heard others preach, but . . .
directly from her own emotions, and under the inspiration of
her own simple faith" is Dinah a speaking subject, or is she sim-

ply the passive medium for a divine message? Her "deep and muffled voice" may at once connote sincerity, sexuality, and concealment.

When the narrator turns to the villagers' point of view, the effect is mixed as well: Dinah elicits "a responsive sigh and groan from her fellow Methodists, but the village mind does not easily take fire" (*AB*, p. 72).

Through Bessy Cranage, Dinah's only dramatic convert, George Eliot confirms the stranger's skepticism. Bessy, who "belonged unquestionably to that unsoaped, lazy class of feminine characters" (*AB*, p. 73), gives up trying to understand Dinah's sermon and falls "to studying Dinah's nose, eyes, mouth, and hair, and wondering whether it was better to have such a sort of pale face as that, or fat red cheeks and round black eyes like her own" (*AB*, p. 73). Like the stranger, she is lulled by the musical tones of Dinah's storytelling, but the harsh-sounding exhortation frightens her.

Though Dinah speaks words of pity as well as remonstrance, the only effect she produces on Bessy is terror. Enjoining Bessy to cast off her jewelry—"they *are* stinging you—they are poisoning your soul—they are dragging you down into a dark bottomless pit, where you will sink for ever, and for ever, and for ever, further away from light and God" (*AB*, p. 75)—Dinah reduces Bessy to frightened sobs. Given what the narrator tells us about Bessy's primitive understanding, Dinah's rhetoric seems cruel, her victory, to us, no victory at all. Dinah here resembles the female writers of conduct books, endlessly scolding other women about their feminine vanities, and looks forward to Savonarola's fanaticism in *Romola*. Indeed, as it turns out, Bessy's repentance is short-lived.

At the point Dinah has ceased to be a Romantic artist appealing primarily to the imagination and has become a propagandist appealing primarily to the will, George Eliot withdraws her sympathy. As the sermon closes we return to the perspective of the traveler, who is literally at a distance from Dinah, on a hill overlooking the field in which she preaches. The traveler records a detached, voyeuristic interest in this spectacle.

> The stranger, who had been interested in the course
> of her sermon, as if it had been the development of

to the evangelical Seth, who would defy male authority in order to guarantee Dinah's right to preach, George Eliot yokes her to Adam, who quietly affirms patriarchal control and removes her to the domestic sphere. His power over Dinah, which stems from a kind of natural or providential order, overcomes even women's spiritually based resistance. Though the precise nature of Adam's power remains obscure in *Adam Bede,* it seems the forerunner of the transcendent, wordless evolutionary forces which clearly dominate George Eliot's characters by the time she writes *Felix Holt.*

The Methodist Conference's prohibition of women's preaching in 1802 and Dinah's silent submission to their will coincide with her marriage in Eliot's narrative. Adam, who supports Dinah's submission, and Seth, who wishes they had "'left the Wesleyans and joined a body that 'ud put no bonds on Christian liberty'" (*AB,* p. 583), carry on the debate while Dinah, now the evangelist of domestic reconciliation, changes the subject. Adam gives as Dinah's reason for abandoning preaching that

> "Most o' the women do more harm nor good with their preaching—they've not got Dinah's gift nor her sperrit; and she's seen that, and she thought it right to set th' example o' submitting, for she's not held from other sorts o' teaching." (*AB,* p. 583)

Adam seems to be quoting from "Silly Novels." Might not the same be said of George Eliot's renunciation of the oracular voice? The claim of an "extraordinary call" could be turned against the woman preacher, as Adam does here, and George Eliot seems to concur.

Rather than continuing her attempt to penetrate a public discourse, Dinah turns, like some of her historical counterparts, to indirect, subversive rhetorical techniques. She continues to engage in a private, hidden practices, "'talking to people a bit in their houses'" (*AB,* p. 583). Where Dinah's sermon resulted in the all-too-brief conversion of the overwrought Bessy Cranage, her ministry to Hetty Sorrel, a ministry hidden in the darkness of a prison cell, elicits the sympathy of both Mr. Irwine, the representative of the patriarchal religion from which her discourse originates, and Arthur Donnithorne, Hetty's ignorant victimizer. But the muted patri-

archal presence, represented in this novel by its titular character, comes increasingly to dominate George Eliot's fiction.

In *Adam Bede,* George Eliot appears to accede to the historical forces which silence the woman preacher, and in her subsequent fiction she gives no female character the opportunity
to speak publicly as Dinah does. Instead, women take on significance as iconographic representations of sympathy and
charity, presumably retaining Dinah's charismatic power without incurring the difficulties inherent in her voice. The
preacher's role is returned to male characters and is eventually
taken over almost entirely by the narrator. And where the narrator speaks in an emphatic, oracular voice, it does so on behalf
of a mythology of transcendent history rather than personal
salvation, a mythology whose essentialist, hierarchical construction of gender George Eliot condones. It is less the case
that George Eliot loses faith in women's ability to engage social
discourses than that she comes to deny the desirability of any
social discourse—any substitution of language for unselfconscious action and the metadiscursive forces of history. In *The
Mill on the Floss,* Maggie's voice does not receive the hearing
it deserves; it is a reversion to the language of childhood
(Tom's "Maggie") that brings about a dubious absolution
before the final silencing of death. In *Romola,* steeped in the
authoritarian patriarchal structures of Renaissance humanism,
Catholicism, and traditional historical narratives, the heroine,
though surviving male discourse, can at best achieve the iconic
status of an earthly Madonna.

Romola: *The Preaching Icon*

Romola's position within a matrix of patriarchal structures
would not, of itself, mark a break with George Eliot's pattern of
developing female characters as I have outlined it thus far.
Janet Dempster and Dinah Morris likewise face problems of
affiliation with and resistance to various forms of patriarchal
language, institutions, and domestic and social relations. Yet
this character has always posed a far more unsettling challenge
to readers than have her predecessors; Mary Wilson Carpenter
begins her summary of twentieth-century responses to *Romola*
by declaring that "the trouble with George Eliot's novel *Romola*

is Romola herself."[43] Treating this novel and its titular character as part of George Eliot's continuing efforts to negotiate her
relationship to the female preaching tradition does, I believe,
offer a reading strategy that clarifies the "trouble with Romola."
Seen within the context of my broader argument concerning
Eliot's ambivalent stance towards a prophetic vocation, Romola
appears rather less anomalous than she has often seemed. At
the same time, this analysis credits the vexation she has evoked,
locating it in discursive and ideological conflicts generated by
the novel's incompatible goals.

Romola brings the novelist face to face with a problem confronted in various forms by other writers we have considered.
For Eliot, the attempt to historicize women's relationship to
evangelical preaching and prophecy runs afoul of the univer-
salizing historiography by which she construes the relationship
between past and present, and women's place in history. The
novel's apparent reconciliation of these goals, symbolized in
the ahistorical iconographic status conferred on Romola by the
conclusion, is disrupted by the consciousness that Romola has
not in fact eluded, but been constructed by, cultural codes of
class and gender behavior. These codes are hardly to be located
in processes of change transcending the political interests so
cynically represented in Tito, or Signor Bardo. In short, to introduce political, material, and discursive histories of women's
difficulties in affiliating with patriarchal structures is to preclude the argument that such affiliations can be recuperated in
a larger, quasi-providential scheme of history. Hannah More
and Charlotte Elizabeth Tonna, arriving at a conflict between
the power that evangelism afforded them as social critics and
the dependence on patriarchal authorization it implied, chose
to bear their sense of betrayal and carry on in the preaching
tradition. Gaskell, as I have argued, found this contradiction
insupportable, and turned to the "illegitimate" prophecies of
fallen women. In *Romola*, Eliot tries once again to bridge the
conflict by redefining its terms. The fallen state from which
Romola must be liberated resembles the humanistic atheism attacked by More and Tonna. However, the evangelical and confessional discourses that effect that liberation, the vocation she
assumes, and extra-linguistic power with which Eliot imbues
Romola's mission, swerve from configurations we have seen

previously, in both their historical particulars and theoretical implications.

The preaching tradition encountered by Romola differs radically from the Protestant evangelicalism which affords limited empowerment to Janet Dempster, Dinah Morris, or the whole range of female preachers, writers, and their characters we have been considering. It is undeniably evangelical insofar as it calls sinners to repentance, but as a phenomenon of quattrocento Florence it likewise partakes of the authoritarianism, clericalism, and misogyny of Renaissance Catholicism. Tonna, it should be remembered, founded her virulent attacks on Roman Catholicism partly on the basis that it denied the laity access to scripture, and thereby to a language of public protest. Savonarola's revival, too, lacks a call to lay prophecy that characterized women's emergence as preachers. Rather than oppose this restriction with an anachronistic version of Dinah Morris, who might rival Savonarola's preaching by turning his ideological contradictions to her advantage, Eliot uses Romola to construct a method of female evangelism that is meant to surpass the historical limitations of preaching. Revising the orthodox practice of icon worship to suggest a Romantic doctrine of ineffable powers which can be intuited through contemplation of the natural world, Eliot makes Romola a preaching icon. As such, she embodies truth to be perceived imaginatively, functioning in much the same way as children, peasant laborers, or the sublime in nature might shadow forth a transcendent reality for Wordsworth or Carlyle, and effecting a similar spiritual reformation in a sympathetic observer.

The possibility of a preaching icon enables Eliot to empower a female character as a reformer while avoiding the discursive practices associated with evangelical repentance which she critiqued in her earlier fictions. However, mounting her attack first on humanist scholarship and then on evangelical prophecy in terms of a historically specified female character undermines the icon as a figure representing an ahistorically-gendered discourse. The problems Romola encounters trying to engage in humanistic or evangelical discourses stem from the fact that Eliot shows them to have been developed to serve masculine interests, and that they are being deployed under particular political circumstances to consolidate power and enforce class and gender hierarchies. Romola masters classical scholarship only to have it invoked against her: "Optimam foeminam nullam esse, alia licet alia pejor sit" (No woman is really good, though one may be worse than another), she is told by her father and teacher.[44] Eliot would reiterate the futility of women's classical learning in *Middlemarch,* where Dorothea Brooke is disabused of her faith in classical languages as the guide to her vocation. In that novel the institutional link between classical learning and a spiritual vocation is represented by the desiccated clergyman, the Reverend Casaubon. While Savonarola may draw followers from all ranks (Romola's brother forsakes his father's scholarly tradition to become the monk, Fra Luca), he maintains a strict clerical control on the movement. He enjoins all to repent, but authorizes few to speak. He is the one who literally turns Romola around and sends her back to her unfaithful husband as she is escaping Florence. The salvation Savonarola offers entails Romola's acceptance of Tito's domestic rule. Moreover, the ecstatic visions of Fra Luca may allude to an "unseen perfection" that transcends the wisdom of men, but Romola rejects her brother's faith as selfish and narcissistic.

If the principal discursive practices in Romola's world are revealed to be entrenched in masculine self-interest and fundamentally unavailable to female speakers, it remains for the narrative itself to provide Romola with her vocation. Yet, if we have been convinced that gender hierarchies are material and historical phenomena, in large measure produced and maintained by discourse, then it is only by sleight of hand that Eliot can make the gendered nature of her own discourse acceptable. For the preaching icon that Romola becomes is itself the product of Eliot's affiliation with Comtean and Feuerbachian doctrines of history, and, moreover, with the foundational text of evangelical revivals: the book of Revelation. Mary Wilson Carpenter has argued that in *Romola* "George Eliot wrote her own 'continuous historical' apocalypse, appropriating the 'scheme of the Apocalypse' in all its fascinating complexity of structure but revising it into a post-Christian and postpatriarchal vision of humanity."[45] Carpenter's elucidation of apocalyptic structures in *Romola* makes good sense of, among other things, the timeless quality of the novel's closing tableau, in which Romola seems to have escaped history and culture. But I would argue that, rather than moving towards a "post-" position, *Romola* takes us forward into the past where, as Deirdre David has put it, female characters "escape from the confinements of their present culture in order to retrieve a more organically coherent time."[46] In other words, Eliot returns us to the past to find structures of coherence that are timeless and universal; preeminent among those structures, having been critiqued only to be recuperated, is gender hierarchy. Romola is its matron saint.

The position Eliot assumes in *Romola* as saint-maker, interpreter of Revelation, and author of narrative providence follows logically from her analysis of female preaching in *Adam Bede*. Taking *Romola* to be representative of Eliot's own status as a female intellectual, Deirdre David sees the novel as "the narrative of an intellectually ambitious woman impeded by male cultural authority and invested with all the immutable, ahistorical autonomy desired by the traditional intellectual."[47] This formulation might also be applied more specifically to describe a particular stage in Eliot's understanding of her "extraordinary call." *Romola* shows Eliot trying to work out a strategy that would allow her simultaneously to affiliate with a female preaching tradition and appropriate the masculine authority that had sought to govern it. She retains in her character those aspects of gender difference that women preachers claimed suited them to be better evangelists than men: for example, moral superiority, refined sensitivities, a heightened sympathy to suffering. Owning these differences, women preachers had attempted to authorize their discourse by appealing over men's heads to the divine sanction of their calling. As Dinah Morris's fate indicates, Eliot found this tactic to be futile. *Romola* goes further, suggesting that the women preachers' strategy should be shunned not for its contradictory, self-defeating stance towards patriarchal power, but for its unwillingness to assume the self-authorizing power claimed by patriarchal discourses. Eliot endows her preaching narrator, in contrast to the iconic Romola, with the decidedly patriarchal power to define difference, hierarchize, construct history while standing outside it, and to effect closure; that is, to impose order rather than plead for reform. The narrator's voice accomplishes the desire that, I

in which the novel was set, and in that sense make a contribution to history as well as fiction. But this purpose inspired a second, and more problematic difference: to feminize her history as had the female historical writers who had preceded her.[52] This second aim seems to have developed in the course of creating her story. Ultimately, what George Eliot needed to "loosen her tongue" was a character, wholly of her own creation—Romola—upon whom she could impose "feminine" history, freeing her narrator to supersede the male preacher, Savonarola. However, her goals, if not incompatible, were not easily reconciled. Repeatedly, she was daunted by the task of presenting Savonarola's life within Romola's story because the historical discourse could not accommodate the suppressed female voice. Eliot's early plot sketches have been lost;[53] therefore, we cannot know the precise role the introduction of Romola's character played in giving voice to Eliot's narrator. Nevertheless, it is not difficult to identify in the finished novel the allegory of authorship being played out in Romola's relationship to the novel's male characters and the patriarchal discourses they represent.

The "proem" to *Romola* reveals conflicts in Eliot's historiography of gender. She begins by evoking a scene of the timeless significance and beauty of Florence, to impress her reader "with the broad sameness of the human lot, which never alters in the main headings of its history—hunger and labour, seedtime and harvest, love and death" (*Rom*, p. 43). By the end of the proem, however, these general mythic categories are shown to be inadequate, masking profound historical changes. Eliot's conception of the muse which finally inspired her historical romance, the "angel of dawn"—a combination of the Holy Spirit, Clio, and a fifteenth-century Florentine nobleman—must be warned not to converse with the present age "for the changes are great and the speech of Florentines would sound as a riddle in your ears" (*Rom*, p. 50). Only architecture and smiling children can be counted on to remain consistent symbols. In effect, George Eliot asks this shade returned from the dead to abandon his memories of battles, political intrigues, shrewd trade—the stuff of which history was traditionally made, wherein irreconcilable divisions occur with oppressive regularity. However, in so doing he would likewise relinquish his peculiarly masculine authority as an observer that makes him useful to Eliot. Standing on the hill of San Miniato, he remembers Savonarola in somewhat the way the stranger in *Adam Bede* might reminisce about Dinah's preaching: "it was a memorable thing to see a preacher move his audience to such a pitch that the women even took off their ornaments, and delivered them up to be sold for the benefit of the needy." In each instance, the aloof masculine observer allows Eliot to establish her own detachment and, therefore, authority as an "objective" writer. Yet she clearly sees a problem with the authoritative observer—and by implication the traditional historian—who under the guise of often specious objectivity renders people, particularly women, as constructs within patriarchal narratives. Discursive authority becomes the focus of this novel in which the male characters are engaged in wars of words, while Romola's feminine contribution remains largely silent.

Romola opens with Tito Melema, who epitomizes the Renaissance revival of pagan mythology and rhetoric, a phenomenon being repeated in George Eliot's own time. He has made his way to Florence after the ship he and his foster-father were sailing on goes down. A Greek scholar, self-interested but not yet ruthless, Tito has a talent for insuring his own survival. When he appears at the Bardi household to offer his scholarly services to Romola's father, Romola is impressed with his Hellenic beauty and eventually captured by his apparent devotion to Signor Bardo's intellectual endeavor and appreciation for her own learning. To Romola, who has spent her life locked in her blind father's library, acting as his amanuensis and translator, and has been trained in the humanism of her age, Tito answers to her ideal of a cultivated, rational thinker. He seems the suitable replacement in her father's life and her own for the brother who betrayed his family's intellectual tradition in order to follow what the Bardi perceive as the superstitions of the fanatical Savonarola. But Tito's learning has not humanized him or caused him to feel the sympathetic bond which should tie all the human community together. Instead, it is for him a temptation to power. From the first, Eliot shows Tito reluctant to forsake his opportunities for advancement in Florence to seek out his foster-father, Baldassarre, to whom he owes not only his learning but his life, and who may have fallen into the hands of slave traders. Tito, the paragon of Hellenistic learning, the realization of Arnold's intellectual ideal, metamorphoses in the course of the novel into a scholarly prostitute, a mere voice for hire to the highest bidder.

The ethical bankruptcy of Tito's learning and its dire consequences for the female characters in *Romola* illuminate George Eliot's relationship to the practices of patriarchal historical narrative. Romola misjudges Tito because she attributes her own moral virtue, quintessentially feminine in Eliot's view, to the rationalism espoused by her father, when in fact she has been blind to the egotism humanism has likewise encouraged in him. As Margaret Homans points out, Bardo's aim in preserving his library is not, as Romola deludes herself, to link one generation to another in an intellectual community, but to secure a lasting fame for himself.[54] Likewise, the humanistic tradition Bardo and Tito represent purports to free all discourses, including history, from the divisive influence of religion. However, pretending to be the disinterested investigator whose voice is the transparent medium for the truth of the past, the historian, as George Eliot discovered, creates a discourse at the service of ideology, or worse, self-interest. Tito's "humanism," like that of the French *philosophes* attacked by Hannah More, employs its expert discourses to control rather than liberate. The tyranny of humanism, with its claim to objectivity, posed a greater threat to female voices than any religious dogma; hence, Tito is the villain whom George Eliot as well as Romola must overcome.

Romola's brother Dino, renamed Fra Luca when he becomes a follower of Savonarola, offers his sister the first challenge to the humanistic discourse in which their father educated his children. Dino secretly calls Romola to his deathbed in the monastery of San Marco to warn her of a vision he has had of the terrible fate which awaits her if she marries her present lover. Romola goes, hoping for a reconciliation between her brother and their father, but instead finds Dino's language alienating. He declares his message comes not from his own heart, but from divine will. In her anger, she responds with a resonant question: "'What is this religion of yours, that places visions before natural duties?'" (*Rom*, p. 211). Romola's indignation stems from what she perceives as Dino's desertion of Signor Bardo for Savonarola at the time when his father was going blind. But her question could have been as aptly directed to members of her own sex as to this feminized and celibate male. Indeed, it had been posed to every woman preacher and woman writer whose spiritual or artistic vision compelled them to resist the tyranny of natural duties.

As a follower of Savonarola, "Fra Luca" espouses religious views analogous to those of the evangelicals of George Eliot's experience. Both groups aimed at a popular revival of a faith grown rigidly hierarchical and authoritarian; both sought to accomplish their goal by converting individuals dead to their own sinfulness as well as to their own spiritual gifts. This conversion would enable them to transcend naturalized social conventions and act as God's messengers. Just as the Methodist preachers had sought an identity that would free them from the control of worldly fathers, so has Dino managed to evade his blind father's constricting intellectual tradition in order to attain his new identity as Fra Luca.

Fra Luca turns Romola's accusations back on her:

> "What were the maxims of philosophy to me? They told me to be strong, when I felt myself weak; when I was ready like the Blessed Saint Benedict, to roll myself among thorns, and court smarting wounds as a deliverance from temptation. For the Divine Love had sought me, and penetrated me, and created a great need in me; like a seed that wants room to grow. . . . Before I knew the history of the saints, I had a foreshadowing of their ecstasy. For the same truth had penetrated even into pagan philosophy: that it is a bliss within the reach of man to die to mortal needs, and live in the life of God as the Unseen Perfectness." (*Rom*, p. 212)

Fra Luca's speech reiterates the pattern of empowering self-renunciation underlying the Reverend Tryan's and Janet's conversions as well as Dinah Morris's vocation, a pattern which dominates George Eliot's later fiction.[55] This celebration of renunciation provides the necessary corrective to egotistical humanism, revealing to Romola her own vulnerability, as well as her potential to achieve knowledge of the transcendent "Unseen Perfectness."

However, despite its power to free the individual from patriarchy, religious fanaticism encourages its own peculiar egotism, and Eliot treats Fra Luca with greater skepticism than she had Dinah. As Fra Luca goes on, he reveals the terrifying isolation that his perfectionism has brought about.

> "But to attain that I must forsake the world: I must have no affection, no hope, wedding me to that which passeth away; I must live with my fellow-beings only as human souls related to the eternal unseen life." (*Rom,* p. 212)

Especially when compared to Dinah's contemplation of duty versus the bond of marriage, the egomania of Fra Luca's desires is clear.

As Romola is caught between her desire for Tito and her brother's warning, her position illuminates George Eliot's as author. In Fra Luca's vision, a priest with the face of death marries Romola to a man ("the Great Tempter") who will bring her "to a stony place where there [is] no water," but instead "parchment unrolling itself everywhere" (*Rom,* p. 215), where their father will die and Romola be abandoned. Romola must choose between her brother, Savonarola's disciple, and Tito, her lover. As author, Eliot likewise locates herself between the visionary polemics of the preacher, which can lead to a monomania she repudiates, and "the Great Tempter," complicity in the authoritative discourse of history, which hides its own ethical vacuity and desire for power behind a facade of objectivity. Both discourses tempt their practitioners to dominate and silence all other voices and thereby recapitulate the literary exclusion of all marginal positions, including women's. As Romola makes this discovery, Eliot begins to sketch out an alternative model of female power.

Romola ignores Fra Luca's warning and proceeds in her fatal relationship with Tito. While Romola imagines a union with a brilliant scholar who appreciates her learning, Tito sets about seducing Tessa, a naive contadina rather like Ruth or Hetty, whom he weds in a sham ceremony, a parody of the marriage rite. But Tito's exploitation of Tessa's ignorance is far more disturbing than Bellingham's of Ruth, or Donnithorne's of Hetty. Bellingham and Donnithorne are, to an extent, carried away by the same romantic fictions with which they dupe Ruth and Hetty. Tito's sophisticated mastery of texts stems from the same disinterestedness George Eliot's contemporaries associated with humanistic culture. Instead, his sophistication enables him to trade in sham texts, represented here by the sideshow marriage rite, to gratify his own desires.[56]

Tito's intellectual prostitution parallels his sexual infidelity, suggesting the connection between linguistic dishonesty and the oppression of women. As Tito becomes more entangled in political intrigue, prostituting his oratorical talents, serving as demagogue and as a double agent who acts as envoy and strategist for opposing groups, he weds Romola, but maintains his liaison with Tessa, becoming increasingly secretive and silent with his wife. His power over her voice prevents Romola from successfully uncovering his deception (he considers confessing to her his betrayal of Baldassarre, but his love of power stays his tongue). She finds it impossible to challenge him outright. Tito's sale of her father's library culminates a growing tension in Romola's relations with her husband. Tito's promise to help Romola ensure that the Bardi's library be preserved intact for future scholars symbolizes the obligation to culture that his learning should impose on him. When he sells the library without Romola's knowledge in order to pay off debts and protect his position in Florence, he betrays Romola, alienating her from her patrimony of language. Just as he betrayed his teacher/father, so does he betray the intellectual tradition of which these texts were a part. At last, Romola must acknowledge that, for Tito, language is solely a tool for self-aggrandizement.

Lacking discursive means to resist Tito, Romola's only hope seems to be in escaping him. Her marriage had been symbolized by Tito's present of a tabernacle on which he had an artisan carve a figure of himself as Bacchus subduing Romola, portrayed as Ariadne. In it Tito had sealed Fra Luca's crucifix, in an effort to confine this threat to his power. Now Romola breaks open that tabernacle and seizes this image of the "Unseen Perfectness" to empower her in her escape.

Of course, Romola cannot escape the web of her cultural

identity. Rather, Eliot shows that she must discover and accept the vocation to which that identity calls her. As she waits for dawn to make her way out of the city, Romola thinks of her brother's vision and recalls the preaching of Savonarola in the Duomo. His "willing sacrifice for the people" (*Rom,* p. 396) had brought her to tears. Yet she cannot commit herself fully to him.

> [S]he shrank from impressions that were alluring her within the sphere of visions and narrow fears which compelled men to outrage natural affections as Dino had done.
>
> This was the tangled web that Romola had in her mind as she sat weary in the darkness. No radiant angel came across the gloom with a clear message for her. In those times, as now, there were human beings who never saw angels or heard perfectly clear messages. Such truth as came to them was brought confusedly in the voices and deeds of men not at all like the seraphs of unfailing wing and piercing vision—men who believed falsities as well as truths, and did the wrong as well as the right. (*Rom,* p. 396)

Eliot's irony clarifies the tangled web Fra Luca's vision has created in Romola's mind, privileging the well-intentioned if imperfect witness of earnest people over the exhortations of visionaries claiming converse with "radiant angel[s]." Such ambiguous guidance would come to Romola from Savonarola himself.

Romola is not far out of Florence when she sees two monks approaching her. More than anyone else she fears meeting them, disguised as she is in nun's garb, because "they might expect some pious passwords of which she knew nothing." Her ignorance of their language would betray her. To Savonarola, however, Romola's disguise is already transparent. In the chapter entitled "An Arresting Voice," Savonarola, one of those two monks on the road from Florence, turns to name her:

> "You are Romola de'Bardi, the wife of Tito Melema." She knew the voice: it had vibrated through

her more than once before; and because she knew it, she did not turn round or look up. She sat shaken by awe, and yet inwardly rebelling against the awe. It was one of those black-skirted monks who was daring to speak to her, and interfere with her privacy: that was all. And yet she was shaken, as if that destiny which men thought of as a sceptered deity had come to her, and grasped her with fingers of flesh.

"You are fleeing from Florence in disguise. I have a command from God to stop you. You are not permitted to flee." (*Rom*, p. 428)

With this arresting voice a new discourse threatens to dominate Romola. "'It is not the poor monk who claims to interfere with you: it is the truth that commands you" (*Rom*, p. 429), Savonarola tells Romola. But just as Romola liberally translated classical texts for her father, she interprets Savonarola's text as an invitation to appropriate the truth.

Savonarola's truth frees her from the false, amoral discourse that makes her Tito's slave, just as Janet Dempster's conversion liberates her from her husband's tyranny. Obeying the command to return to Florence and accept her vocation enables Romola to construct an identity independent of her patriarchal roles as wife and daughter. Though George Eliot assigns to Romola "works of womanly sympathy" (*Rom*, p. 463)—acts of charity to the city's poor—she does so to establish traditionally feminine morality as a universal ideal. Likewise, Romola avoids Dinah Morris's mistakes in seeking her power through religion. Instead, she eschews its prophetic discourse, "the wearisome visions and allegories" (*Rom*, p. 463) of Savonarola's followers, while allowing the "passionate sympathy and the splendour of [Savonarola's] aims" (*Rom*, p. 464) to empower her. Just as Maggie Tulliver had been inspired by Thomas à Kempis's *Imitation of Christ,* so does Romola attempt to imitate Savonarola, who "held up the conditions of the Church in the terrible mirror of his unflinching speech, which called things by their right names and dealt in no polite periphrases" (*Rom*, p. 521). Romola's repentance becomes her emancipation from the prison of her "privacy," an opportunity to escape the isolation of humanist individualism.

Yet through the redeemed Romola, George Eliot once again appropriates the preacher's power for a woman only to silence her. Romola possesses all of Janet's or Dinah's charisma, but not the preacher's oracular voice. Her power is almost wholly iconographic, her benign influence emenating almost mystically from her mere physical presence rather than her speech. A woman's status as spectacle, used to undercut Dinah's power in *Adam Bede,* is celebrated in *Romola* as language itself is more directly impugned as corrupting. Describing Romola's ministry to the poor, the narrator dwells on her appearance and its healing effect and includes little dialogue. She might be described as appearing in a series of frescoes, like Fra Angelico's in Savonarola's San Marco, through which George Eliot establishes woman's power. Romola appears to represent the sort of public ministry for women of which Eliot could approve: extraordinary *and* silent.

The chorus of "'Bless you, madonna! bless you!'" (*Rom,* p. 462) that sustains Romola in her service to the sick, comes to describe her literally. In two chapters, one of which George Eliot originally entitled "The Unseen Mother" rather than "The Unseen Madonna," she establishes Romola as the visible manifestation of the qualities of compassion, generosity, and strength the Florentines worship in "the image of the Pitying Mother" (*Rom,* p. 455), the Virgin Mary. The grateful cries of "'Bless you, madonna!'" resonate in this context with attributions of sainthood in Eliot's religion of humanity. Though she appears in many "frescoes" as redemptress—as Tito's good angel (*Rom,* p. 492), or as a priest-like figure who brings "the refreshment of bread and wine to Baldassarre" (*Rom,* p. 493)—none is so important as her appearance to Tessa as "the Holy Madonna" (*Rom,* p. 511). By treating with all the kindness of a sister the woman whom she has every cause to hate, Romola will become the redemptress of woman George Eliot thought the woman preacher could never be.

Romola first meets the contadina on a Florence street, where a group of Savonarola's young followers is badgering her to give up her sinful baubles. Tessa, like Bessy Cranage under Dinah's preaching, is overcome with awe and terror.

> Suddenly a gentle hand was laid on her arm, and
> a soft, wonderful voice, as if the Holy Madonna

were speaking, said, "Do not be afraid; no one shall harm you."

Tessa looked up and saw a lady in black, with a young heavenly face and loving hazel eyes. She had never seen any one like this lady before, and under other circumstances might have had awe-struck thoughts about her; but now everything else was overcome by the sense that loving protection was near her. (*Rom*, p. 511)

The role of this redemptress is to save women from terror, regardless of its source. She does not discover Tessa's relation to Tito immediately, but seems drawn to Tessa by providence operating on her compassion.

Even when the horror of Fra Luca's vision comes to pass, and Romola seeks oblivion by setting out to sea in a fisherman's small boat, it is her special duty to women that calls her back to fulfill her role as redemptress. Romola comes on shore near a village that has been stricken with the plague. The cries of a baby belonging to a Jewish family, whose other members died after having been expelled from the village, attracts Romola's attention, and she carries the child to the village to find assistance. When this striking woman carrying a child appears to a plague-weakened villager, she immediately believes her to be the Virgin Mary sent to save them. The local padre, a cowardly man, reacts likewise, and in part it is the authority this image confers upon Romola that enables her to enforce the priest's duty on him. With his help, Romola indeed becomes the redemptress of this village, nursing its inhabitants back to health. In gratitude, they accept her "son," the Jewish baby, into their village. This almost miraculous experience of human community convinces Romola of her continued duty in Florence, and she returns there to create a community of women with Tessa and Mona Brigida. All this Romola accomplishes almost silently.

Deeply suspicious of the language Savonarola's vision inspires, George Eliot guards her heroine's integrity by limiting her speech. Ultimately, the mad utterance of Camilla, the prophetess, and Savonarola's preaching may derive from the same source, a proposition the narrator describes as haunting the preacher.

by his fellow-men to all time" (*Rom,* p. 666), Eliot concludes of Savonarola. In his torture, she imagines his thought: "'I count as nothing: darkness encompasses me: yet the light I saw was the true light'" (*Rom,* p. 667).

Throughout this trial Romola waits for some inspiring word from her spiritual guide, but none comes. Instead she hears rumors: Savonarola requests that the Dominicans of San Marco pray for him, "'for God has withdrawn from me the spirit of prophecy'" (*Rom,* p. 668); he retracts his confession, committing himself to suffer for the truth; and finally, he is unable to uphold that commitment under torture. The great preacher never speaks on his own behalf as Romola hopes, vindicating himself with the words "'O people, I was innocent of deceit.'" But in the moment of his execution, Romola knows "that Savonarola's voice had passed into eternal silence" (*Rom,* p. 671).

Savonarola's voice has not passed into the void, but has transcended language by passing into the life of the redemptress, Romola, and thereby into history. That "eternal silence," Fra Luca's "Unseen Perfectness," is manifested in an enduring picture of human community. One can imagine the scene described in the Epilogue to *Romola* as George Eliot's fresco of the Holy Family. There she paints this peaceful scene.

> At one end of the room was an archway opening into a narrow inner room, hardly more than a recess, where the light fell from above on a small altar covered with fair white linen. Over the altar was a picture, discernible at the distance where the little party sat only as the small full-length portrait of a Dominican Brother . . . part of the floor was strewn with a confusion of flowers and green boughs, and among them sat a delicate blue-eyed girl of thirteen, tossing her long light-brown hair out of her eyes, as she made selections for the wreaths she was weaving, or looked up at her mother's work in the same kind, and told her how to do it with a little air of instruction. . . .
> Monna Brigida was asleep at this moment, in a straight-backed arm-chair, a couple of yards off. . . .

The other two figures were seated farther off, at
the wide doorway that opened on to the loggia.
Lillo . . . held a large book. . . . of Petrarch which
he kept open at one place, as if he were learning
something by heart.

Romola sat nearly opposite Lillo, but she was not
observing him. Her hands were crossed on her lap
and her eyes were fixed absently on the distant
mountains: she was evidently unconscious of anything around her. An eager life had left its marks
upon her: the finely-moulded cheek had sunk a
little, the golden crown was less massive; but there
was a placidity in Romola's face which had never belonged to it in youth. It is but once that we can know
our worst sorrows, and Romola had known them
while life was new. (*Rom*, p. 672)

That small party includes Tessa and her two children, Lillo and
Ninna, Monna Brigida, and their redemptress, Romola. This
woman has transcended the roles assigned to her by philosopher and preacher to fulfill the roles of husband, father,
teacher, provider, moral guide—in short, savior. Tito's scholarship became a means of dividing each against all, and
Savonarola's prophecy isolated him as the omniscient voice.
Whereas both modes of discourse established destructive relations of dominance, Romola invites other speakers into dialogue. Significantly, however, the final example of Romola's
domestic ministry shows her eliciting the voice of Tito's son.

"Mama Romola's" first two lines in the epilogue are questions
she asks of Lillo. Rather than answer his question "'What am I
to be?'" Romola responds with another question: "'What
should you like to be, Lillo?'" (*Rom*, p. 674). The guidance the
cynical Tito, or even the visionary Savonarola, might have offered, contrasts with Romola's "sermon," in which she turns
the boy's attention from his own desires to some wider goal.

"There are so many things wrong and difficult in
the world, that no man can be great—he can hardly
keep himself from wickedness—unless he gives up
thinking much about pleasure or rewards, and gets
strength to endure what is hard and painful. My fa-

ther had the greatness that belongs to integrity; he chose poverty and obscurity rather than falsehood. And there was Fra Girolamo—you know why I keep to-morrow sacred: *he* had the greatness which belongs to a life spent in struggling against powerful wrong, and in trying to raise men to the highest deeds they are capable of. And so, my Lillo, if you mean to act nobly and seek to know the best things God has put within reach of men, you must learn to fix your mind on that end, and not on what will happen to you because of it." (*Rom*, p. 674)

Romola would have Lillo be part of the tradition which included her father and Savonarola, but would have him renounce self, as she has done, to avoid their fate.

Romola's final role should be compared with that of Dinah Morris at the close of *Adam Bede*. Privately, Romola continues to encourage, exhort, rebuke, and catechize her spiritual charges as did the women preachers in their more intimate ministries. But unlike Dinah, she is the unchallenged head of this family of women and children. She rescues the innocent Tessa from abandonment, and saving her from the stigma of her true status as Tito's mistress, and she saves her children from the stigma of bastardy. Even Monna Brigida finds a safe home here, free from the fears and vanity which marked her life, she spends a peaceful old age. From each of these characters, Romola has drawn out her better self—she is the source of their power. What role did the preaching of Savonarola play in this? As Romola concludes, "'Perhaps I should never have learned love of him if he had not helped me when I was in great need'" (*Rom*, p. 676). His voice called her to a repentance, a renunciation of self, that empowered her action because it revealed her necessary role in an interdependent community. Romola succeeds where Savonarola failed because she never assumes the prophetic voice, the voice asserting absolute authority over its audience and a unique rather than universal vision. She is not Jeremiah, but a redeeming Madonna.

Even more significant is the role George Eliot as narrator has assumed in describing this scene. The novel's heroine virtually silenced, its orator, Tito, drowned, and its prophet, Savonarola, burned at the stake, the narrator alone remains to deliver this edifying message. She does so in restrained, unemphatic language, much as Dinah recounted her childhood memories of Wesley's preaching. This is showing as well as telling; the "Holy Family" is not only an aesthetic object but one of instruction, its iconography clearly comprehensible. The novel's conclusion might be taken out of a saint's life, or the biography of an "eminently pious woman," with its scene of domestic beatitude. George Eliot has achieved her own authoritative voice. Yet this voice seems to confirm an "extraordinary calling" rather than provide a strategy for empowering women's public voices. As that voice evolves in *Felix Holt,* its unfortunate consequences for women dramatically emerge.

Felix Holt: *George Eliot as Preacher of Patriarchy*

In its romance plotting and character development, *Felix Holt* completes the sexual division of social and discursive labor to which George Eliot increasingly resorted in her efforts to come to terms with the female preaching tradition. While she continues to attack some forms of patriarchal discourse, especially those employed in legal, political, and religious institutions, she defends the legitimacy of conventional gender roles cast in the rhetoric of religious humanism's mythology. The result is a conventional hero, Felix Holt, and heroine, Esther Lyon, the former domineering, rational, and vocal, the latter submissive, sentimental, and silent. At the same time, her narrator assumes a rather Miltonic mission to illuminate the providential course of history, and to justify the ways of men to women.

The novel that became *Felix Holt* may have begun as a politically far different work: a treatment of female marginality and silence, the tragedy of Mrs. Transome.[57] Mrs. Transome's story, a significant subplot in the completed novel, tells the dismal fate of a woman married to an imbecile, deserted by a cruel lover, and tyrannized over by their son, whose illegitimacy is a secret enforcing her isolation and silence. George Eliot suppressed this plot and muted its potential denunciation of patriarchy, turning instead to history and the election riots of 1832. This shift in focus cannot be construed as a displacement of feminist concerns onto class struggle as, for example, in

Charlotte Brontë's *Shirley.* The tragedy of Mrs. Transome
serves not as an indictment of female exploitation but as a cautionary tale, warning Esther of the desolation awaiting women
who transgress against the patriarchy, in search of pleasure,
power, or love.

Through Esther Lyon and Mrs. Transome, George Eliot ad-
monishes women for their inability to obtain and wield authority, and their propensity for being victimized or acting the fool.
Except for their ridiculous susceptibility to political rhetoric
and evangelical preaching, female characters play only a supporting role in Eliot's discussions of social reform, a departure
from her earlier attacks on institutions and attitudes which
served to enforce the oppression of women. In *Felix Holt* she
offers the heroine's renunciation of power and desire as
woman's salvation. The only authoritative "female" voice in this
novel is the narrator's, and she has become an evangelist of religious humanism, complete with that role's emphatic, oracular
rhetoric. This narrative returns us to the discursive politics
typical of Hannah More and Charlotte Elizabeth Tonna as
preachers of patriarchy.

Despite this shift in attitude towards women, George Eliot
loses none of her scorn for more obviously authoritarian forms
of rhetoric as they have been deployed by men: political, legal,
religious, and sexual/romantic. Skillfully transferring the
attack she made in *Romola* on the opportunistic, mercenary,
amoral practitioners of political rhetoric from the proscenium
stage of quattrocento Florence to the "parrot house" of provincial England, she accomplishes a devastating indictment of political discourse. While Tito Melema's crimes attain a villainous
grandeur, the machinations of his counterparts in *Felix Holt,*
the political agents Messrs. Putty and Johnson, appear despi-
cable for their banality as well as reprehensible for their unscrupulous intent. The occupation of political agent reveals in
the most cynical terms the reduction of the power of language
to mere commodity. Putty's protégé, Mr. Johnson, praises his
mentor's talent "for saving a candidate's money—does half the
work with his tongue" (*FH*, p. 281).

> He'll talk of anything, from the Areopagus, and
> that sort of thing down to the joke about "Where are

you going, Paddy?" . . . Putty understands these things. He has said to me, "Johnson, bear in mind there are two ways of speaking an audience will always like: one is, to tell them what they don't understand; and the other is, to tell them what they're used to." (*FH,* pp. 281–82)

Johnson continues by noting Putty's particular skill at manipulating women, who, like Eve, will then convince their unwitting husbands of the veracity of this tempter's message.

Such an indictment of a debased political discourse which treats the Areopagus and crude jokes as equal in value does not, however, incline Eliot to empathize with its victims. Instead, she adopts something of the Machiavellian cynicism her politicos display towards their audiences, sharing their contempt for the objects of their seduction, the polis. For the characters, it is impossible to participate in political discourse, even passively, and escape the taint of complicity. All are implicated: from Mr. Putty to the candidate Harold Transome (Mrs. Transome's son), to the electorate, even to Felix Holt himself.

Eliot applies an analogous argument to religious discourse, although she allows a greater degree of sympathy for its practitioners. Originally motivated by a desire to give expression to his fervor, Mr. Lyon, the dissenting minister, falls prey to the temptation to use his eloquence to achieve personal glory. As the descendent of Huguenots, Lyon is accustomed to the tyranny of an authoritative discourse, of the sort which drove his ancestors from their homeland. But he seems compelled to create an authoritative discourse of his own rather than be silent. Eliot describes him as a "zealous preacher, with whom copious speech was not a difficulty but a relief" (*FH,* p. 258). The lust for power with which religious discourse infects this otherwise generous, selfless man becomes clear when he contemplates the opportunity of debating his village's rector, the the Reverend Augustus Debarry. "It would be an argumentative luxury," he imagines, "to get into close quarters with him, and fight with a dialectic short-sword in the eyes of the Treby world" (*FH,* p. 259). Here zeal for God has been replaced by desire for rhetorical domination.

Interestingly, Eliot distinguishes between this rhetoric of

theological debate and the sermon, the language of the Spirit, revealing a persistent nostalgia for some form of human language that would communicate directly between the transcendent and the finite. Lyon contrasts the personal satisfaction of sophisticated debate with the uncertainty and irrationality of sermonizing. He thinks that

> [v]ice was essentially stupid—a deaf and eyeless monster, insusceptible to demonstration: the Spirit might work on it by unseen ways, and the unstudied sallies of sermons were often as the arrows which pierced and awakened the brutified conscience; but illuminated thought, finely-dividing speech, were the choicer weapons of the divine armoury, which whoso could wield must be careful not to leave idle. (*FH*, p. 259)

The irony of this passage belies Lyon's judgment: it is precisely his ability to act as a medium for a transcendent spirit that saves him from the scorn George Eliot heaps on the manipulators of the political discourse. However, though Lyon—and apparently, the narrator—associate this ability with the sermon, one can find no evidence in the novel that such sincerity in communication is achieved discursively, or even consciously. What in fact constitutes Lyon's heroism has to do with his unconscious obedience to the transcendent spirit of history, not to his homiletic skills.

In opposition to the discourses of politics and religion, Eliot, like Carlyle, posits the force of history, which transcends reason and language, and escapes control by any discourse. The attempt to contain this force within language is both futile and self-defeating—a sin against "Nature." Harold Transome attempts precisely that, and his failure to avoid his own past and the destiny dictated by its consequences, by means of Johnson's rhetorical skill, reveals the ineluctability of history. "At present," the narrator remarks as Transome launches his campaign,

> it seems to me that the . . . illusion lay with Harold Transome, who was trusting in his own skill to shape the success of his own morrows, ignorant of what

many yesterdays had determined for him beforehand. *(FH,* p. 277)

Humans do not control history; instead, like the evangelicals'
God, history works mysteriouly through human agents. When
Lyon attempts to influence the candidate Harold Transome to
behave ethically, the narrator defends his unspoken intention
rather than his action.

> If a cynical sprite were present, riding on one of the
> motes in that dusty room, he may have made him-
> self merry at the illusions of the little minister who
> brought so much conscience to bear on the produc-
> tion of so slight an effect. I confess to smiling
> myself, being skeptical as to the effect of ardent
> appeals and nice distinctions on gentlemen who are
> got up and out, as candidates in the style of the
> period; but I never smiled at Mr Lyon's trustful en-
> ergy without falling into penitence and veneration
> immediately after. For what we call illusions are of-
> ten, in truth, a wider vision of past and present
> realities—a willing movement of a man's soul with
> the larger sweep of the world's forces—a movement
> towards a more assured end than the chances of a
> single life. *(FH,* p. 276)

The attitude of this narrator resembles that of the traveler who
observed Dinah Morris's field preaching. He credited Dinah
with the effect, at least, of supernatural vision, and was en-
thralled by the transcendent quality of her presence, viz. both
her appearance and the musical quality of her speech. Like the
narrator of this passage, he repented of his original cynicism,
but through him Eliot also expressed her skepticism regarding
the efficacy of a patriarchal discourse. Neither the doctrine of
Dinah's sermon nor the argument of Lyon's "brief writing"
possesses more than illusory power.

Instead, the heroism of both characters lies in actions far
from their conscious goals, and therefore, their egos. As the
narrator continues:

> We see human heroism broken into units; and say,
> this unit did little—might as well not have been. But

in this way we might break up a great army into
units; in this way we might break the sunlight into
fragments, and think that this and the other might
be cheaply parted with. Let us rather raise a monument to the soldiers whose brave hearts only kept
the ranks unbroken, and met death—a monument
to the faithful who were not famous, and who are
precious as the continuity of the sunbeams is precious, though some of them fall unseen on barren-
ness. (*FH*, pp. 276–77)

This is the standard Carlylean stance towards history: the
unconscious contributions of the sort of people celebrated in
Gray's churchyard elegy constitute heroism as much as those of
the acknowledged great men. Doubtless many unrecognized
women preachers and writers so consoled themselves. However, whereas Carlyle never questions the ability of history's
great men to embody the spirit of the age, Eliot comes increasingly to deny this possibility. Wesley looms behind Dinah as the
charismatic hero of a bygone age, and Savonarola, though he
dies a martyr's death, effects a permanent change in the lives of
individuals and therefore in the course of history. Neither man
is truly silenced. But beginning with *Felix Holt*, no such presence exists in George Eliot's novels (though Daniel Deronda
revives its promise, if not its actuality). The reason for this
depletion lies in the dilemma Eliot faces when she simultaneously confronts the oppressive power of authoritative
discourse and yet rejects the possibility or desirability of an
alternative discourse that would liberate marginal voices, especially those of silenced females. By producing a silenced hero
and heroine in *Felix Holt*, George Eliot retains the preacher's
role for herself. It is no coincidence that, at the end of her
career, she would have dispensed with fiction altogether in
Impressions of Theophrastus Such, a collection of meditative essays
in which she could address herself to the ills of her world by
speaking in her own distinctive voice.

Again, the narrator of *Felix Holt* achieves discursive pre-
eminence by leading the characters through false, fractious
rhetorical exercises towards a wise silence attained once
they "discover" their places in an organic social system. That

organicism depends on a stable gender hierarchy, thematized in the novel's romance plot. The heterosexual domestic unit, which provides the melancholy close of *Adam Bede,* and which is displaced onto Romola's "family" after the deaths of Bardo, Baldassare, Tito, and Savonarola, becomes the symbol of political harmony as the marriage of Christ and the church represents the happy ending of time.

As the prophet of such a providential scheme, Eliot's narrator brooks no rival. Felix Holt, who shares with Dinah Morris both reformist zeal and rhetorical powers, must, like Dinah, be silenced. By contrast with Tito Melema and Savonarola, who do not survive their contests with Eliot's narrator, Felix must learn the futility of discursive dominance in time to take up his place in the social hierarchy. George Eliot subjects this character to criticism for his participation in political discourse as Dinah was criticized as a public evangelist. When Holt's convictions draw him into a public debate, ego immediately begins to overcome sympathy, and he distorts his message as Rufus Lyon had his.

Felix's speech to the Treby Magna crowd begins in a fashion much like those of the women preachers and fictional characters we have been examining. After a trades-union speaker has tried to stir up the working-class members of his audience to support electoral reform as a panacea for their problems, the irate Felix spontaneously expresses his indignation. At first, he simply blurts out an objection. Soon, however, he accepts an invitation that no female would have received from a male rival: to address the crowd himself. His unconscious charisma as a speaker is as immediately apparent as Dinah's had been. Without being asked, he steps up onto the stone from which the trades-union man had been speaking, and removes his cap "by instinctive prompting that always led him to speak uncovered" (*FH,* p. 398).[58]

This guileless sincerity is enhanced by Felix's physical appearance:

> The effect of his figure against the stone back-
> ground was unlike that of the previous speaker. He
> was considerably taller, his head and neck were
> more massive, and the expression of his mouth and

eyes was something very different from the mere
acuteness and rather hard-lipped antagonism of the
trades-union man. Felix Holt's face had the look of
the habitual meditative abstraction from objects of
mere personal vanity or desire, which is the peculiar
stamp of culture, and makes a roughly-cut face
worthy to be called "the human face divine." (*FH*,
p. 398).

Thus, before Felix begins to speak, Eliot attributes to him the
same charismatic presence possessed by Dinah. However, unlike Dinah or the trades-union man, Felix does not appear to be
genuinely a marginal character. He is a cultured male; even his
lower-class status is mitigated by his trade: he is not a mere
wage laborer. Spiritual gifts would be superfluous additions to
the secular gifts he already possesses. Consequently, "Felix at
once [draws] the attention of persons comparatively at a distance" (*FH*, p. 399), as well as those who had already been attending to the previous speaker.

Nevertheless, his speech, which even employs some of
Dinah's most effective strategies—identification with his audience, story-telling, plain, sometimes colloquial diction—fails
to effect any conversions. Instead, his audience, including
many who would be his political foes, is "attracted by Felix
Holt's vibrating voice" (*FH*, p. 400), and many abandon him after they perceive that they have heard the best of his speech: a
joke at the expense of Transome's agent, Johnson. Felix's
speech serves only to sully the value of his beliefs and to an extent his own integrity. He has supplied his "well-dressed
hearers" with an anecdote for dinner conversation, but far
more damning is the opportunity he has given his audience to
label his message according to categories of political discourse.
"'That tremendous fellow . . .'" one of his listeners declares,
"'is some red-hot Radical demagogue, and Johnson has offended him, I suppose; else he wouldn't have turned in that
way on a man of their own party'" (*FH*, p. 403). Translating
one's inner voices into public speech inevitably results in reductive misinterpretations. Such speech may briefly fascinate an
audience, as Dinah entranced the traveler with her sincerity,
but it will not convert them. This is a stiff-necked generation,

George Eliot seems to say, which refuses to comprehend its prophets. "There is hardly any mental misery worse than that of having our own serious phrases, our own rooted beliefs, caricatured by a charlatan or a hireling" (*FH*, p. 226), the narrator remarks. Such is the fate of the rejected prophet. The act of speech-making has caused Felix to forfeit the disinterested status conferred on him by the transcendent value of culture in the same way unrestrained rhetoric might cause George Eliot to be labeled as a "Silly Lady Novelist."

Though Eliot in no way undercuts the content of Felix's speech, as she had Dinah's sermon, her criticism of its medium—the discourse itself—is far stronger. She refrained from attacking the source of Dinah's preaching, divine inspiration, because it was necessary leverage in her provisional argument in favor of woman's independence from the roles of wife and mother. Felix's indignation, the same inspiration he shares with a host of preachers, real and fictional, Eliot characterizes as a masculine desire for personal domination. "In spite of his cooling meditations an hour ago," the narrator comments in the middle of Felix's speech, "his pulse was getting quickened by indignation and the desire to crush what he hated was likely to vent itself in articulation" (*FH*, p. 402). This is the conclusion about public speech suggested in *Adam Bede* and offered explicitly at the point of Savonarola's death in *Romola*. In the former novel, George Eliot presents the possibility that alternatives exist to authoritarian discourses; in *Romola*, the female icon silently offers redemption. In both, there is a profound anxiety about expressing one's "inner voices" in "letters of flame." With *Felix Holt*, George Eliot eliminates the option of a nonauthoritarian discourse for her characters, resorting instead to gender roles in a humanist myth of history that conceal their ideological origins.

The stifling quality of woman's role in this scheme of history is clear if one compares Esther with Margaret Hale in *North and South*. As frustrating as Margaret's final silence is, it is not freighted with positive universal or mythological significance. Her renunciation of power and speech satisfies nothing more than the conventions of the romance plot. No transcendent force demands her silence, no destiny is fulfilled by it. Esther's submission, on the other hand, takes on a quasi-divine status, her marriage representing obedience to destiny, and her vow being one of silence.

Namesake of the queen who successfully pleaded the Israelites' cause before the Persian king, that favorite subject of biographical sketches by evangelical women writers, this English Esther should possess great charisma and oratorical power. George Eliot's "sweet-voiced Queen Esther" (*FH*, p. 160) of Malthouse Yard shares more than a name with the biblical queen. She too is an orphan brought from her native land (in this case France), to be raised by a foster father. As Queen Esther pled for her people, she too will plead before the law of the land to save an innocent man, Felix Holt, from execution for murder; only this man will rule over her as her husband. The secular sainthood George Eliot confers on her character changes utterly the nature of her power.

Evangelical conversion had afforded women a short-lived freedom from conventional gender roles, enabling them to gain access to a sphere from which they had been hitherto excluded. In secularizing the evangelical conversion model, George Eliot shows her heroine repenting of unwomanly desires for power, sex, adventure, and turning not to Christianity but to the transcendent values of a natural social order. She must relinquish ego in favor of sympathy. This humanistic counterpart of religious conversion, though it avoids some of the pitfalls of orthodox Christian doctrine, still mystified the elevation of conventional gender roles to universals by locating its ideal in the gender-bound concept of "human." We can easily recognize that Esther's vision of the world beyond her ego reveals not "Spirit," or history but "Nature," from which those oppressive conventions, "natural duties," derive. Esther, like other female characters in the novel, has no direct influence on political events. The political forces with which Felix acquaints Esther merely enable her to attain some fraction of the broader, transcendent vision of history necessary to the heroine. In the history of Esther, the bildungsroman plot, these events do play a significant role. But the goal of this bildungsroman is to create a woman who accepts her destiny as heroine, the silent helpmeet of the hero.

Esther's progress towards the silence of ideal womanhood can be charted by reflections she makes on heroism and language, beginning when Felix challenges her taste for Byron's poetry, and culminating in her marriage to the hero. In their first encounter, Felix, who has come to visit Rufus Lyon, startles Esther with his blunt speech. The narrator's description of Felix's "brusque openness that implied the absence of any personal intention" (*FH,* p. 149) reminds the reader that his rhetoric is the near relative of the evangelical sincerity of Dinah Morris's speech. Esther's taste has been so corrupted by the Romantic literature represented by Byron's poetry that rather than admiring Felix's plain speech, as Romola did Savonarola's, she finds him merely rude. This conflict in taste and its moral implications becomes obvious when Felix inadvertently upsets Esther's workbasket and, finding among its contents a volume of Byron's poetry, declares with disgust, "'What! do you stuff your memory with Byron, Miss Lyon?'" (*FH,* p. 150). Undeterred by Esther's expression of admiration of Byron, Felix continues like a preacher, "holding the book open in the air":

> "A misanthropic debauchee . . . whose notion of a hero was that he should disorder his stomach and despise mankind. His corsairs and renegades, his Alps and Manfreds, are the most paltry puppets that were ever pulled by the strings of pride." (*FH,* p. 151)

The narrator concurs with Felix's assessment of Byron, snidely remarking that at one point his books "embodied the faith and ritual of many young ladies and gentlemen" (*FH,* p. 151). But unlike Carlyle, whose Teufelsdröckh enjoins us "'close thy Byron'" so as to "open thy Goethe,'" George Eliot turns this exchange into an attack on Esther's verbal power. Though Esther can hold her own in a war of words with Felix, and Felix is undoubtedly rude, nevertheless his "licence in . . . language" (*FH,* p. 155) produces a feeling of "great enlargement" in Rufus Lyon, while Esther's wit earns her a rebuke from her father ("'Esther, my dear . . . let not your playfulness betray you into disrespect'" [*FH,* p. 153]). Indeed, it is her wit that provokes Felix's desire to master her: "'I should like to come and scold her every day, and make her cry and cut her fine hair off'" (*FH,* p. 154). This is meant as a sure clue to the reader that

Felix "loves" Esther, though at this point he is only conscious of his disgust at trivial-minded girls who would distract him from his vocation.

This initial encounter between hero and heroine makes an interesting contrast to that between Margaret and Thornton in *North and South*. Despite his own attempts to reduce Margaret's power, Thornton's first response is one of admiration. He is clearly the more limited character of that pair. Esther's power, by way of contrast, seems almost wholly contingent on direction from male characters. Its only appropriate outlet is in the duties of daughter, wife, and mother. The first sign that Felix has begun to dominate and domesticate Esther comes when she acknowledges her failure as a daughter. Shocked into sympathy by the distraught appearance of Rufus Lyon when he returns home after learning of Esther's legal claim to the Transome estates through her natural father, Esther repents of her selfishness and assumes the daughter's duty of ministering to Lyon: serving his porridge, making him comfortable, offering to sit up with him. Lyon does not inform Esther of the cause of his sorrow, but is moved to exclaim, "'you have become the image of your mother to-night'" (*FH*, p. 245), thus marking Esther's first step towards realizing her vocation.

The narrator's comments on the scene unmistakably identify it as a kind of conversion:

> When Esther was lying down that night, she felt as if the little incidents between herself and her father on this Sunday had made an epoch. Very slight words and deeds may have a sacramental efficacy, if we can cast our self-love behind us, in order to say or do them. And it has been well believed through many ages that the beginning of compunction is the beginning of a new life; that the mind which sees itself blameless may be called dead in trespasses—in trespasses on the love of others, in trespasses on their weakness, in trespasses on all those great claims which are the image of our own need. (*FH*, p. 246)

This passage resonates with rhetorically effective evangelical language: "sacramental efficacy," "cast . . . behind us," "believed through the ages," "new life," and "trespasses." Esther is Felix's—and George Eliot's—potential convert to humanism. The narrator continues by remarking that Esther "persisted in assuring herself that she was not bending to any criticism from Felix" (*FH,* p. 246), yet making clear that indeed she is.

By contrast to Esther's conversion, Margaret Hale overcomes her prejudice against Thornton and defends him because that action is consistent with principles she already holds. She consequently is justified in deeply resenting the perception that desire motivates her defense. Margaret thus enjoys an autonomy George Eliot denies Esther. Granted, Margaret's authority derives from the patriarchal structure itself: she owes her principles to her minister father, not to another woman or her own authority. Esther has accepted authority too, but of the wrong kind, taking as her ideals the heroes and heroines of Byronic romance, a mistake that could lead her to reenact Mrs. Transome's tragic role. Eliot is not concerned that this literary ideology might exploit women; instead, she perceives it as a threat to the patriarchal structure of society, as Mrs. Transome's adultery and its "illegitimate" offspring make obvious. It is to a version of this very structure that Esther is being converted.

Felix calls Esther not to heroism but to "heroinism" in his patriarchal plot. For him, she becomes an iconic representation of feminine virtue. When he declares that she is beautiful, he looks at her "very much as a reverential Protestant might look at a picture of the Virgin, with a devoutness suggested by the type rather than the image" (*FH,* p. 364). The narrator's comment aligns Esther with Romola, but whereas the reader reveres a final picture of that character in her virginal self-sufficiency (with the image of Savonarola fixed in its own shrine), Esther's virgin status is symbolic only: a "type" which inspires men. To suit herself to that patriarchal function, she must learn to construct her own identity symbolically. "Her life," Esther muses,

> was a heap of fragments, and so were her thoughts: some great energy was needed to bind them together. Esther was beginning to lose her complacency at her own wit and criticism; to lose the sense

of superiority in an awakening need for reliance on
one whose vision was wider, whose nature was purer
and stronger than her own. (*FH*, p. 264)

Felix's vision of Esther may include political and historical
forces she has ignored; nevertheless, it is elevated to the status
of a universal imperative despite the fact that it remains limited
by the perspective of his gender. Eliot chooses not to interrogate these limitations.

Esther triumphs over false authority when she renounces
the temptation to realize her fantasies about becoming the
mistress of Transome Court, a somewhat hollow victory as it
signals only the exchange of aristocratic "decadence" for bourgeois domesticity. However, her choice is represented according to the model of an evangelical calling, in which worldly law
is opposed to the gifts of the spirit, in particular, the gift of prophetic speech. When it comes to light that Esther has a legal
claim to Transome Court, her romantic dreams lie within her
reach. So too does Harold Transome, with his stereotypical villain's desire to possess a beautiful woman and enhance his own
power. Esther's progressive disillusionment with Harold and
her life at Transome Court is primarily rendered in literary
terms that deceptively suggest a mastery of language and life.
When Harold finds her contemplating a portrait of a former
mistress of Transome Court, he is pleased with the aesthetic
effect: "'Don't move, pray'" he tells her; "'you look as if you
were standing for your own portrait'" (*FH*, p. 498). Esther in-
stinctively resists being co-opted into the traditions of "My Last
Duchess," responding with a laugh, "'that fair Lady Betty looks
as if she had been drilled into that posture, and had not will
enough of her own ever to move again unless she had a little
push given to her'" (*FH*, p. 498). We are to understand that
Felix has given Esther that push to escape the confinement of
artifice in order to experience life, to take her destiny into her
own hands. "Esther found it impossible to read in these days"
the narrator tell us; "her life was a book which she seemed herself to be constructing—trying to make character clear before
her, and looking into the ways of destiny" (*FH*, p. 498). Though
effacing the patriarchal origins of her own conception of history and morals, George Eliot vigorously attacks the obvious
exploitation of women as objects of lust and greed.

Esther's noble-sounding reflection on the incompatibility of poetry and life conceals more significant contradictions. Just at the point where Esther might achieve authorship of her own identity and acquire her own prophetic vocation, she must renounce her power and submit to "the ways of destiny," or less poetically, the gender role assigned her in history. She merely chooses between two male-authored plots, one overtly exploitive, the other more subtly so.

Eliot describes Esther's rejection of Harold (the gift of the law) in sublime terms, suggesting the spiritual nature of her alteration:

> [Esther] had begun to feel more profoundly that in accepting Harold Transome she left the high mountain air, the passionate serenity of perfect love forever behind her, and must adjust her wishes to a life of middling delights, overhung with the languorous haziness of motiveless ease, where poetry was only literature, and the fine ideas had to be taken down from the shelves of the library when her husband's back was turned. (*FH*, p. 547)

Surely the reader is pleased to witness Esther's rejection of the merely decorative. Still, even though Eliot implies that this new-found taste for sublimity will enable Esther to become a heroine, that status is limited by a patriarchal definition of what constitutes the sublime: her taste is reformed, her progress complete, as soon as she perceives Felix as her sublime hero.

The language with which Eliot treats this transformation precludes irony. To see Felix as hero means to experience transcendent truth. Commenting on Esther's contemplation of Felix, she writes:

> It is terrible—the keen bright eye of a woman when it has once been turned with admiration on what is severely true. . . . (*FH*, p. 529)

What Esther has just seen is not God, or the good, but the superiority of Felix Holt to Harold Transome, and in so doing, has discovered her own essence.

The power of this myth of the heroine to silence women becomes clear when the heroine is at last moved to speak. The scene in which Esther speaks on behalf of Felix, on trial for a murder committed during an election riot, follows the pattern of female speech we have encountered throughout this study. In a moment of crisis, a woman is overcome by some transcendent force—be it God, virtue, love—to act as its medium. George Eliot begins building the dramatic tension which will culminate in Esther's testimony with what can only be described as a vision. Before the trial, Harold remarks to Esther about Felix's eccentricity, whereupon she spontaneously leaps to his defense:

> "If it is eccentricity to be very much better than other men, he is certainly eccentric; and fanatical too, if it is fanatical to renounce all small selfish motives for the sake of a great unselfish one. I never before knew what nobleness of character really was before I knew Felix Holt!"
>
> It seemed to Esther as if, in the excitement of this moment, her own words were bringing her a clearer revelation. . . .
>
> Esther at that moment looked perfectly beautiful, with an expression which Harold had never hitherto seen. All the confusion which had depended on personal feeling had given way before the sense that she had to speak the truth about the man whom she felt to be admirable. (*FH*, p. 537)

This ecstatic vision of Felix's transcendent worth provides Esther with her inspiration and vocation. "'This is not like love,'" Harold thinks to himself, and it comes as no surprise that this visionary sympathy lies outside his experience with women. But it is the myth of redemptive romantic love as the moving force of human history that comes to replace inspired speech as the medium of women's empowerment in George Eliot's fiction.

In her description of Esther's testimony, the culmination of that character's verbal power, one can detect Eliot's persistent resentment over the failure of the preaching voice. She begins by undercutting the validity of all testimony: "man cannot be defined as an evidence-giving animal" (*FH*, p. 563), tempted as he is by "private motive," comments the narrator. The context for Esther's speech will be the same pharisaical legal discourse which enslaved Janet Dempster and condemned Hetty Sorrel and Savonarola; it is tainted by the degrading political discourse of Tito Melema and Mr. Putty. The testimony against Felix is damning, and though the narrator attributes to Felix "the sublime delight of truthful speech" in delivering his defense, he manages only to cheer himself without influencing his judges. From all indications, Harold Transome is correct in deeming Felix's brilliant peroration an abysmal mistake. The jury will misunderstand it and the judge resent it, he tells Esther, and his assessment is borne out. For his part, Harold manages only slightly better in his attempt to impress the judge and jury, and when the questioning turns to his own political activities, Harold's temper gets the better of his oratory. As in the trial scenes in Eliot's earlier novels, testimony which might reveal the ambiguous complexities of reality proves to be irrelevant to the legal proceedings, a judgment having been reached even before the trial has begun. With a sinking sense of the futility of this word game as a means for discovering the truth, Esther is inspired to speak.

The description of Esther's thoughts leading up to this decision reveals the extent of the novel's reworking of the evangelical call:

> When a woman feels purely and nobly, that ardour of hers which breaks through formulas too rigorously urged on men by daily practical needs, makes one of her most precious influences: she is the added impulse that shatters the stiffening crust of cautious experience. Her inspired ignorance gives a sublimity to actions so incongruously simple that otherwise they would make men smile. Some of that ardour which has flashed out and illuminated all poetry and history was burning to-day in the bosom of sweet Esther Lyon. (*FH*, p. 571)

Unfortunately, despite Eliot's clear attempt to celebrate women's contributions to the pursuit of truth under the influence of a transcendent power, one might also read this passage as suggesting that, thanks to her own marginality, ignorance, and impracticality, a woman can offer an original perspective.

Recalling Eliot's own cutting remarks in "Silly Novels" on the inspiration of idiots who have only their passionate intensity to recommend them, the reliability of this perspective seems dubious. Nevertheless, the narrator confers upon such inspiration the sublimity of great poetry and epic actions—the same which Eliot's preaching foremothers claimed. Yet at the same time, this revision of the model of inspiration excludes the possibility that it could disguise the fact that women spoke consciously, of their own volition, with considerable preparation and forethought, and frequently, like Felix, out of a sense of indignation and frustration.

Superficially, Esther's testimony itself follows the model of the female witnesses in earlier fictions by Tonna and Gaskell. She is unselfconscious of her own beauty as well as of the chance that she might look ridiculous. Her speech is sincere and plain: "her clear voice sounded as it might have done if she had been making a confession of faith" (*FH*, p. 572), and in a sense, she is. She testifies to the nobility of Felix's sentiments, concluding with her confession of faith in Felix: "'he could never have had any intention that was not brave and good'" (*FH*, p. 573). Esther's audience is entranced by her "naive and beautiful" action. She has been transformed from a beautiful "toy or ornament" (*FH*, p. 573) by serving as the medium for some transcedent force. "Some hand had touched the chords, and there came forth music that brought tears" (*FH*, p. 573). And, still true to the earlier model, the "acting out of that strong impulse . . . exhaust[s] her energy" (*FH*, p. 573), so that Esther returns to her place in a daze.

Yet despite the narrator's efforts to extol Esther's action, the content of her testimony signifies little in terms of the verdict she meant to influence. Rather, it is the essentially chivalrous desire to please a "'modest, brave, beautiful woman'" (*FH*, p. 576) like Esther that moves a man like Sir Maximus Debarry to exert his influence on Felix's behalf. As Harold later tells Esther, "'I think your speaking for him helped a great deal. You made all the men wish what you wished'" (*FH*, p. 589). This seems a rather sad anticlimax to so "sublime" a speech. Esther, the "essentially feminine" character, has been robbed of her voice to become an icon whose power depends wholly on her status as an object of desire. Woman is either the medium of a quasi-divine redemptive force, or she is a vessel of sexual power that makes men willing to relinquish their political power.

At the same time, Eliot's development of the novel's climax and closure obscures what may in fact constitute a genuine act of heroism on Esther's part. Esther's dramatic testimony at the trial seems to lead almost without interruption to her union with Felix: "'I am weak,'" she confesses to Felix in her final dialogue, "'my husband must be greater and nobler than I am'" (*FH,* p. 603). The utopian scene of Esther's future provided in the epilogue, which begins with her marriage and ends with the information that she has borne her husband "a young Felix," thus ensuring the continuation of the patriarchy, confirms the wisdom of the heroine's submission to destiny. "I will only say that Esther has never repented," the narrator concludes. However, in the penultimate chapter, George Eliot returns to the tragedy of Mrs. Transome. The conclusion of this plot deals one last blow to the adulteress's attempt to subvert patriarchy. As ineluctable as the force of history, with which it is perhaps synonymous, patriarchal authority reasserts itself. When the lawyer Jermyn, the father of the illegitimate child, returns to the world of Transome Court, it is to destroy both mother and child. Mrs. Transome allowed herself to become his victim by failing to renounce her desires as Esther has done. Unknowingly, Harold too has sold his soul to this incarnation of self-interest and exploitation by adopting Jermyn's own unscrupulous behavior, thereby following in his father's footsteps.

Esther alone has the power to rescue Mrs. Transome from despair and restore the son to his mother. Isolated from her husband, her former lover, and now her son, Mrs. Transome still remains impenitent, absorbed by self-pity and frustration. Then she thinks of Esther.

> The proud woman yearned for the caressing pity that must dwell in that young bosom. . . . She had never yet in her life asked for compassion—had never thrown herself in faith on an unproffered love. . . . And she might have gone on pacing the corridor like an uneasy spirit without a goal, if

Esther's thought, leaping towards her, had not
saved her from the need to ask admission. . . . (*FH,*
p. 596)

Like the Reverend Tryan in "Janet's Repentance," Esther immediately intuits Mrs. Transome's need and her sympathy
goes out to her. But no implicit vindication of Mrs. Transome's
rebellion can be found in the ensuing exchange, a significant
contrast to the effect of Hetty's confession to Dinah, or Tessa's
naive reliance on Romola.

Rather, Esther's missionary role apparently requires that she
justify the ways of men to women. When Mrs. Transome tells
Esther that all men are "selfish and cruel," and that all they
"care for is their own pleasure and their own pride," her words
fall on Esther "with a painful jar." "Not at all," she replies (*FH,*
p. 597). Esther's sympathy is tinged with horror as she contemplates "the dreary waste of years empty of sweet trust and affection" (*FH,* p. 597) suggested by Mrs. Transome's bitterness
and Esther's vague understanding of her past. Nevertheless,
she tends to her with a daughter's tenderness, and exerts her
sexual power over Harold in order to restore the son's affection
to his mother.

Esther tells Harold that she loves Felix, renounces her claim
to the Transome estates, and wishes "to go back to her father"
(*FH,* p. 599). Clearly, Esther relinquishes wealth in exchange
for Felix and her place in the patriarchy: she returns to her father. Yet she has also told Harold that she "'would bear a great
deal of unhappiness to save [Mrs. Transome] from having any
more'" (*FH,* p. 598). What Mrs. Transome most desires is for
Esther to become her daughter-in-law. Although Esther cannot redeem the tainted world of Transome Court according to
the law, by marrying Harold, her renunciation of her claim (the
sign of Esther's own spiritual redemption) reestablishes Mrs.
Transome as mistress of Transome Court and guarantees that
this surrogate mother will not be further exiled.

In so doing, Esther enacts a variation on the biblical story of
Esther. The ancient Esther reclaimed her natural heritage to
save her people from the nation that had made her queen. The
English Esther renounces a claim passed to her through the
natural patriarchal line in order to save a member of her

people—the female sex—who had rebelled against patriarchal control. Having acted the part of angel of mercy, Esther
is then free to join Felix as his heroine.

Even if we grant the possibility that Esther acts heroically
with respect to Mrs. Transome, it cannot be denied that her
power is far more limited by patriarchy than any previous
George Eliot heroine considered here.[59] Further, the preaching voice itself becomes irrelevant to social reform. Felix, who
assumed the preacher's role in this novel, retires, like Esther, to
quiet domesticity, silenced as Dinah was by the law, but with no
hint that he will continue to carry out his mission by subversion.
The myth of transcendent historical forces—silent, ineluctable
patriarchy—overwhelms the individual voice.

When John Blackwood called Felix Holt out of retirement in
November 1867 to address the working class in the pages of his
magazine, George Eliot complied against the objections of
Lewes. Did her mentor fear the revival of this reforming voice?
Did she long for history to vindicate her where words seemed
to fail? Her "Address to Working Men," published in January
1868, certainly suggests that the economically and politically
disenfranchised ought to bide their time. "The nature of things
in this world has been determined for us beforehand" (*FH*,
p. 617), George Eliot wrote in Felix's voice. The real struggle is
against madness, as it was for Janet, Dinah, Romola, and Mrs.
Transome.

> Let us, I say, show that our spirits are too strong to
> be driven mad, but can keep that sober determina
> tion which alone gives mastery over the adaptation
> of means. (*FH*, p. 619)

This counsel has great poignancy when applied to the
struggles of women to author politically effective discourses.
When George Eliot asks in the preface to *Middlemarch*, where
are the St. Theresas of yesteryear? she seems to question the
very historical forces in which she had placed her faith. Why
must she denigrate her own authoritative voice as sounding
like one speaking "from a campstool in a parrot house"? "'You
are a poem,'" Will declares to Dorothea. For all the poetry
in Dorothea's character—or Esther's, Romola's, Dinah's, or
George Eliot's—nothing authorizes their voices. Dorothea is

condemned to play the muse and end in silent obscurity. St. Theresa's daughters abounded among Eliot's contemporaries. Was not Florence Nightingale, or Elizabeth Fry, the equal of a St. Theresa? Their absence from Eliot's fiction suggests that her ultimate acquiescence to a patriarchal mythology could undermine their voices as surely as George Benson or Jabez Bunting had silenced Elizabeth Hurrel.

When George Eliot turns to Zionism as her theme in *Daniel Deronda,* she shows historical forces slowly moving to restore to power through a modern messiah a people whose disenfranchisement is ancient. The restoration she imagines is, of course, that of an ancient patriarchy, and if Mirah is any indication, one in which women would continue to play their mythic role. It is as if *Felix Holt* had put to rest the possibility that preaching discourse would ever bring about a reader's repentance, but that the novelist's extraordinary calling remained to bear witness to the mysterious movements of history, and to maintain faith in their benevolence.

As the fortuitous union of evangelical spirituality, political reform, and romantic poetics, which marked the period of religious revival in England, gave way in the later decades of the century to religious humanism, aestheticism, and mythologizing, preaching discourse lost much of its potential to empower the disenfranchised. The dominant discourse of Modernism eschewed social criticism which aimed at its reader's repentance, replacing it with patriarchal modes of "culture" and "tradition," not unlike those resisted by Hannah More, Charlotte Elizabeth Tonna, and Elizabeth Gaskell. George Eliot's career testifies to this transition, both resisting it and hastening its coming— creating the most memorable woman preacher in fiction, yet also preventing the creation of a better.

Afterword

"Here I would stop," wrote Virginia Woolf in *A Room of One's Own* (1929),

> but the pressure of convention decrees that every speech must end with a peroration. And a peroration addressed to women should have something, you will agree, particularly exalting and ennobling about it. I should implore you to remember your responsibilities, to be higher, more spiritual; I should remind you how much depends upon you, and what an influence you can exert upon the future. But those exhortations can safely, I think, be left to the other sex, who will put them, and indeed have put them, with far greater eloquence than I can encompass. When I rummage in my own mind I find no noble sentiments about being companions and equals and influencing the world to higher ends. I find myself saying briefly and prosaically that it is much more important to be oneself than anything else. Do not dream of influencing other people, I would say, if I knew how to make things sound exalted. Think of things in themselves.[1]

Is this a highly self-conscious twentieth-century Mary Bosanquet writing to the single women of the Methodist Society? Or perhaps Sarah Crosby reincarnated in 1929, remembering Wesley's advice to her back in 1761 that she should "nakedly tell . . . what is in [her] heart"? Now she will say "briefly and prosaically" what is on her mind. The ironic treatment Virginia Woolf gives the woman preacher's voice testifies to its persistent power. Over a century and a half after the first Methodist women preachers "addressed [themselves] to women" seeking to exalt, ennoble, and empower them, and eighty years after Gaskell came to the realization in her work on *The Life of Charlotte Brontë* that "it is much more important to be oneself than anything else," Virginia Woolf still had to work to distance herself from the preacher's voice. This very passage, with its dialogic relation to the reader, its disingenuous claims of inadequacy, its anxious suggestions that women rid their language of heroic rhetoric and their thought of romantic ideals, shows that the motifs and strategies of the preaching tradition remained alive in women's writing. In mocking the tradition, Woolf reveals her indebtedness to it.

On the basis of *A Room of One's Own*, Virginia Woolf has been seen as taking George Eliot as her principal precursor. This may be true in a way Woolf might not have anticipated, for, like Eliot, she became an ambiguous preacher of a patriarchy—in her case, of the myths of Modernism. Woolf castigated the women writers of the nineteenth century for having allowed overt complaints against patriarchal control of discourse to enter into their fiction. However, Modernism did not sweep away the source of such complaints. Its discourse merely resorted to new forms by which to disguise its misogyny. As Hannah More had warned a century earlier, pagan and secular myths claimed authority without offering accessibility as Christian scripture did. The woman writing these myths became like George Eliot's Mirah: a voice singing a song that was not her own.

For a woman writer of the nineteenth century who genuinely swerved from the preaching tradition, we could turn to Gaskell's subject, Charlotte Brontë, on whom Woolf heaps considerable abuse in *A Room of One's Own*. In her *Life of Charlotte Brontë*, Gaskell quotes Brontë's letter to George Henry Lewes, responding to his review of her social-problem novel *Shirley*. Brontë complains, not about Lewes's criticisms of the novel, but of his consideration of her as a woman writer rather than as a writer.

> I will tell you why I was so hurt by that review in the
> "Edinburgh"; not because its criticism was keen or

its blame sometimes severe; not because its praise
was stinted (for, indeed, I think you give me quite as
much praise as I deserve), but because after I had
said earnestly that I wished critics would judge me
as an *author*, not as a woman, you so roughly—I even
thought so cruelly—handled the question of my
sex. I dare say you meant no harm, and perhaps you
will not now be able to understand why I was so
grieved at what you will probably deem such a trifle;
but grieved I was, and indignant too.[2]

Why did Brontë's first, and only, social-problem novel inspire
Lewes to treat the subject of the author's sex? By 1850 the tradition of the woman preacher as the writer of the social narrative
had been thoroughly integrated into Victorian culture. Women
were expected to place their literary talents in the service of social reform, and deliver a predictable, ameliorist message.
Brontë already saw what Gaskell was soon to learn: that so long
as a woman was an evangelist of reconciliation she would have
no trouble gaining access to social discourse; but as soon as she
began to discover the irreconcilable differences between her
interests and those of male authorities, when she became a
feminist prophet, she would be silenced.

Political questions are in fact only incidental in *Shirley*. The
novel's primary interest was clearly in matters of sexual relations among people of the middle and upper ranks. Brontë ex-
plored female sexuality and desire, and continued to develop
the psychosexual symbolism she introduced in *Jane Eyre*.
Brontë was hardly irreligious; on the contrary, she frequently
experimented with matriarchal or androgynous images for
God. But she would not be a preacher. Rather, it was her biographer, Elizabeth Gaskell, whom Woolf altogether ignored in
her 1929 essay, who managed to maintain the paradox of a
language both privileged and accessible. Through constant innovations in her narrative technique, she created new modulations of the woman preacher's voice that neither debased the
notion of an authoritative discourse nor denied women's ability
to write it. She continued to have faith that the community of
literary women would produce a discourse, to which God, if no
other father, would listen, and a discourse which could, to use
Woolf's words, "exert" some "influence . . . upon the future."

Finally, it was changes in the law—the discourse demonized in the women's preaching tradition—that brought about material improvements in the lot of women preachers. In 1869, Louisa Lowe, the wife of an Anglican priest, who had to that point led an unexceptional life, was converted to Spiritualism. She began engaging in "Passive Writing," a Spiritualist practice in which the believer was thought to act as the medium for a spirit's message. The spirit who chose to communicate with Lowe was, according to its medium, none other than Christ. From her extensive "dialogues" with Christ, Lowe learned "to cast off the trammels of authority, and let my mind admit new ideas, and, according to its powers, grapple fearlessly with every doubt as it arises."[3] Science, rather than patriarchal religious dogma, was to be her new guide. As Alex Owen summarizes Lowe's position,

> Her interpretation of these words made her position crystal clear: she must turn her back on the conventional authority of church and husband—both, of course, represented by the one man—and begin to make her own way. . . . Louisa was rejecting Anglicanism and husband in one clean sweep.[4]

Within the year, the Reverend Lowe had his wife confined to a lunatic asylum. Despite the fact that the Lunacy Commissioners eventually considered her appeals for freedom to be valid, they, like King Darius in Hannah More's *Daniel*, felt themselves to have no legal authority to intervene. Not until the Reverend Lowe brought the case to public trial in Chancery in order to gain control of Louisa's property by means of a Lunacy Commission decision was the court involved. In the course of a lunacy inquisition, Louisa was examined by Dr. George Fielding Blandford, who testified to her competence, and the Lunacy Commission ordered her release, which, however, was not final until April of 1872.

Louise Lowe eventually returned to the Spiritualist circles and separated from her husband. But conscious that her own fate had depended utterly on the benevolence of one man with medical and legal authority, she began to agitate for lunacy reform, founding the Alleged Lunatic's Friend Society. Lowe's activities proved crucial to Georgina Weldon, a successful singer and Spiritualist sympathizer, whose debt-ridden husband attempted to obtain his wife's property by having her incarcerated for lunacy. Louisa Lowe hid Weldon from the authorities long enough to secure legal aid to prevent the incarceration. However, Weldon's freedom remained precarious until the passage of the Married Women's Property Act in 1882.

The Married Women's Property Act, reluctantly supported by Elizabeth Gaskell and George Eliot, enabled Weldon to sue her husband and the influential alienist, Dr. Lyttleton Stuart Forbes Winslow, who had certified Weldon's lunacy, alleging she claimed to be an instrument of Providence. Acting for herself in court, she won cases against both men, and launched something of a second career in the law, bringing over a dozen suits in the next decade. Thanks to the passage of the Married Women's Property Act, a woman preacher no longer needed to stand outside the law, dependent on a husband, father, or male mentor, but could preach on her own behalf, and obtain satisfaction from the law.

Notes

Part One: Introduction

1. Among the most significant examples I would cite are Louis Cazamian, *The Social Novel in England, 1830–1850,* trans. Martin Fido (London: Routledge and Kegan Paul, 1973 [1903]); John Holloway, *The Victorian Sage* (New York: Macmillan, 1953); Kathleen Tillotson, *Novels of the Eighteen-Forties* (Oxford: Clarendon Press, 1954); Raymond Williams, *Culture and Society, 1780–1950,* rev. ed. (New York: Columbia University Press, 1983), chap. 5; Valentine Cunningham, *Everywhere Spoken Against: Dissent in the Victorian Novel* (Oxford: Clarendon Press, 1975); and Elizabeth Jay, *The Religion of the Heart: Anglican Evangelicalism and the Nineteenth Century Novel* (Oxford: Clarendon Press, 1979).

2. Joseph Kestner, *Protest and Reform: The British Social Narrative by Women, 1827–1867* (Madison: University of Wisconsin Press, 1985).

3. Deborah M. Valenze, *Prophetic Sons and Daughters: Female Preaching and Popular Religion in Industrial England* (Princeton: Princeton University Press, 1985). Other modern discussions of the Methodist women preachers follow Leslie Church's model in *More About Early Methodist People* (London: Epworth Press, 1949). In the one chapter of that work devoted to women's preaching, Church divides his attention among the activities of more than a dozen preachers and Wesley's attempts to deal with them. Earl Kent Brown reviewed Church's sources in "Women of the Word: Selected Leadership Roles of Women in Mr. Wesley's Methodism," his contribution to *Women in New Worlds,* ed. Hilah F. Thomas and Rosemary Skinner Keller (Nashville: Abingdon Press, 1981), pp. 69–87. Brown adds helpful classifications of women's activities, but no reassessment. The most recent reiteration of this history is D. Colin Dews, "Ann Carr and the Female Revivalists of Leeds," in *Religion in the Lives of English Women, 1760–1930,* ed. Gail

Malmgreen (Bloomington: Indiana University Press, 1986).

4. Deirdre David, *Intellectual Women and Victorian Patriarchy: Harriet Martineau, Elizabeth Barrett Browning, George Eliot* (Ithaca: Cornell University Press, 1987), p. 14.

5. As Marie Maclean has argued in a related context, feminist critics must reject as definitive all androcentric interpretations of women's speech, in "Oppositional Practices in Women's Traditional Narrative," *New Literary History* 19 (Autumn 1987):37–50.

6. See Judith Fetterly, *The Resisting Reader* (Bloomington: Indiana University Press, 1978), and Mary Poovey, *The Proper Lady and the Woman Writer* (Chicago: University of Chicago Press, 1984), both of whom analyze what Fetterly has aptly named the "immasculation" of female readers of male texts. Patrocinio P. Schweickart offers an alternative view in "Reading Ourselves: Towards a Feminist Theory of Reading," in *Gender and Reading: Essays on Readers, Texts, and Contexts,* ed. Elizabeth A. Flynn and Patrocinio P. Schweickart (Baltimore: Johns Hopkins University Press, 1986), pp. 31–62. She sees women as potentially oppositional and revisionary readers.

7. For important discussions of this issue, see Poovey, *The Proper Lady and the Woman Writer;* Nina Auerbach, *Woman and the Demon: The Life of a Victorian Myth* (Cambridge: Harvard University Press, 1982); and Françoise Basch, *Relative Creatures: Victorian Women in Society and the Novel, 1837–1867,* trans. Anthony Rudolf (London: Allen Lane, 1974).

8. Nancy Armstrong, *Desire and Domestic Fiction: A Political History of the Novel* (Oxford: Oxford University Press, 1987).

9. Thomas Timpson, *Female Biography of the New Testament* (London: T. Ward, 1834), p. 35.

10. Leonore Davidoff and Catherine Hall, *Family Fortunes: Men and Women of the English Middle Class, 1780–1850* (Chicago: University of Chicago Press, 1987), p. 114.

11. Bernard Semmel, *The Methodist Revolution* (New York: Basic Books, 1973), p. 14.

12. See E. P. Thompson, *The Making of the English Working Class* (New York: Pantheon Books, 1963) for an analysis of the role of Methodism in working-class formation.

13. Patricia Meyer Spacks, *Imagining a Self: Autobiography and Novel in Eighteenth Century England* (Cambridge: Harvard University Press, 1976). p. 57.

14. For the limitations George Eliot places on her heroine's voice, see chapter 9, p. 249.

15. See M. H. Abrams, *The Mirror and the Lamp: Romantic Theory and*

the Critical Tradition (Oxford: Oxford University Press, 1953); and for the relationship of romantic poetics to Methodism, see Richard E. Brantley, *Wordsworth's "Natural Methodism"* (New Haven: Yale University Press, 1975), intr. and pp. 66–78.

16. Margaret Homans, *Bearing the Word: Language and Female Experience in Nineteenth-Century Women's Writing* (Chicago: University of Chicago Press, 1986).

17. Elaine Showalter, *A Literature of Their Own: British Women Novelists from Brontë to Lessing* (Princeton: Princeton University Press, 1977), p. 7.

18. Olivia Smith, *The Politics of Language: 1791–1819* (Oxford: Clarendon Press, 1984), pp. 3–34.

19. Quoted in ibid., p. 31. For her discussion of the use of language theories by Parliament to suppress obnoxious petitions, see pp. 30–34.

20. Rev. T. E. Owen, *Methodism Unmasked, or the Progress of Puritanism, from the Sixteenth Century to the Nineteenth Century: Intended as an Explanatory Supplement to "Hints to Heads of Families"* (London: J. Hatchard, 1802). p. v.

21. See for example Sandra Gilbert and Susan Gubar, *The Madwoman in the Attic* (New Haven: Yale University Press, 1979), p. 116; and Thompson, *The Making of the English Working Class*. Marilyn Butler omitted More entirely from *Romantics, Rebels, and Reactionaries: English Literature and Its Background, 1760–1830* (Oxford: Oxford University Press, 1982).

22. Ivanka Kovaccvic, *Fact Into Fiction* (Leicester: Leicester University Press, 1975), p. 101.

23. Monica Correa Fryckstedt, "The Early Industrial Novel: *Mary Barton* and Its Predecessors," *Bulletin of the John Rylands University Library of Manchester* 63 (Autumn 1980):24–29.

24. See Margaret Anne Doody, who has constructed George Eliot's link with another set of literary mothers in "George Eliot and Her Eighteenth Century Predecessors," *Nineteenth Century Fiction* 35 (1980):260–91.

25. Gillian Beer, *George Eliot* (Bloomington: Indiana University Press, 1986), p. 6.

26. Cunningham, *Everywhere Spoken Against,* pp. 158ff.

27. Sandra Gilbert, "Life's Empty Pack: Notes toward a Literary Daughteronomy," *Critical Inquiry* 11(1985):357.

28. U. C. Knoepflmacher, *George Eliot's Early Novels: The Limits of Realism* (Berkeley: University of California Press, 1968), p. 30.

29. Gilbert, "Life's Empty Pack," p. 384, n. 66.

Chapter One

1. Ole E. Borgen, *John Wesley on the Sacraments* (Zurich: Publishing House of the United Methodist Church, 1972), p. 46.

2. Sarah Crosby to Frances Mortimer Pawson, October 11, 1784, Methodist Archives, John Rylands University Library of Manchester (all subsequent citations of materials from these archives will be to Methodist Archives).

3. William Law, "A Serious Call to a Devout and Holy Life," *Works of the Reverend William Law* (London, 1893), p. 192. All emphases in this passage are Law's.

4. Ibid., pp. 192–93.

5. Ibid., p. 193.

6. Hester Ann Rogers (1756–94) was the daughter of an Anglican clergyman and married a Methodist preacher; Frances Mortimer Pawson's brother was rector of Lincoln College, her first husband an Anglican clergyman, and her second a Methodist preacher; after she had established herself as the most famous female preacher, Mary Bosanquet married the Reverend John Fletcher, who would eventually lead the Methodist Connexion; finally, the marriage of George Eliot's preacher aunt, Elizabeth Evans, to the preacher Seth Evans is represented in *Adam Bede*.

7. John Wesley, "Female Course of Study," *The Arminian Magazine* 3 (1790):602.

8. Ibid., p. 602.

9. Ibid., p. 604.

10. Ibid., p. 604.

11. John Lyth, *The Living Sacrifice, or a Short Biographical Notice of Sarah Bentley of York* (York, 1848), p. 21.

12. Ibid., p. 21.

13. John Lyth, *The Blessedness of Religion in Earnest, a Memorial of Mrs. Mary Lyth* (London, 1861), p. 279.

14. Ibid., p. 280.

15. Abel Stevens, *The Women of Methodism* (New York, 1866), pp. 26, 38.

16. Ibid., pp. 56–57.

17. Annie Keeling, *Eminent Methodist Women* (London, 1899).

18. Joseph Sutcliffe, *The Experience of Mrs. Pawson* (London: Conference Office, 1813), p. 6.

19. Daniel Defoe, *The Family Instructor* (Oxford, 1841), e.g., 1: 108ff., 203ff.

20. Leonore Davidoff and Catherine Hall, *Family Fortunes: Men and Women of the English Middle Class, 1780–1850* (Chicago: University of Chicago Press, 1987), pp. 335–48.

21. Elizabeth Jay, *The Religion of the Heart: Anglican Evangelicalism and the Nineteenth Century Novel* (Oxford: Clarendon Press, 1979), pp. 142–43.

22. Zechariah Taft, *Biographical Sketches of the Lives and Public Ministry of Various Holy Women* (Leeds, 1825), 1: 15–16.

23. Ibid., pp. 16–17.

24. Ibid., p. 17.

25. Hester Ann Rogers, *A Short Account of the Experience of Hester Ann Rogers* (Dublin, 1803), p. 21.

26. Henry Moore, *The Life of Mrs. Mary Fletcher* (New York, n.d.), p. 22.

27. Sarah Crosby to Frances Mortimer, Methodist Archives.

28. Moore, *Life*, p. 32.

29. Ibid., *Life*, p. 26.

30. Ibid., *Life*, p. 27.

31. Bosanquet quotes Isaiah 52:11. The context of this verse significantly shades the tone of what might otherwise sound rather squeamish. "The Lord hath made bare his holy arm in the eyes of all the nations; and all the ends of the earth shall see the salvation of our God. Depart ye, depart ye, go ye out from thence, touch no unclean *thing;* go ye out of the midst of her; be ye clean, that bear the vessels of the LORD. For ye shall not go out with haste, nor go by flight: for the LORD will go before you; and the God of Israel *will be* your reward" (Is. 52:10–12).

32. Taft, *Biographical Sketches*, 1: 156–57.

33. Stevens, *Women of Methodism*, p. 115.

34. For example, the heroine Maria's confinement in Mary Wollstonecraft's 1798 novel *The Wrongs of Woman*, ed. Gary Kelly (London: Oxford University Press, 1976), pp. 183–85. In *The Darkened Room: Women, Power and Spiritualism in Late Victorian England* (Philadelphia: University of Pennsylvania Press, 1990), Alex Owen documents the alarming frequency with which women were incarcerated for lunacy on the grounds of their religious activities for over a century after Murray's experience.

35. The titular character in Mary Wollstonecraft's *Mary, a Fiction* (1788) yearns after a similar utopia. "In moments of solitary sadness, a gleam of joy would dart across her mind—She thought she was hastening to that world *where there is neither marrying* nor giving in marriage" (*Mary, a Fiction,* ed. Gary Kelly [London: Oxford University Press, 1976], p. 185).

Chapter Two

1. Henry Moore, *The Life of Mrs. Mary Fletcher* (New York, n.d.), p. 42.

2. Ibid., p. 42.

3. Joseph Sutcliffe, *The Experience of Mrs. Pawson* (London: Conference Office, 1813), p. 22.

4. Ibid., p. 27.

5. Sarah Crosby to Frances Mortimer, June 17, 1780, Methodist Archives.

6. Sutcliffe, *Experience*, pp. 77–78.

7. Grace Bennet, diary fragment, Methodist Archives.

8. Sutcliffe, *Experience*, pp. 78–79.

9. Ibid., p. 79.

10. John Lyth, *The Blessedness of Religion in Earnest, A Memorial of Mrs. Mary Lyth* (London, 1861), p. 283.

11. Whitefield did not approve women's preaching in his Connexion, and the most notable women among the Calvinist-Methodists were aristocrats who served instead as benefactresses. Though the countess of Huntingdon, and others, evangelized through conversation and letters, they were not encouraged to do so; neither, perhaps, were they inclined to violate rules of decorum to preach.

12. Anne Dutton, *A Letter from Mrs. Anne Dutton to the Rev. George Whitefield* (Philadelphia, [1743]), pp. 6–7.

13. Agnes Bulmer, *Memoirs of Elizabeth Mortimer* (London: John Mason, 1836), p. 52.

14. Sarah Crosby to Frances Mortimer Pawson, May 22, 1802, Methodist Archives.

15. Ann Freeman, *A Memoir of the Life and Ministry of Ann Freeman* (London, 1826).

16. Elizabeth Gaskell, *Mary Barton* (1848). See below, p. 174.

Chapter Three

1. Leslie Church, *More About the Early Methodist People* (London: Epworth Press, 1949), pp. 162–63.

2. Ibid., p. 164.

3. Grace Bennet, diary fragment, Methodist Archives.

4. Taft, *Biographical Sketches*, 2: 142–43.

5. Agnes Bulmer, *Memoirs of Elizabeth Mortimer* (London: John Mason, 1836), p. 53.

6. Taft, *Biographical Sketches*, 1: 98.

7. Ibid., 1: 73–74.

8. Ibid., 1: 150.

9. Wesley, *Letters*, 8: 15n.

10. Taft, *Biographical Sketches*, 1: 84.

11. Ibid., 1: iii, iv, vi.

12. Ibid., 1: 50.

13. Ibid., 2: p. 54.

14. Edith Rowley, *Fruits of Righteousness in the Life of Susanna Knapp* (London, 1866), p. 63.

15. Joanna Southcott's sensational prophecy in 1802 that she would give birth to the second Christ literalizes this metaphor. In his prose preface to *Don Juan*, Byron ridiculed Southcott for claiming she had been divinely impregnated when in fact she was suffering from dropsy. Byron's characteristic objection to poetic afflatus could be particularly devastating when aimed at a woman.

16. Moore, *Life*, p. 43.

17. Ibid., p. 103.

18. Wesley, *Letters*, 4: 164.

19. Ibid., 4: 133.

20. John Lyth, *Lyth*, p. 119.

21. Brown, "Women of the Word," p. 171.

Chapter Four

1. See Suzanne Graver's excellent analysis of the analogous tensions in positivist social theory between the desire for community and for individual liberty as they inform George Eliot's narrative techniques in *George Eliot and Community: A Study in Social Theory and Fictional Form* (Berkeley: University of California Press, 1984), especially pages 8–13, 140–48, and 277–88.

2. For example, Miriam (Ex. 15:20), Deborah (Judg. 4:4), Huldah (2 Kings 22:14 and 2 Chron. 34:22), and Anna (Luke 2:36).

3. Sarah Crosby to Frances Mortimer, June 17, 1780, Methodist Archives.

4. George Eliot, in "Silly Novels by Lady Novelists," disparaged the addiction of certain of her female colleagues to capitals and underlining for emphasis, as if by such practices they hoped to make a thing true. She may have failed to appreciate their attempts to persuade in a preacher's voice.

5. Wesley, *Letters*, 5: 133. I have not yet discovered the fate of Hannah Harrison.

6. Brown, "Women of the Word," p. 72.

7. Ibid.

8. Diary entry dated August, 1776, in Moore, *Life*, p. 116.

9. Church, *More About the Early Methodist People*, p. 173.

10. Brown, "Women of the Word," p. 70.

11. Ibid., p. 71.

12. Taft, *Biographical Sketches*, 1: 69.

13. Moore, *Life*, p. 46.

14. Ibid.

15. Paul Sangster, *Pity My Simplicity: The Evangelical Revival and the Religious Education of Children, 1738–1800* (London: Epworth Press, 1963), p. 110.

16. Wesley, *Letters*, 6: 290–91.

17. Bosanquet to Wesley, quoted in Taft, *Biographical Sketches*, 1: 23.

18. Taft, *Biographical Sketches*, 1: 19–21.

Chapter Five

1. Sutcliffe, *Experience*, pp. 110–11.

2. Hester Ann Rogers, *Spiritual Letters* (Dublin, 1803), publishers' note, title page.

3. Ibid., p. 24.

4. Bosanquet, *Jesus, Altogether Lovely* (Bristol, 1766), p. 3.

5. Ibid., p. 4.

6. Ibid.

7. "As Moses lifted up the serpent in the wilderness, so must the Son of Man be lifted up: That whosoever believeth in him shall not perish, but have everlasting life." John 3:5, in Mary Bosanquet, *An Aunt's Advice to a Niece* (Leeds, 1780), p. 24.

8. Ibid., pp. 24–26.

9. Ibid., pp. 58–59.

10. Taft, *Biographical Sketches*, 1: i.

11. For example, Bosanquet, *Advice*, Rogers, *Spiritual Letters*, and Mary Tooth, *A Letter to the Loving and Beloved People of the Parish of Madeley* (Ironbridge: Will Smith, 1816).

12. Church, *More About the Early Methodist People*, p. 174.

13. Ibid.

14. Taft, *Biographical Sketches*, 1: v.

15. John Wesley, *The Journal of the Rev. John Wesley* (London: J. M. Dent, 1907), 7: 446n.

16. See *The Arminian Magazine* 7 (1784):671; 8 (1785):437ff.; 10 (1787):383ff.

17. Ibid., 16 (1793): 145. This is precisely what Charlotte Elizabeth Tonna's character Helen Fleetwood does in the factory (see below, p. 104).

18. Elizabeth Gaskell reported that Charlotte Brontë was, as a child,

a faithful reader of the *Methodist Magazine*. See Gaskell, *Life of Charlotte Brontë*, ed. Alan Shelston (Harmondsworth: Penguin, 1975), p. 124.

19. Church, *More About Early Methodist People*, p. 172.

20. Taft, *Biographical Sketches*, 2 (1828):53.

21. Ann Tripp to Mary Bosanquet Fletcher, June 13, 1805, Methodist Archives.

22. As far as I can discover, that manuscript was lost.

23. Wesley's collected letters include twenty-one to Crosby, an especially impressive number given that Wesley protected Crosby's privacy by burning her letters to him after transcribing those portions he wished to preserve (see Wesley to Crosby, May 11, 1780, Wesley, *Letters*, 7:18). Their correspondence was so extensive that it caused Wesley's wife considerable anxiety.

24. Letters of Joseph Benson to Mary Bosanquet Fletcher, 1787–1789, Methodist Archives.

25. Joseph Benson to Mary Tooth, March 28, 1816, Methodist Archives.

26. Mary Tooth to Joseph Benson, April 15, 1816, Methodist Archives.

27. Tooth, *Letter*, pp. 10–12.

28. Gordon S. Haight, *George Eliot: A Biography* (Oxford: Oxford University Press, 1968), p. 24.

29. Annie Keeling, *Eminent Methodist Women* (London, 1899).

30. Ibid., pp. 154–58.

31. Agnes Bulmer, *Memoirs of Elizabeth Mortimer* (London: John Mason, 1836), p. 184.

32. Ibid., p. 145.

33. Ibid., p. 103.

34. Edith Rowley, *Fruits of Righteousness in the Life of Susanna Knapp* (London, 1866), p. 88.

Part Two: Introduction

1. See M. H. Abrams, *Natural Supernaturalism* (New York: Norton, 1971).

2. See, e.g., Louis Cazamian, *The Social Novel in England, 1830–1850*, trans. Martin Fido (London: Routledge and Kegan Paul, 1973); Robert Colby, *Fiction with a Purpose* (Bloomington: Indiana University Press, 1967); Catherine Gallagher, *The Industrial Reformation of English Fiction: 1832–1867* (Chicago: University of Chicago Press, 1985); U. C. Knoepflmacher, *Religious Humanism and the Victorian Novel* (Princeton: Princeton University Press, 1965).

3. See, e.g., Rosemarie Bodenheimer, *The Politics of Story in Victorian*

Fiction (Ithaca: Cornell University Press, 1988); Elaine Showalter, *A Literature of Their Own* (Princeton: Princeton University Press, 1977); Margaret Homans, *Bearing the Word* (Chicago: University of Chicago Press, 1986).

4. Sandra Gilbert and Susan Gubar, *The Madwoman in the Attic* (New Haven: Yale University Press, 1979); Margaret Homans, *Women Writers and Poetic Identity* (Princeton: Princeton University Press, 1980); Alan Richardson, "Romanticism and the Colonization of the Feminine," in *Romanticism and Feminism*, ed. Anne K. Mellor (Bloomington: Indiana University Press, 1988), pp. 13–25.

5. A. W. Schlegel, *Vorlesungen über schöne Literatur und Kunst* (1801–4); William Wordsworth, Preface to the second edition of *Lyrical Ballads;* and Byron, letter to Miss Milbanke, November 10, 1813, all quoted in M. H. Abrams, *The Mirror and the Lamp* (Oxford: Oxford University Press, 1953), pp. 47–49.

6. George P. Landow, "Aggressive (Re)interpretations of the Female Sage: Florence Nightingale's *Cassandra*," in *Victorian Sages and Cultural Discourse: Renegotiating Gender and Power*, ed. Thaïs E. Morgan (New Brunswick: Rutgers University Press, 1990), p. 32.

7. Alex Owen, *The Darkened Room: Women, Power and Spiritualism in Late Victorian England* (Philadelphia: University of Pennsylvania Press, 1990), see especially chapter 6, "Medicine, Mediumship and Mania," and chapter 7, "Louisa Lowe's Story."

8. Landow, "Aggressive (Re)interpretations," p. 33.

9. Carol T. Christ, "'The Hero as Man of Letters': Masculinity and Victorian Nonfiction Prose," in *Victorian Sages and Cultural Discourse: Renegotiating Gender and Power*, ed. Thaïs E. Morgan (New Brunswick: Rutgers University Press, 1990), p. 26.

10. For an extended discussion on the forces inspiring the rise of Anglical Evangelicalism, see Davidoff and Hall, *Family Fortunes*, pp. 81–99.

11. Among the most notable of the many nineteenth-century articulations of "Woman's Mission" are: Sarah Lewis, *Woman's Mission* (London, 1982); J. A. James, "Woman's Mission," *Works*, 4; and Anna Jameson, "Woman's Mission and Woman's Position," *Memoirs and Essays Illustrative of Art, Literature and Social Morals* (London, 1846). See also Alex Tyrrell, "'Woman's Mission' and Pressure Group Politics in Britain (1825–1860)," *Bulletin of the John Rylands University of Manchester Library* 63 (Autumn 1980): 194–230.

12. Harriet Taylor Mill, "The Enfranchisement of Women," in *Essays on Sex Equality*, ed. Alice S. Rossi (Chicago: University of Chicago Press, 1970), p. 198. See also F. K. Prochaska, *Women and Philanthropy in Nineteenth-Century England* (Oxford: Oxford University Press, 1980).

13. Tyrrell, "'Woman's Mission,'" pp. 214–16, for a discussion of the strategic use of women by the leadership of the Anti-Corn Law League.

14. Elizabeth Gaskell, *The Life of Charlotte Brontë*, ed. Alan Shelston (Harmondsworth: Penguin, 1975), p. 348.

Chapter Six

1. Rosemarie Bodenheimer, *The Politics of Story in Victorian Social Fiction* (Ithaca: Cornell University Press, 1988), pp. 21ff.

2. William Roberts, *Memoirs of the Life and Correspondence of Mrs. Hannah More*, 2d. ed. (New York: Harper and Brothers, 1834), 2: 371.

3. Ivanka Kovacevic, *Fact Into Fiction* (Leicester: Leicester University Press, 1975); Joseph Kestner, *Protest and Reform: The British Social Narrative by Women, 1827–1867* (Madison: University of Wisconsin Press, 1985); Richard Altick, *The English Common Reader: A Social History of the Mass Reading Public, 1800–1900* (Chicago: University of Chicago Press, 1957); and Olivia Smith *The Politics of Language, 1791–1819* (Oxford: Clarendon Press, 1984).

4. Mary Alden Hopkins, *Hannah More and Her Circle* (New York: Longmans, 1947), p. 45.

5. Roberts, *Memoirs*, 1: 127.

6. Hannah More, *Daniel*, pt. 4, in *Her Bible Dramas, Poems and Tragedies Complete* (London: Thynne and Co., 1931), pp. 227–28.

7. Roberts, *Memoirs*, 2: 37.

8. Horne to More, August 16, 1786, in ibid., p. 38.

9. Hannah More, Prefatory Letter to *Poems on Several Occasions by Ann Yearsley* (London, 1785), p. vii.

10. Hannah More, *The Works of Hannah More* (London: Cadell and Davies, 1818), 6: iv.

11. Ibid., p. v.

12. Hannah More, "Thoughts on the Manners of the Great," *Works*, 6: 25.

13. Ivanka Kovacevic credits More with pioneering propagandistic fiction, in *Fact Into Fiction*, p. 147.

14. Hannah More, "Village Politics," in ibid., p. 166.

15. More, "Village Politics," in ibid., pp. 166–67.

16. R. K. Webb, *The British Working Class Reader, 1790–1848* (London: Allen and Unwin, 1955), p. 43.

17. Mary Gwladys Jones, *Hannah More* (New York: Greenwood Press, 1968), p. 134.

18. Charlotte M. Yonge, *Hannah More* (Boston: Roberts Brothers, 1888), p. 124.

19. Quoted in Kovacevic, *Fact Into Fiction*, p. 149.

20. More, *Works*, 6: 296–97.

21. Ibid., p. 282.

22. Charlotte Elizabeth Tonna, "Hannah More," *Christian Lady's Magazine* 4 (October 1835):375.

23. More, *Works*, 6: 302.

24. Kovacevic, *Fact Into Fiction*, p. 149.

25. More, *Works*, 6: 57–58.

26. Jones, *Hannah More*, p. 148.

27. Kovacevic, *Fact Into Fiction*, p. 152.

28. Jones, *Hannah More*, p. 148.

29. More, *Works*, 6: x.

30. More, *Estimate of the Religion of the Fashionable World*, 3d ed. (Dublin, 1791), pp. 91–92.

31. More, *Works*, 5: 247.

32. Much of Wollstonecraft's *Vindication of the Rights of Woman* is devoted to making precisely this argument about women's education; in 1851, Harriet Taylor Mill would be making the same point in *The Enfranchisement of Women*.

33. More, *Works*, 6: 250–51.

34. See Jones, *Hannah More*, pp. 170–83.

35. Quoted in ibid., p. 176.

36. Roberts, *Memoirs*, 2: 94.

37. Ibid., 2: 101.

38. Jones, *Hannah More*, p. 196. Fifty years later, these sentiments would be echoed by Elizabeth Rigby reviewing *Jane Eyre*, who doubted that a woman could have produced that novel, and who maintained that if one did, it was a woman unfamiliar with the society of her sex (Elizabeth Rigby, *"Jane Eyre," The Quarterly Review* [December 1848] in Charlotte Brontë, *Jane Eyre*, ed. Richard J. Dunn [New York: Norton, 1971], p. 453).

39. Jones, *Hannah More*, pp. 197–98.

40. Roberts, *Memoirs*, 2: 158.

Chapter Seven

1. Charlotte Elizabeth Tonna, *Personal Recollections*, in *The Works of Charlotte Elizabeth Tonna*, intr. Harriet Beecher Stowe (New York: M. W. Dodd, 1848), 1: 15.

2. *Christian Lady's Magazine*, ed. Charlotte Elizabeth Tonna, 1 (January 1834): 12. Hereafter cited as *CLM*.

3. Tonna, *Works*, 1: 15.

4. Tonna, *Personal Recollections*, in *Works*, 1: 38, 44.

5. Ibid., p. 44.
6. Ibid., pp. 72–73.
7. Ibid., p. 94.
8. Ibid.
9. Ibid.
10. Ibid., p. 96.
11. Ibid., p. 99.
12. *CLM*, 1 (January 1834):ii.
13. Ibid.
14. Ibid.
15. Ibid., p. 73.
16. Ibid.
17. Ibid., p. 74.
18. *CLM*, 1 (February 1834), p. 154.
19. Ibid., p. 157.
20. *CLM*, 1 (March 1834):250.
21. *CLM*, 1 (June 1834):540–41.
22. *CLM*, 4 (October 1835):374–75.
23. *CLM*, 12 (December 1839):513.
24. Ibid., p. 515.
25. Tonna, *Personal Recollections*, in *Works*, 1: 1.
26. Louis Tonna, *Memoir of Charlotte Elizabeth*, in Tonna, *Works*, 1: 115–26.
27. Kestner, *Protest and Reform*, p. 91.
28. Charlotte Elizabeth Tonna, *The Perils of the Nation: An Appeal to the Legislature, the Clergy, and the Higher and Middle Classes* (London: Seeley, Burnside and Seeley, 1848), pp. 18–19.
29. Ibid., pp. 18–19.
30. Ibid., p. 263.
31. Ibid., pp. 259–60.
32. Louis Tonna, *Memoir*, quoted in Kestner, *Protest and Reform*, pp. 91–92.
33. Tonna, *Works*, 2: 398–99.
34. I am adapting this analysis from M. M. Bakhtin, *The Dialogic Imagination*, ed. Michael Holquist, trans. Caryl Emerson and Michael Holquist (Austin: University of Texas Press, 1981), p. 68.
35. *CLM*, 6 (July 1836):28–29.
36. *CLM*, 14 (February 1841):129.
37. See Elizabeth Gaskell, *The Life of Charlotte Brontë*, ed. Alan Shelston (Harmondsworth: Penguin, 1975), p. 348.

Chapter Eight

1. "The Lady Novelists of Great Britain," *Gentleman's Magazine* 40 (July 5, 1853):18–25.

2. In a letter to Eliza Fox, Gaskell quotes this as the reason given by a lending library for withdrawing the book. *The Letters of Mrs. Gaskell,* ed. J. A. V. Chapple and Arthur Pollard (Manchester: Manchester University Press, 1966), 151, [? early February] 1853. *The Letters of Mrs. Gaskell* will hereafter be cited as *GL.*

3. *GL,* 150 [? early February] 1853.

4. Quoted by Gaskell, *GL,* 151, [? early February] 1853.

5. Patsy Stoneman argues that "Elizabeth Gaskell's unfamiliarity with patriarchy at close quarters may account for her exaggeration, in *The Life of Charlotte Brontë,* of Patrick Brontë's authoritarianism and her astonishment at Charlotte's 'patient docility . . . in her conduct towards her father'" (*Elizabeth Gaskell* [Bloomington: Indiana University Press, 1987], p. 25).

6. Gaskell went so far as to counsel William's sister Elizabeth, who was soon to be married, to prevent her husband from initiating this custom, at the same time begging Lizzy not to "notice [my advice] in your answer," lest it be read by William. *GL,* 13, [August 19, 1838].

7. Homans, *Bearing the Word,* p. 224.

8. See, for example, Valentine Cunningham, *Everywhere Spoken Against,* p. 40.

9. For a discussion of the evolving relationships between religious ideology and the cult of domesticity in the first half of the nineteenth century, see Davidoff and Hall, *Family Fortunes,* pp. 114–18, 180–192. Nancy Armstrong argues that domestic ideology could also be deployed in order to control women's writing. As in the economic division between male and female spheres, women's writing might be understood as complementary to men's, rather than adversarial (*Desire and Domestic Fiction,* pp. 28–58).

10. *GL,* 12 [August 18, 1838].

11. See letter to Miss Elizabeth Gaskell, *GL,* 8 [May 12, 1836].

12. Webb, *The British Working Class Reader,* pp. 83–102.

13. *GL,* 68 [c. February 1850].

14. Webb, *The British Working Class Reader,* pp. 109–11.

15. George Eliot, *Essays of George Eliot,* ed. Thomas Pinney (New York: Columbia University Press, 1963), p. 310.

16. "Lizzy Leigh" appeared in Charles Dickens' *Household Words* in 1850. However, Winifred Gérin and Aina Rubenius both concur with A. W. Ward's dating of "Lizzy Leigh" as prior to *Mary Barton.* See Winifred Gérin, *Elizabeth Gaskell* (Oxford: Oxford University Press, 1980), p. 106; Aina Rubenius, *The Woman Question in Mrs. Gaskell's Life*

and Works (Cambridge: Harvard University Press, 1950), p. 66 n.1; A. W. Ward, "Biographical Introduction" to *Mary Barton,* The Knutsford Edition (New York: AMS, 1972), 1: xxviii–xxxix.

17. As we shall see, Gaskell explores the destructive potential of such idolatry in *Sylvia's Lovers* (below, p. 229).

18. Stoneman, *Gaskell,* p. 63.

19. Aina Rubenius locates the beginning of Gaskell's feminism in this story (*The Woman Question,* p. 66 n. 1.).

20. Letter of Thomas Carlyle to Elizabeth Gaskell, quoted in Gérin, *Gaskell,* pp. 89–90.

21. Mary Howitt claimed that William Howitt's inspiration "led to the production of the beautiful story of 'Mary Barton', the first volume of which was sent in MS. to my husband, stating this to be the result of his advice. We were both delighted with it, and a few months later Mrs. Gaskell came up to London, and to our house, with the work completed. Everybody knows how rapturously it was received; and from that time she became one of the favorite writers of fiction" (Mary Howitt, *Autobiography* [New York: Appleton, 1844], 2: 28–29).

22. *GL,* 28, [October 19, 1848].

23. Gaskell protested when correspondents badgered her to own *Mary Barton.* When her friends Catherine and Susanna Winkworth confronted Gaskell with their suspicions, the author ducked under a table, pretending to search for a lost napkin. She intentionally misled Emily Winkworth by attributing the novel to Miss Stone. *GL,* 30, November 11, 1848.

24. *GL,* 24, March 21, [1848].

25. *GL,* 25, April 13, 1848.

26. As noted above, Gaskell complained to William Gaskell's sister Elizabeth that "the sort of consciousness that Wm may at any time and does generally see my letters makes me not write so naturally & heartily as I think I should do" (*GL,* 26 [August 19, 1838]).

27. Stoneman, *Gaskell,* p. 41.

28. Coral Lansbury, *Elizabeth Gaskell: The Novel of Social Crisis* (New York: Harper, 1975), p. 25.

29. Monica Correa Fryckstedt first identified Gaskell's borrowings from these and other factual documents in *Elizabeth Gaskell's Mary Barton and Ruth: A Challenge to Christian England.* (Stockholm: Alinquist and Wiksell International, 1982).

30. Quoted in ibid., p. 93.

31. Patsy Stoneman makes this point, along with the intriguing observation that Esther's appearance to Mary, silhouetted by the moon, bears a striking resemblance to the moon over the moor scene in *Jane Eyre,* which Gaskell had not yet read (*Gaskell,* p. 79).

32. Tonna, *Helen Fleetwood,* p. 560. See above, p. 141.

33. Thomas Carlyle, whose *Sartor Resartus* appeared in 1833–34, greatly admired *Mary Barton.*

34. Stoneman, *Gaskell,* p. 80.

35. Literally, the hedge, where Barton's gun-wadding lodges after he shoots Carson (*MB,* p. 225).

36. Homans, *Bearing the Word,* p. 234.

37. An upper-class child accidentally pushed down by a ragged errand boy "makes peace" by asking him to kiss her (*MB,* p. 348).

38. Stoneman points out the same limitations in *Ruth,* noting that Gaskell abandons her evangelical rhetoric in subsequent novels (*Gaskell,* pp. 111–17).

39. See Elaine Showalter, *A Literature of Their Own,* pp. 5–8.

40. Patrocinio P. Schweickart. "Reading Ourselves: Towards a Feminist Theory of Reading," p. 46.

41. *GL,* 39, January 5 [1849].

42. *GL,* 29, January 5 [1849].

43. Patsy Stoneman offers a corrective reading in *Gaskell,* pp. 100–103.

44. In *The Subjection of Women* (1869), a propensity to reason intuitively rather than systematically is the one feature of women's character Mill assigns to nature rather than nurture. See J. S. Mill, *The Subjection of Women,* in *Essays in Sex Equality,* intro., ed. Alice S. Rossi (Chicago: University of Chicago Press, 1970), pp. 190–91.

45. See Nina Auerbach, *Woman and the Demon: The Life of a Victorian Myth* (Cambridge: Harvard University Press, 1982) pp. 196–98, for a discussion of women's faces as icons in Victorian fiction.

46. *Christian Observer* (July 1857), quoted in Rubenius, *The Woman Question,* p. 213.

47. Catherine Gallagher, in *The Industrial Reformation of English Fiction: Social Discourse and Narrative Form, 1832–1867* (Chicago: University of Chicago Press, 1985), complains that "Margaret tends to turn all issues, even the most personal, into questions of abstract morality," reproducing a tendency of domestic magazine tales, "where private territory was often completely colonized by social considerations, and strictly personal or romantic motives were abolished" (p. 174). Whereas Gallagher seems to consider "romantic motives" as being untainted by social expectations, or more broadly, by patriarchal ideology, I would argue that Gaskell's point is that the distinction between a private and public discourse is itself a means of marginalizing women's political activity.

48. I borrow this phrase from Luce Irigaray, *Speculum of the Other Woman,* trans. Gillian C. Gill (Ithaca: Cornell University Press, 1985), pt. 1, "The Blind Spot of an Old Dream of Symmetry."

49. Gérin, *Gaskell*, p. 150.

50. See above, p. 190.

51. Cf. Mill, *The Subjection of Women*, pp. 185–89.

52. Gérin, *Gaskell*, p. 160.

53. See Bosanquet, *Jesus Altogether Lovely.*

54. *Gentleman's Magazine* 40 (July 5, 1853):24.

55. Ibid., pp. 24–25.

56. See, for example, Gaskell, *Life*, p. 263.

57. This argument originates with Aina Rubenius, in *The Woman Question*, pp. 60–61.

58. Christine L. Krueger, "The 'Female Paternalist' as Historian: Elizabeth Gaskell's *My Lady Ludlow*," in *Rewriting the Victorians*, ed. Linda Shires (London: Routledge, 1992), pp. 166–83, and "'Speaking Like a Woman': or, How to Have the Last Word on *Sylvia's Lovers*," in *Famous Last Words*, ed. Alison Booth (Charlottesville: University Press of Virginia, forthcoming).

59. Armstrong, *Desire and Domestic Fiction*, p. 41.

60. Letter from Charlotte Brontë to George Henry Lewes, January 19, 1850, quoted in Elizabeth Gaskell, *The Life of Charlotte Brontë*, p. 348.

61. *GL*, 515, September 25, 18[62].

Chapter Nine

1. U. C. Knoepflmacher, *George Eliot's Early Novels: The Limits of Realism* (Berkeley: University of California Press, 1968); Mary Wilson Carpenter, *George Eliot and the Landscape of Time: Narrative Form and Protestant Apocalyptic History* (Chapel Hill: University of North Carolina Press, 1986); Valentine Cunningham, *Everywhere Spoken Against: Dissent in the Victorian Novel* (Oxford: Clarendon Press, 1975).

2. Jennifer Uglow, *George Eliot* (New York: Pantheon, 1987), p. 23.

3. Ibid., p. 75.

4. Gillian Beer, *George Eliot* (Bloomington: Indiana University Press, 1986), p. 26.

5. Ibid., pp. 26–27.

6. Deirdre David, *Intellectual Women and Victorian Patriarchy: Harriet Martineau, Elizabeth Barrett Browning, George Eliot* (Ithaca: Cornell University Press, 1987), p. 162.

7. Ibid., p. 163.

8. For an analysis of George Eliot's adaptations of Comte and Feuerbach, see Suzanne Graver, *George Eliot and Community: A Study in Social Theory and Fictional Form* (Berkeley: University of California Press, 1984).

9. George Eliot, *Essays of George Eliot,* ed. Thomas Pinney (New York: Columbia University Press, 1963), p. 301.

10. Eliot, *Essays,* p. 311.

11. Ibid., p. 310.

12. George Eliot, *The George Eliot Letters,* ed. Gordon S. Haight (New Haven: Yale University Press, 1954), 3: 198–99.

13. Eliot, *Essays,* p. 163.

14. Eliot, *Letters,* 1: 11–12.

15. See Carpenter's discussion of Eliot's response to Cumming's millenarianism, in *George Eliot and the Landscape of Time,* pp. 23–25.

16. Homans, *Bearing the Word,* pp. 177–78.

17. Ibid., p. 197.

18. For an alternative analysis of George Eliot's gender identification, see Gillian Beer's discussion the turmoil wrought by the author's attempt "to slough off the contextuality of her own name and enter a neutral space for her writing," in *George Eliot,* p. 25.

19. Eliot, *Letters,* 2: 190.

20. Beer, *George Eliot,* p. 26.

21. See chapter 1, pp. 38–39, for a discussion of Elizabeth Evans.

22. Eliot, *Letters,* I, p. 75.

23. Ibid., p. 19.

24. Gordon S. Haight, *George Eliot: A Biography* (Oxford: Oxford University Press, 1980), p. 24. Jennifer Uglow also comments that Mary Ann "devoured books, especially evangelical biographies and essays" (*George Eliot,* p. 20).

25. For a discussion of Mary Bosanquet Fletcher's memoirs, see chapter 3, pp. 56–57.

26. Eliot, *Letters,* 1: 18–19.

27. Uglow, *George Eliot,* p. 21.

28. Jennifer Uglow suggests these biographical sources for Eliot's fiction in ibid., p. 18.

29. See the discussions of George Eliot's relation as an adult to the evangelicalism of her childhood in Valentine Cunningham, *Everywhere Spoken Against,* and U. C. Knoepflmacher, *Religious Humanism and the Victorian Novel: George Eliot, Walter Pater and Samuel Butler* (Princeton: Princeton University Press, 1965).

30. Homans, *Bearing the Word,* p. 190.

31. George Eliot to Blackwood, quoted in Haight, *George Eliot: A Biography,* p. 219.

32. Quoted in ibid., p. 219.

33. Uglow, *George Eliot,* p. 89.

34. Knoepflmacher *George Eliot's Early Novels,* p. 57; Gilbert and Gubar, *Madwoman,* p. 484; Beer, *George Eliot,* p. 55; Uglow, *George Eliot,* p. 86.

35. Haight, *George Eliot: A Biography*, p. 234.

36. George Eliot, *Scenes of Clerical Life*, ed. David Lodge (Harmondsworth: Penguin, 1973), p. 284.

37. See *Adam Bede*, intr. Stephen Gill (Harmondsworth: Penguin, 1980), p. 586.

38. Armstrong, *Desire and Domestic Fiction*, pp. 68–69.

39. In his chapter on women preachers in *More About the Early Methodist People*, Leslie Church consistently conflates Elizabeth Evans and Dinah.

40. Eliot, *Letters*, 1: 19.

41. Carpenter, *George Eliot and the Landscape of Time*, p. 32.

42. Eliot, *Adam Bede*, p. 497.

43. Mary Wilson Carpenter, "The Trouble With Romola," in *Victorian Sages and Cultural Discourse: Renegotiating Gender and Power*, ed. Thaïs E. Morgan (New Brunswick: Rutgers University Press, 1990), p. 105.

44. George Eliot, *Romola*, ed. Andrew Sanders (Harmondsworth: Penguin, 1980), pp. 101, 699 n. 26.

45. Carpenter, *George Eliot and the Landscape of Time*, pp. 61–62.

46. David, *Intellectual Women and Victorian Patriarchy*, p. 179.

47. Ibid., p. 180.

48. Haight, *George Eliot: A Biography*, p. 326.

49. Journal entry for July 30, August 12, 1861, quoted in ibid., p. 350.

50. Ibid., p. 353.

51. Eliot, *Letters*, 3: 339.

52. See Margaret Anne Doody, "George Eliot and Her Eighteenth-Century Predecessors," *Nineteenth Century Fiction* 35 (1980). 260–91.

53. Haight, *George Eliot: A Biography*, p. 352.

54. Homans, *Bearing the Word*, p. 199.

55. See Gilbert and Gubar, *Madwoman*, pp. 539–80, for a discussion of this pattern in nineteenth-century women's writing generally.

56. Tessa depends totally on her seducer, first to rescue her from her violent stepfather, and then to maintain her and her children. Though Gaskell bore much criticism for Ruth's innocence, George Eliot's choice of a fifteenth-century Italian peasant girl saved her from the same complaints, for Tessa never suspects Tito's duplicity. Further, her innocence is happily preserved by her redemptress, Romola.

57. Fred C. Thomson, "The Genesis of *Felix Holt*," *PMLA* 74 (December 1959):576–84.

58. This is an instinct of a speaker in a Christian culture. Paul prescribes in 1 Corinthians that men always speak in church with their heads uncovered; George Eliot may have recalled that, in the same passage, Paul discusses women speaking in church. He appears to as-

sume the acceptability of this practice, stipulating only that the woman's head be covered.

59. An obvious exception would be Maggie Tulliver, who comes to a tragic end.

Afterword

1. Virginia Woolf, *A Room of One's Own* (London: Hogarth Press, 1967), pp. 166–67.

2. Letter from Charlotte Brontë to George Henry Lewes, January 19, 1850, quoted in Elizabeth Gaskell, *The Life of Charlotte Brontë,* ed. Alan Shelston (Harmondsworth: Penguin, 1975), p. 348.

3. Louisa Lowe, "How an Old Woman Obtained Passive Writing and the Outcome Thereof," in *Quis Custodiet Ipsos Custodes?,* no. 3 (London: James Burns, 1873); idem, Epilogue, quoted in Alex Owen, *The Darkened Room: Women, Power and Spiritualism in Late Victorian England* (Philadelphia: University of Pennsylvania Press, 1990), p. 175. I am indebted to Owen's study for the stories of Louisa Lowe and Georgina Weldon.

4. Owen, *The Darkened Room,* p. 175.

Bibliography

Unpublished Sources in the Methodist Archives, John Rylands University Library of Manchester

Bennet, Grace. Diary fragment.
Benson, Joseph. Letters to Mary Bosanquet Fletcher, 1787–1789.
Benson, Joseph. Letters to Mary Tooth, 1816.
Crosby, Sarah. Letters to Frances Mortimer Pawson.
Tooth, Mary. Letter to Joseph Benson, 15 April 1816.
Tripp, Ann. Letters to Mary Bosanquet Fletcher.

Published Sources

Abrams, M. H. *The Mirror and the Lamp: Romantic Theory and the Critical Tradition.* Oxford: Oxford University Press, 1953.
———. *Natural Supernaturalism.* New York: Norton, 1971.
Adburgham, Alison. "Educating 'the Poor' and Family Magazines," *Women in Print.* London: George Allen and Unwin, 1972.
Altick, Richard. *The English Common Reader: A Social History of the Mass Reading Public, 1800–1900.* Chicago: University of Chicago Press, 1957.
The Arminian Magazine 7–16 (1790–93).
Armstrong, Nancy. *Desire and Domestic Fiction: A Political History of the Novel.* Oxford: Oxford University Press, 1987.
Auerbach, Nina. *Communities of Women: An Idea in Fiction.* Cambridge: Harvard University Press, 1978.
———. *Woman and the Demon: The Life of a Victorian Myth.* Cambridge: Harvard University Press, 1982.
Bakhtin, M. M. *The Dialogic Imagination.* Edited by Michael Holquist.

Translated by Caryl Emerson and Michael Holquist. Austin: University of Texas Press, 1981.

Basch, Françoise. *Relative Creatures: Victorian Women in Society and the Novel, 1837–1867*. Translated by Anthony Rudolf. London: Allen Lane, 1974.

Bauman, Richard. *Let Your Words Be Few: Symbolism of Speaking and Silence Among Seventeenth Century Quakers*. Cambridge: Cambridge University Press, 1983.

Beer, Gillian. *George Eliot*. Bloomington: Indiana University Press, 1986.

Bodenheimer, Rosemarie. *The Politics of Story in Victorian Social Fiction*. Ithaca: Cornell University Press, 1988.

Booth, Wayne C. *The Rhetoric of Fiction*. Chicago: University of Chicago Press, 1961.

Borgen, Ole. *John Wesley on the Sacraments*. Zurich: Publishing House of the United Methodist Church, 1972.

Bosanquet, Mary. *An Aunt's Advice to a Niece*. Leeds, 1780.

———. *Jesus Altogether Lovely*. Bristol. 1766.

Branca, Patricia. *Women in Europe Since 1750*. Princeton: Princeton University Press, 1978.

Brantley, Richard E. *Wordsworth's "Natural Methodism."* New Haven: Yale University Press, 1975.

Brown, Earl Kent. "Women of the Word: Selected Leadership Roles in Mr. Wesley's Methodism." In *Women in New Worlds*, edited by Hilah F. Thomas and Rosemary Skinner Keller. Nashville: Abingdon Press, 1981.

Bulmer, Agnes. *Memoirs of Elizabeth Mortimer*. London: John Mason, 1836.

Burder, Samuel. *Memoirs of Eminently Pious Women*. London, 1815.

Butler, Marilyn. *Romantics, Rebels, and Reactionaries: English Literature and Its Backgrounds, 1760–1830*. Oxford: Oxford University Press, 1982.

Carlyle, Thomas. *The Works of Thomas Carlyle*. New York: AMS Press, 1969.

Carpenter, Mary Wilson. *George Eliot and the Landscape of Time: Narrative Form and Protestant Apocalyptic History*. Chapel Hill: University of North Carolina Press, 1986.

———. "The Trouble With Romola." In *Victorian Sages and Cultural Discourse: Renegotiating Gender and Power*, edited by Thaïs A. Morgan. New Brunswick: Rutgers University Press, 1990.

Cazamian, Louis. *The Social Novel in England, 1830–1850*. Translated by Martin Fido. London: Routledge and Kegan Paul, 1973.

Christ, Carol T. "'The Hero as Man of Letters': Masculinity and Victorian Non-Fiction Prose." In *Victorian Sages and Cultural Discourse: Renegotiating Gender and Power,* edited by Thaïs A. Morgan. New Brunswick: Rutgers University Press, 1990.

The Christian Lady's Magazine. London: R. B. Seeley and W. Burnside, 1834.

Church, Leslie. *More About the Early Methodist People.* London: Epworth Press, 1949.

Colby, Robert. *Fiction with a Purpose.* Bloomington: Indiana University Press, 1967.

Cole, Joseph. *Memoirs of Miss Hannah Ball.* York, 1796.

Cunningham, Valentine. *Everywhere Spoken Against: Dissent in the Victorian Novel.* Oxford: Clarendon Press, 1975.

David, Deirdre. *Intellectual Women and Victorian Patriarchy: Harriet Martineau, Elizabeth Barrett Browning, George Eliot.* Ithaca: Cornell University Press, 1987.

Davidoff, Leonore, and Catherine Hall. *Family Fortunes: Men and Women of the English Middle Class, 1780–1850.* Chicago: University of Chicago Press, 1987.

Davie, Donald. *A Gathered Church: The Literature of the English Dissenting Interest, 1770–1930.* New York: Oxford University Press, 1978.

Defoe, Daniel. *The Family Instructor.* Oxford, 1841.

Dews, D. Colin. "Ann Carr and the Female Revivalists of Leeds." In *Religion in the Lives of English Women, 1760–1930,* edited by Gail Malmgreen. Bloomington: Indiana University Press, 1986.

Doody, Margaret Anne. "George Eliot and Her Eighteenth-Century Predecessors." *Nineteenth Century Fiction* 35 (1980):260–91.

Dutton, Anne. *A Letter from Mrs. Anne Dutton to the Rev. Mr. G. Whitefield.* Philadelphia, 1743.

Eliot, George. *Adam Bede.* Introduction by Stephen Gill. Harmondsworth: Penguin, 1980.

———. *Essays of George Eliot.* Edited by Thomas Pinney. New York: Columbia University Press, 1963.

———. *Felix Holt.* Edited by Peter Coveney. Harmondsworth: Penguin, 1973.

———. *The George Eliot Letters.* Edited by Gordon S. Haight. New Haven: Yale University Press, 1954.

———. *Romola.* Edited by Andrew Sanders. Harmondsworth: Penguin, 1980.

———. *Scenes of Clerical Life.* Edited by David Lodge. Harmondsworth: Penguin, 1973.

"Elizabeth Fry." Biographical Notice. John Wild Collection, Firestone Library, Princeton University, n.d.

Evans, John. *Lancashire Authors and Orators.* London: Houlston and Stoneman, 1850.

The Family Magazine. London, 1788–89.

The Female Instructor. Liverpool, [1815].

Fetterly, Judith. *The Resisting Reader.* Bloomington: Indiana University Press, 1978.

Freeman, Ann. *A Memoir of the Life and Ministry of Ann Freeman.* London, 1826.

Fryckstedt, Monica Correa. "The Early Industrial Novel: *Mary Barton* and Its Predecessors." *Bulletin of the John Rylands University Library of Manchester* 63 (Autumn 1980): 11–30.

———. *Elizabeth Gaskell's Mary Barton and Ruth: A Challenge to Christian England.* Stockholm: Alinquist and Wiksell International, 1982.

Gallagher, Catherine. *The Industrial Reformation of English Fiction: Social Discourse and Narrative Form, 1832–1867.* Chicago: University of Chicago Press, 1985.

Gaskell, Elizabeth. *Cousin Phillis and Other Tales.* Edited by Angus Easson. Oxford: Oxford University Press, 1981.

———. *Cranford.* New York: E. P. Dutton, 1906.

———. *The Letters of Mrs. Gaskell.* Edited by J. A. V. Chapple and Arthur Pollard. Manchester: Manchester University Press, 1966.

———. *The Life of Charlotte Brontë.* Edited by Alan Shelston. Harmondsworth: Penguin, 1975.

———. *Mary Barton.* London: Everyman, 1971.

———. *Ruth.* London: Everyman, 1982.

———, and William Gaskell. "Sketches Among the Poor, no. 1." *Blackwood's Magazine* 41 (January 1, 1837): 255.

———. *Sylvia's Lovers.* Edited by Andrew Sanders. Oxford: Oxford University Press, 1982.

———. *The Works of Mrs. Gaskell.* 7 vols. Edited by A. W. Ward. New York: AMS Press, 1972.

Gérin, Winifred. *Elizabeth Gaskell.* Oxford: Oxford University Press, 1980.

Gilbert, Sandra. "Life's Empty Pack: Notes Towards a Literary Daughteronomy." *Critical Inquiry* 11 (1985):355–84.

———, and Susan Gubar. *The Madwoman in the Attic.* New Haven: Yale University Press, 1979.

Gill, Frederick C. *The Romantic Movement and Methodism.* London: Epworth Press, 1937.

Graver, Suzanne. *George Eliot and Community: A Study in Social Theory and Fictional Form.* Berkeley: University of California Press, 1984.

Haight, Gordon S. *George Eliot: A Biography.* Oxford: Oxford University Press, 1968.

Halévy, Elie. *The Birth of Methodism in England.* Translated and edited by Bernard Semmel. Chicago: University of Chicago Press, 1971.

———. *England in 1815.* Translated by E. I. Watkin and D. A. Barker. London: T. F. Unwin, 1924.

Holloway, John. *The Victorian Sage.* New York: Macmillan, 1953.

Holt, Raymond. *The Unitarian Contribution to Social Progress in England.* London: Allen and Unwin, 1938.

Homans, Margaret. *Bearing the Word: Language and Female Experience in Nineteenth-Century Women's Writing.* Chicago: University of Chicago Press, 1986.

———. *Women Writers and Poetic Identity.* Princeton: Princeton University Press, 1980.

Hopkins, Mary Alden. *Hannah More and Her Circle.* New York: Longmans, 1947.

Howitt, Mary. *Autobiography.* 2 vols. New York: Appleton, 1844.

———, and William Howitt. *Howitt's Journal of Literature and Popular Progress.* 3 vols. London, 1847–48.

Irigaray, Luce. *Speculum of the Other Woman.* Translated by Gillian C. Gill. Ithaca: Cornell University Press, 1985.

Jay, Elizabeth. *The Religion of the Heart: Anglican Evangelicalism and the Nineteenth Century Novel.* Oxford: Clarendon Press, 1979.

Jones, Mary Gwladys. *Hannah More.* New York: Greenwood Press, 1968.

Keeling, Annie. *Eminent Methodist Women.* London, 1899.

Kestner, Joseph. *Protest and Reform: The British Social Narrative by Women, 1827–1867.* Madison: University of Wisconsin Press, 1985.

Knoepflmacher, U. C. *George Eliot's Early Novels: The Limits of Realism.* Berkeley: University of California Press, 1968.

———. *Religious Humanism and the Victorian Novel. George Eliot, Walter Pater and Samuel Butler.* Princeton: Princeton University Press, 1965.

Kovacevic, Ivanka. *Fact Into Fiction.* Leicester. Leicester University Press, 1975.

———, and S. Barbara Kanner. "Blue Book Into Novel: The Forgotten Industrial Fiction of Charlotte Elizabeth Tonna." *Nineteenth Century Fiction* 25 (September 1970): 152–73.

Krueger, Christine L. "The 'Female Paternalist' as Historian: Elizabeth Gaskell's *My Lady Ludlow.*" In *Rewriting the Victorians: Theory, History, and Politics,* edited by Linda Shires. London: Routledge, 1992.

———. "'Speaking Like a Woman,' or How to Have the Last Word on *Sylvia's Lovers.*" In *Famous Last Words,* edited by Alison Booth. Charlottesville: University Press of Virginia, forthcoming.

"The Lady Novelists of Great Britain." *Gentleman's Magazine* (London) 40 (July 5, 1853) 18–25.

Landow, George P. "Aggressive (Re)interpretations of the Female Sage: Florence Nightingale's *Cassandra*." In *Victorian Sages and Cultural Discourse: Renegotiating Gender and Power,* edited by Thaïs E. Morgan. New Brunswick: Rutgers University Press, 1990.

Lansbury, Coral. *Elizabeth Gaskell: The Novel of Social Crisis.* New York: Harper and Row, 1975.

Law, William. "A Serious Call to a Devout and Holy Life." *Works of the Reverend William Law,* vol. 4. London, 1893.

Lyth, John. *The Blessedness of Religion in Earnest, a Memorial of Mrs. Mary Lyth.* London, 1861.

———. *The Living Sacrifice, or a Short Biographical Notice of Sarah Bentley of York.* York, 1848.

Maclean, Marie. "Oppositional Practices in Women's Traditional Narrative." *New Literary History* 19 (Autumn 1987): 37–50.

Mill, Harriet Taylor. "The Enfranchisement of Women." In *Essays on Sex Equality,* edited by Alice S. Rossi. Chicago: University of Chicago Press, 1970.

Mill, J. S. "The Subjection of Women." In *Essays on Sex Equality,* edited by Alice S. Rossi. Chicago: University of Chicago Press, 1970.

Miller, J. Hillis. *The Disappearance of God: Five Nineteenth-Century Writers.* Cambridge: Harvard University Press, 1963.

Minto, W. "Mrs. Gaskell's Novels." *Fortnightly Review* 24 (July–December): 353–69.

Moore, Henry. *The Life of Mrs. Mary Fletcher.* New York, n.d.

More, Hannah. *Estimate of the Religion of the Fashionable World.* 3d edition. Dublin, 1791.

———. *Her Bible Dramas, Poems and Tragedies Complete.* London: Thynne and Co., 1931.

———. Prefatory Letter to *Poems on Several Occasions by Ann Yearsley.* London, 1785.

———. *The Works of Hannah More.* 18 vols. London: Cadell and Davies, 1818.

Neff, Wanda Fraiken. *Victorian Working Women.* New York: Columbia University Press, 1929.

Owen, Alex. *The Darkened Room: Women, Power, and Spiritualism in Late Victorian England.* Philadelphia: University of Pennsylvania Press, 1990.

Owen, Rev. T. E. *Methodism Unmasked, or the Progress of Puritanism, from the Sixteenth Century to the Nineteenth Century: Intended as an Explanatory Supplement to "Hints to Heads of Families."* London: J. Hatchard, 1802.

Perry, Ruth. *Women, Letters, and the Novel.* New York: AMS Press, 1980.

Poovey, Mary. *The Proper Lady and the Woman Writer.* Chicago: University of Chicago Press, 1984.

Prior, Mary, ed. *Women in English Society, 1500–1800.* New York: Methuen, 1985.

Prochaska, F. K. *Women and Philanthropy in Nineteenth-Century England.* Oxford: Oxford University Press, 1980.

Richardson, Alan. "Romanticism and the Colonization of the Feminine." In *Romanticism and Feminism,* edited by Anne K. Mellor. Bloomington: Indiana University Press, 1988.

Rigby, Elizabeth, *"Jane Eyre." The Quarterly Review* (December 1848). In Charlotte Brontë, *Jane Eyre,* edited by Richard J. Dunn. New York: Norton, 1971.

Roberts, William. *Memoirs of the Life and Correspondence of Mrs. Hannah More.* 2 vols. Second edition. New York: Harper and Brothers, 1834.

Rogers, Hester Ann. *A Short Account of the Experience of Hester Ann Rogers.* Dublin, 1803.

———. *Spiritual Letters.* Dublin, 1803.

Rowley, Edith. *Fruits of Righteousness in the Life of Susanna Knapp.* London, 1866.

Rubenius, Aina. *The Woman Question in Mrs. Gaskell's Life and Works.* Cambridge: Harvard University Press, 1950.

"Ruth." *Leader* 6 (January 22, 1853): 89.

Sangster, Paul. *Pity My Simplicity: The Evangelical Revival and the Religious Education of Children, 1738–1800.* London: Epworth Press, 1963.

Schweickart, Patrocinio P. "Reading Ourselves: Towards a Feminist Theory of Reading." In *Gender and Reading: Essays on Readers, Texts, and Contexts,* edited by Elizabeth A. Flynn and Patrocinio P. Schweickart. Baltimore: Johns Hopkins University Press, 1986.

Scott, Sarah. *Journey Through All the Stages of Life.* London, 1745.

Semmel, Bernard. *The Methodist Revolution.* New York: Basic Books, 1973.

Shaen, Margaret, ed. *Memorials of Two Sisters, Susanna and Catherine Winkworth.* London: Longmans, 1908.

Showalter, Elaine. *A Literature of Their Own: British Women Novelists from Brontë to Lessing.* Princeton: Princeton University Press, 1977.

Smith, Olivia. *The Politics of Language, 1791–1819.* Oxford: Clarendon Press, 1984.

Spacks, Patricia Meyer, *Imagining a Self: Autobiography and Novel in Eighteenth Century England.* Cambridge: Harvard University Press, 1976.

Stevens, Abel. *The Women of Methodism*. New York, 1866.

Stoneman, Patsy. *Elizabeth Gaskell*. Bloomington: Indiana University Press, 1987.

Sutcliffe, Joseph. *The Experience of Mrs. Pawson*. London: Conference Office, 1813.

Taft, Zechariah. *Biographical Sketches of the Lives and Public Ministry of Various Holy Women*. 2 vols. Leeds, 1825.

Thompson, E. P. *The Making of the English Working Class*. New York: Pantheon, 1963.

Thomson, Fred C. "The Genesis of *Felix Holt*." *PMLA* 74 (December 1959): 576–84.

Tillotson, Kathleen. *Novels of the Eighteen-Forties*. Oxford: Clarendon Press, 1954.

Timpson, Thomas. *Female Biography of the New Testament*. London: T. Ward, 1834.

Tonna, Charlotte Elizabeth. *The Perils of the Nation: An Appeal to the Legislature, the Clergy, and the Higher and Middle Classes*. London: Seeley, Burnside and Seeley, 1848.

———. *The Works of Charlotte Elizabeth Tonna*. 2 vols. Intr. H. B. Stowe. New York: M. W. Dodd, 1848.

Tooth, Mary. *A Letter to the Loving and Beloved People of the Parish of Madeley*. Ironbridge: William Smith, 1816.

Tyrrell, Alex. "'Woman's Mission' and Pressure Group Politics in Britain (1825–1860)." *Bulletin of the John Rylands University Library of Manchester*. 63 (Autumn 1980): 194–230.

Uglow, Jennifer. *George Eliot*. New York: Pantheon, 1987.

Valenze, Deborah M. *Prophetic Sons and Daughters: Female Preaching and Popular Religion in Industrial England*. Princeton: Princeton University Press, 1985.

Walsh, Elizabeth Miller. *Women in Western Civilization*. Cambridge, Mass.: Schenkman, 1981.

Webb, R. K. *The British Working Class Reader, 1790–1848*. London: Allen and Unwin, 1955.

Wesley, John. *The Journal of the Rev. John Wesley*. 4 vols. London: J. M. Dent, 1907.

———. *The Letters of John Wesley*. 8 vols. Edited by John Telford. London: Epworth Press, 1931.

———. *The Works of John Wesley*. 14 vols. London: Wesleyan Conference Office, 1878.

Wheeler, Michael David. "The Writer as Reader in *Mary Barton*." *Durham University Journal* 67 (1974–75): 92–102.

Williams, Raymond. *Culture and Society, 1780–1950*. Revised edition. New York: Columbia University Press, 1983.

Wollstonecraft, Mary. *Mary, A Fiction.* Edited by Gary Kelly. London: Oxford University Press, 1979.

———. *Vindication of the Rights of Woman.* Edited and with an introduction by Miriam Brody Kramnick. Harmondsworth: Penguin, 1982.

———. *The Wrongs of Woman.* Edited by Gary Kelly. London: Oxford University Press, 1976.

Woolf, Virginia. *A Room of One's Own.* London: Hogarth Press, 1967.

Yonge, Charlotte M. *Hannah More.* Boston: Roberts Brothers, 1888.

Index

Abrams, M. H., 55, 87
Anglican: clergy, 27, 36, 104, 127, 139, 206, 310; Church, 22, 36, 310
Anglican Evangelicals, 8, 91, 92, 96, 103, 109, 118, 123, 125, 126, 127, 130, 155, 158; Clapham Sect, 91, 111
Anti-Jacobin Review, 116
Arminian Magazine (Methodist Magazine), 27, 48, 76
Armstrong, Nancy, 6, 118, 248, 326 n. 9
Arnold, Matthew, 3, 272, 281
Audience, 46, 57, 113, 287; and class, 46, 88, 104–6, 111, 118, 126, 144, 150, 162, 292, 305; female, 74, 97, 152–55, 165, 176, 181, 182; and gender, 46, 57, 113, 114, 133, 134, 141, 150, 158, 162, 178; male, 302
Auerbach, Nina, 314 n. 7, 328 n. 45
Austen, Jane, 123, 205, 206, 209, 220
Authors: evangelicalism and women as, 19, 20, 30, 44, 55, 56, 85, 86, 88, 96, 97, 110, 114, 123, 146–47, 149, 150, 155, 156, 165, 168, 186, 194, 195, 235, 240, 243; *ad feminam* attacks on women as, 3, 10, 19, 105–6, 170, 226, 324 n.

38; suppression of women as, 186, 188, 230–31; women's discursive authority, 181, 196, 215, 219, 241, 248–58, 263, 266–68, 278, 281, 285, 286, 295, 299, 300

Bakhtin, M. M., 325 n. 34
Ball, Hannah, 36, 67
Barritt, Mary. *See* Taft, Mary Barritt
Basch, Françoise, 314 n. 7
Beer, Gillian, 330 n. 18
Bennet, Grace Murray, 39, 43, 4, 51, 66, 109
Benson, Joseph, 77, 78, 81, 82, 306
Bentley, Sarah, 28
Best, Sibyl, 52
Bible. *See* Scripture
Biographies, and gender, 75, 76, 78–81, 137–38, 144, 151, 221–28, 234, 242, 285
Blackwood, John, 305
Blackwood, William, 269
Blackwood's Magazine, 159, 160, 243
Blandford, George Fielding, 310
Bodenheimer, Rosemary, 93, 95
Bodichon, Barbara Smith, 282
Bosanquet, Mary. *See* Fletcher, Mary Bosanquet
Boscawen, Mrs., 109
Boyce, Sarah Mallet, 38
Bradsley, Samuel, 32
Brantley, Richard E., 314 n. 15